Most of the Germans were now running helter-skelter down the slope—heading for the groves, going back toward the mine fields, fleeing in disarray. The machine guns kept firing, and the mortars kept up their pounding until not one live German was in sight. Then the heavy weapons were given the order to cease fire, and our artillery began. Every gun we had within twenty miles must have opened up, plastering the groves, the village, the top of the ridge. Two more flights of P-47s came in over the groves and flew on to strafe the village.

Soon it looked like the whole ridge was on fire, and the village was fast disappearing. For about a half hour the planes kept dropping their bombs. After they stopped, B-25s came in and bombed behind the ridge.

I was sure then the fight was over. It had accomplished nothing but killing men, destroying a lot of equipment, and making one set of generals happy and another set sad. But what else was war . . . ?

THE GREAT NAZI BATTLES OF WORLD WAR II

BRAVE MEN ALL

NOBLE PAUL ROTH

ZEBRA BOOKS

KENSINGTON PUBLISHING CORP.

ZEBRA BOOKS

are published by

KENSINGTON PUBLISHING CORP.
475 Park Avenue South
New York, N.Y. 10016

Printed in the United States of America

This novel is dedicated to Teresa Murray Roth, of Mohill, County Leitrim, Republic of Ireland, and to the three children she, as my wife has given me: Michael Phillip Roth, Anne Marie Good, and Theresa Belinda Gillespie; and to my two grandchildren, Teresa Belina Good, and Michael A. Roth.

Chapter 1

It was 1975, the thirtieth anniversary of the end of World War II. The Division was having its sixth reunion. After the war, some of the members had decided they did not want to give up the comradeship we had established during the war. We also did not want the memory of those who had fallen to be forgotten, so the Division Association had been formed.

They came from all parts of the United States; and from Italy, even one who now calls Germany his home. There was Russ, a successful advertising executive from New Jersey; MacLean, a successful real estate broker from Colorado; the colonel, who was regular army and had stayed in until retirement. We four had arrived a day before the official reunion, and many others came in the day of the reunion.

It so happened that the four of us were assigned to the same lodge, and naturally the talk was about the war and about comrades who had not made it.

The Division had been assigned late to a war theater, but we did manage to receive 1,386 medals and other citations, one of which was the Congressional Medal of Honor, awarded posthumously. It went to Les, from Illinois. The talk now turned to the exploits which had earned him the medal.

7

This was the first reunion I had been to that the colonel attended. Until very recently, I'd believed he had been killed back then. The last time I saw him he had been machine-gunned, and had also been hit by shrapnel while awaiting the litter bearers. At that time he was nothing but a bloody pulp, so bloody you could not tell where the blood was coming from.

I said to him, "Colonel, I'd thought you were dead. How did you ever survive all that?"

His thin lips curled in a thoughtful half-smile before he spoke. "I had eight slugs in me, and then while I was still lying back there, a mortar shell came in and I was hit again. I remember all of this happening and I said, 'This is it . . .' Well, by God, this is the only scar I have." And he rolled his sleeve up to show a long white line down the lower part of his right arm.

MacLean was a lieutenant when the Division went overseas and later became our second captain when Captain Bear was promoted to battalion. He was now sixty years old and still took skiing trips almost every weekend during the winter when he could get away from his business. He was one of the lucky ones: He had not even been wounded.

Russ was only forty-eight now, and had been a mere lad of eighteen when the war ended. He had won the Silver Star, the Bronze Star with Clusters, and the Purple Heart. He had become quite heavy, had three ulcers, and drank too much. Russ was one of the most successful advertising men in New Jersey, but had reached a point where he wondered if it was worth it all. This was his fourth reunion, and he was looking forward to doing some good drinking with his buddies and just relaxing. Of course, he had left his telephone number with his office so they could get in touch with him in case of an emergency.

The colonel was the first one to give in after a few drinks. "I'm seventy-five years old," he announced "and I flew in from Fort Benning today. Plus that auto trip of a hundred twenty-five miles. I'm going to bed. You guys can stay up all night and drink if you want to, but I have to save some of my strength for the rest of the boys coming in." With that, he strode from the room in the military manner a lifetime of soldiering had taught him. MacLean was next to leave, but Russ wanted to stay for a nightcap, so I stayed on with him since he obviously wanted to talk.

The bartender set up fresh drinks, and after a few sips Russ asked, "What are you doing these days?"

I told him I had returned to Indiana after the war, back to my father's eighty acres to cool off and decide what I wanted to do with my life. I had in mind to go to college, but I did not know what I wanted to study. Time went on and I was still farming; my father started giving me more and more responsibilities. Before I knew it I was running the farm and he had all but retired. I decided that if I was to be a farmer, I could handle more than the eighty acres, with the modern equipment a farmer now has at his disposal. So I leased two more eighty-acre farms from neighbors who were ready to retire. I have since bought these parcels and two others, so I now farm four hundred acres, have two hundred head of cattle and other livestock, and am making out very well.

"I understand you went into advertising when you left the army. I remember you always used to talk about it when we were in Italy."

"Yes." Russ nodded. "When I was discharged, I went to the University of Pennsylvania. I took up journalism and advertising on the GI Bill. After I graduated I took a job in the advertising department of a Philadelphia newspaper, and worked there for five years. I made a living, but it didn't do anything for my pride. I'd been around long enough to see where the excitement was, the advertising agencies. I had a good friend who worked for an agency in north Jersey, so I gave him a call. At first, he laughed and said, 'You poor sucker, you're just a babe in the woods. Why, Christ, the first time you approached a client with your newspaper background he'd laugh you out of his office.' But there I was, bored to death, divorced and married a second time, and hung up with a newspaper job that I hated to death. So I said to Cy, my friend, 'Do you think I could get a job at the bottom? I don't give a damn about the money, but I have to get the hell out of this job or I'll go nuts.' So Cy said he'd talk to his boss. 'Maybe Old Hard Guts will consider you for the office boy.' That's what he said. Well, as it turned out Old Hard Guts did hire me. I also started at the bottom, and I mean the bottom! Hell, the office boy was about two steps above me. But, by God, I learned, and I did it the hard way, by taking hard knocks from Old Hard Guts.

"When I'd finally scrambled up to a junior account exec job, the old man picked the toughest accounts for me to handle. Then one day I hit it lucky with one of these hardies. The guy was as mean and tough to please as they come. He said he had a good product, but no one could promote it. His profits then were seventy-five thousand a year, but I knew he should have been making a profit of at least five hundred thousand. He told me that if I could come up with a good promotion that would make him a profit of two hundred fifty thousand, half of that profit would be mine. He also said if I failed he'd run me out of the advertising business and I would never get another job in advertising, not even sweeping floors.

"Well, I decided to do some research into his product and its competitors, to see what he had. I hired a business investigator, and after two weeks he reported back to me and told me this was the greatest product on the market, none of the competitors could touch it. So I worked up an ad and promotion program in the most minute detail. You know, it was like working out a detail of an infantry attack, calculating where the enemy was and how to get to him without his knowing it. I guess I don't have to tell you the thing worked out like a charm. The year's profits turned out to be four hundred grand. I got my half and with it I bought a small percentage of the agency. Of course, I got to be the hot shot. Everyone wanted me, I was the greatest, and I could pick and choose who my clients would be. Now that I owned a piece of the business Old Hard Guts made me a full-fledged partner, a vice-president, and put me third in command, after Cy. My salary also went up. Then, as it turned out, Old Hard Guts was a bachelor, and one day he up and died. He had no living relatives, so he left me—yes, me—everything. I became the largest stockholder in the agency, and consequently the president, making money like it was going out of style. I also went through another divorce and another marriage, which is now on the rocks. Not to mention the ulcers, a near heart attack, a threat of getting shot by a jealous lover, and a hell of a lot of booze."

He shook his head, as if he could barely believe the story he'd just told was actually his own. We sat and drank in silence until the bartender let us know it was time to leave.

Chapter 2

The next day was the first day of the reunion. Registration was being held at the main lodge. After a good heavy mountain breakfast, I wandered up the hill. When I arrived, the colonel was sitting at the table with Miss Reed, the only paid person in the Division Association, who was taking the registrations. Miss Reed's father had been a member of another regiment in the Division, and had been killed in Italy. She was very dedicated to us and to the unit. Captain Reed had received the Distinguished Service Cross posthumously. Many thought he should have had the Medal of Honor.

"Good morning, and I hope you slept well," said the colonel.

"A hell of a lot better in that bed than I used to, lying on the ground in a rainstorm under a shelter in Italy," I said. "But then, thirty years makes you yearn for a little more comfort."

I finished my registration and was leaving when in walked Lieutenant Studebaker with Sergeant Levin, the former platoon guide. I hadn't seen either of these fellows for the past two reunions.

"Nice to see you guys again," I said, shaking hands with both and doing a little backslapping. "You don't look ten years older, so you must be doing something right."

Fritz Studebaker looked me over and said, "That farming you're doing must be agreeing with you. By God, you don't look a day over thirty-five, and I know damn well you have to be fifty. Now, me—the reason I look so good is because of women and good booze. Lawyers have to do something to take away the tension, you know."

Levin and I laughed and gave old Fritz a bang on the arm. Levin said, "I stay young worrying about my three ex-wives and how I'm going to meet those alimony payments every month."

"You and Russ!" I said. "He's working on his third divorce too. Can't any of you guys live with one woman and be satisfied?"

"Well, Ike, you should know I like variety, after all the time we spent in a foxhole together," Levin replied.

We said we would meet later at the company headquarters, which was set up at the Ale Hoffbrau, about halfway down the hill.

It was such a nice day, I decided I would take a ride on the cable car, and maybe even go all the way up on a ski lift. I walked toward the cable-car station, and who did I spot coming my way but old Willie, the fighting Austrian. Willie had been wounded twice and walked with a limp. That and his long nose made it impossible not to recognize him, no matter how much time had passed. Willie had left Austria in the early thirties, before all that Hitler business in his native country. His father and mother had been killed during the war by an American bombing raid, but he did not find this out until after the war, when he went back to his village. His sister had survived, and it was a grand reunion they had, although sad. Willie later brought his sister to America. She had adjusted quite well, married and now lives in Long Island with her own family. Willie himself became a stockbroker on Wall Street, and according to all the stories, is loaded. He never married, always said he had too many girlfriends and he didn't want to offend any of them by marrying one of them.

"Nice to see you. How long has it been?" he asked.

"Ten long years."

Willie said, "I don't believe you've changed one bit since I last saw you. I'd recognize you anywhere! My goodness, you're the youngest looking person here. I think I'll give up Wall Street and go back to the farm, too." Willie had been born a farmer in Austria, but his father wanted him to have an education so he wouldn't have to work with his people had always done. He had made a lot of money and helped as many of his relatives in Austria as he could find. He is a good man, Willie is. Traditional and purposeful, a church-goer. Now he was saying, "I go to church, I ask God to guide me, but so far, no answer. Do you think I'll get the answer before I die, Ike?"

I replied, "I think you've done very well with your life, Willie. There are some much richer men than you in this association, but I know you've given far more than any of them. I know what this outfit means to you." Any money that comes into the association is used to help the orphans of the men who were killed, to see to good educations, to make sure we do the job their fathers could not finish. Willie has donated thousands. "I think you've done wonders," I said. "I wouldn't have any doubts, my friend."

Willie said, "Thanks, but I still have the lingering feeling that there's something I must do. I know God will tell me when He's ready, but it's a nagging feeling that's with me constantly, I just can't get away from it, no matter where I go or what I do."

I said, "Willie, if the Almighty wants you to do more, He'll let you know. I'll see you at the Ale Hoffbrau later on." Turning back to the cable-car station, I walked on up the hill. There was a car waiting to go up. The attendant asked me if I wanted to go by myself, or wait for someone else. I told him I'd go alone. He closed me up and sent the car on its way.

Chapter 3

It was a nice ride, all by myself. It was quiet up above the beautiful aspens and oaks, and brought back memories of Italy, where I had had my first ride in a cable car—not quite so modern as this, and the scenery had not been as spectacular as what I was seeing here, but it was still a warm memory. I remembered how we had been given a three-day pass. We could do anything we wanted as long as we stayed within a hundred miles of our bivouac. Several of the fellows and myself had decided to go to Florence. We had been there before, and we wanted to go into some of the galleries and possibly pick up something we could take home with us. The war was over, everyone had his mind on getting back home, but the good old army said to wait.

The war with Japan was still going on and the rumors were that our Division was going to be in on the landing there in October. They would take us east, not west, and so we wouldn't get a chance to go home before the invasion. When we arrived at the departure point, we found that the trucks going to Florence were filled. But the lieutenant in charge told us they had organized a three-day trip up into the Alps, to a very famous skiing resort, and we took it.

17

We rode past Lake Garda, where so many of our comrades had died in those goddamned tunnels. We saw the villas across the lake, where all those famous fascists hung out with their girlfriends, and up to the north end of the lake were Riva and Torbole, where the assistant Division commander had been killed. A very famous and daring soldier, he died just before the war ended—like so many others of our buddies. God bless them. We came into Bolzano. The last time we had been there, Germans were all over the place, and we didn't know if they had heard of the surrender or not. We were on our way to the customs station on the Austrian-Italian-Swiss border, one battalion with tank support. In fact we were riding the tanks, hanging on for dear life. It seemed different now, with Italian people out on the streets, stores open, dogs, pigs, chickens, and cattle everywhere, and the Italian police directing traffic. We went past places that had been bombed and shelled out, and the bridges which were not there just a few weeks ago were back in place, thanks to the United States Army Engineers. When we left Bolzano, we took the road to the northeast, which was not familiar to us, since we had taken the road to the northwest when we came through here on our way to the customs station. Two hours more and we were at the resort, where only the very wealthy had skied before the war. It was something to see—no war damage, ski lifts, cable cars, the whole deal. And believe it or not, no soldiers. The lieutenant said it had been reserved for our Division and quite a few civilians: Italians, Austrians, Germans—the wealthy, who could travel anywhere they wished regardless of war. This disgusted me some. After all, a couple of weeks ago we were firing at each other. I don't hate anyone, and I am of German stock: my mother was born in Germany, and my grandfather was a captain in the German army during the Franco-Prussian War in 1870, but I could not believe I was ready to sit down and break bread with these people yet. These were the people who stood and cheered Hitler when he made his blood-curdling speeches. It wasn't the soldiers we had been fighting; these were the people who now said, "I was never a Nazi. I was against Hitler." Maybe they were, but how did they make enough money so that just a few weeks after the war they could come to an expensive place like this, living a life of luxury, while back in Germany people were starving to death? It just didn't figure.

The lieutenant advised us that these people had all been passed by army intelligence and were free to congregate wherever they wanted. He said to forget the war and have a good time for the two days we would be here. So we did, being civil to the Germans when the occasion called for it, but not going out of our way to be over friendly with them. They had money, they were always trying to buy us drinks and inviting us up to their suites for cocktail parties, but I don't think any of us accepted one of those invitations.

I arose early the next morning. The night before I had not drunk as much as some of the other guys, so I had a clear head when I awoke. I dressed quickly and took a walk around to see what this place had to offer. I remembered the cable car; I had always wanted to take a ride in one, but being from the state of Indiana, I didn't think I would ever have that chance. I walked down to the station, and to my surprise an attendant was there. He said I could go up now, spend as much time as I wanted, and come down when I felt like it. He also told me not to stay up too long because I would freeze my ears and not even know they were frozen. I knew about frostbite. After all, it gets pretty cold in Indiana. I'd had a frozen ear before.

The car started out with a lurch that almost threw me off the seat, and up and up and away we went. It was a nice feeling, yet I was a bit on the apprehensive side, just a little afraid to look out. Finally, I scooted to one side of the car and bent over, looking out the other side. It was beautiful. The snow was laced with ski tracks, the pine trees were magnificent against the whiteness. After about ten minutes we came to a halt at the top station. An attendant let me out and advised me that it was ten degrees below zero up here, so to bundle up good. The restaurant would not open for another hour yet, but if I got too cold I could come into the station. It was warm in there, and he could manage a cup of hot tea. I thanked him and started out of the station. It was absolutely beautiful up here, with a beauty beyond words. It made me forget about the war, home, and even the possibility of the invasion of Japan, the possibility of facing death again. I was glad that I had made the trip by myself. I'm not sure some of the other fellows would have enjoyed this scene as much as I had.

I walked up to the ski start. Many tracks were there. It had not snowed since the day before. I knew that soon the place would be crowded. I went back to the attendant at the station and borrowed a pair of skis, the most ancient pair of skis that I'd ever seen.

It had been some time since I was on skis. Although

we were trained to ski, mountain climb, and all the rest, it had been ages since I had actually skied. I was going along at a good clip, dodging the trees and rocks, the skis surprisingly smooth and responsive—even more responsive than the American-made GI skis—when another skier came from nowhere and almost crashed into me. I gave a yell, and the other skier peeled off just in time to avoid a collision. I called out, "Damn you, can't you see where the hell you're going?"

The other skier looked back and waved. "I'll apologize at the end of the run," called a distinctly female voice.

We went down the trail, both of us skiing very gracefully, the woman in the lead. I had noticed that she had a very heavy accent that sounded German. I thought to myself, my first encounter with one of those hated people that just a few weeks ago I would have shot and not even given it a second thought.

We reached the end of the trail and skied to the finish line. She was waiting for me as I came to a stop. "I am very sorry that I cut you off as I did. You see, usually there are no skiers on the trail this early in the morning. Most of them at the chalet are too drunk and not clear-headed enough to get up this early." She was breathing heavily, a slight girl of about twenty: blonde, blue eyes, and despite her heavy suntan, quite fair of complexion. "The least I can do for you is buy you a hot chocolate, after I almost ran you down on the trail."

We returned to the chalet and ordered our drinks, and then she began to tell me something of herself. She was German born, but held a Swiss passport. Her father had been a very well known German journalist, a publisher, who could stand neither the Nazi nor the Communist ideas, and had stood up against both. "He is dead now," she said, "but he was wise enough to see what was going to happen, so he sent me out of Germany with my mother, to Switzerland, to school. He also sent money to a Swiss account in a trust fund, so my mother and I would never have to worry about financial matters. Shortly after we left Germany, in 1937, my father was arrested. After years of waiting, we were told by the Swedish consul that he had died of a heart attack while he was a prisoner near Stuttgart. Of course, we don't believe he died of a heart attack. Knowing how stubborn my father was, we are sure he did not give in to them and was eliminated." She said that her name was Erica Von Hoffman. "What is yours?"

I said, "Just call me Ike."

We walked further into the dining room so we would be near the large windows. She led the way, as if she were very well acquainted with the resort.

I said, "Do you come here often?"

"Oh yes. You see, my mother's brother is a part owner of this resort. My mother is Austrian, from the Tyrol, so our roots are here. This is my country."

We sat at a table near the large windows overlooking the ski trail we had just descended. It was really a beautiful sight—the light mountains covered with snow; the valley between, green with the new spring grass; the pines; the sheep and cattle grazing lazily in the warm sun.

"Were you active in any way in the war?" I asked Erica.

"No, not really. Oh, we had pressure placed on us many times by the German agents in Switzerland. They were constantly reminding my mother that we still had relatives in Germany and northern Italy, the Tyrol. But we just never gave in. My father had made Mother promise before we left Germany that regardless of what happened, even his death, we would not involve ourselves when war broke out, and we did not. It was hard at times. There were many refugees in Switzerland, many who had relatives in Germany, many Jews from Germany and other countries that had been invaded by the Germans.

"My mother died in 1944, and since that time I have gone to school, had many vacations here, and have lived a very comfortable life. I do not want it to change."

The waiter brought our hot drinks. Erica asked me what I would do now that the war was over. I told her only that I was a farmer back home, that my father was getting up in years and would need help on the farm. When I said that the farm was in northern Indiana, near South Bend, and the University of Notre Dame, she said she had heard of this school, and of St. Mary's. She was even considering going to America after the war, to study at St. Mary's. "I understand that it is one of the most outstanding girls' schools in America."

Other people were now coming into the dining room for their breakfast, but none of the GIs with my party had yet shown up. I know they had been hitting the bottle pretty good when I left them. I had had a few beers and let it go at that.

I said to Erica, "If you're really thinking of coming

to St. Mary's in Indiana, I'll give you my address. I'd be pleased to show you around South Bend, and take you back to our farm. You could tell my mother about Germany. She knows only about the Germany her mother and father left so long ago."

Erica said she would be very happy to do this. "It may be some time before I am able to get to the United States. I am sure I would have to be checked very carefully before they would let me come."

I wrote my address on a paper napkin and handed it to Erica, who said she would put this away and when she came to America she would definitely get in touch with me. I thought to myself, yeah, when hell freezes over! A rich and beautiful European woman getting in touch with a dirt farmer from Indiana.

We sat in silence sipping our hot chocolate. After a while, Erica said, "Sometimes, I like to take a walk up along the trails on the mountain for a few hours. Would you like to come along?"

I told her that it sounded like a great idea. She had to get into her walking boots, and asked me to tell the waiter to make up a lunch for two and to put it on her chalet while she changed. When the waiter came back with the lunches in a backpack, I went outside to wait for Erica.

She came out about five minutes later. She had put on a little makeup, lipstick. It was very slight. She didn't really need makeup, she was such a beautiful girl. Actually, this was the first time I had noticed her beauty.

"Are you ready for our great adventure?" she asked.

"I sure am. By the weight of this backpack, that waiter must have packed some lunch."

"I know a beautiful spot where we can stop. It is about three hours walking. We should be ready to eat by that time."

We walked up the trail to the north. This was up a very large mountain which Erica said had no name. It was more than ten thousand feet high, but not near the height of the highest mountain in Italy, Mount Rosa, or the Dufourspitze, which is more than fifteen thousand feet.

I said, "You seem to know quite a bit about mountains."

"Yes, I studied them. The Swiss make a very big fuss about mountains, and they have many courses in their schools about mountains. The Alps are not the highest in the world, but they *are* the most beautiful. Of course, I have never seen your Rockies. They are supposed to be quite beautiful, too." She wanted to know more about the geography of my home, and as we walked and I described the flat rolling land to her, she became thoughtful, and finally remarked that Indiana must be much like the Po Valley. The more we talked, the more I felt a vague sense of homesickness, and realized how much I wanted to be getting back to the States—how much I was secretly hoping that there would be no invasion, no more war.

We were now heading up the trail at a mountaineer's pace. It was wide enough for a small car, and every two or three hundred yards a pullout had been made in the pine forest, so one car could wait until another coming toward it could pull to the side. There did not seem to be many tracks of cars or carts on the gravel road. I asked Erica, "Didn't the Germans use this mountain?" She answered, "Only a small crew of

Germans were up here, three or four men. I think they had a radar station or some kind of observation post up at the summit."

"When did they leave?"

"Three or four weeks ago. The people at the chalet told me. I was not here when they left."

"I'm glad I didn't have to do too much fighting in the Alps. We did do a lot along Lake Garda. Those tunnels . . . We lost a lot of men. But after we got to the north end the fighting was about over. We'd expected the Germans to put up a real defense here. Most of us figured it'd take at least another year. We figured Hitler would take the elite of his SS troops and hold out at the Eagle's Nest—and us being a mountain unit, we'd have to take the brunt of the attack. We really thought that this was why we were sent over here, and that the fighting in Italy was just a warmup for what was to come. I'm glad we were all wrong, that it's over and we can get back to living again."

"Being a soldier in war must be a horrible experience. Killing and destroying, never doing anything to help build up a society, just destroying it," Erica said quietly.

"Well, it *is* a little hard for an Indiana boy to figure out. But I'd studied a lot about the world situation back in high school, and I had a feeling when I graduated that it wouldn't be long before everything blew up and I'd be getting into a uniform and carrying a gun across the ocean. I've read quite a lot about Europe—mostly about its wars, and it seemed to me that until Europe got this one out of its system, the world would always be in danger. But now, I'm very worried about the Russians. I don't think Joe Stalin

26

can be trusted. And I don't know what to think about that man Tito in Yugoslavia. They shot down an American plane and he's threatening to march into Fiume. We were up there for a couple of weeks. Orders were not to shoot, but those bastards could shoot at us. It doesn't really make any sense to me. I'm just a sergeant. The generals and the politicians make the decisions."

Erica had been listening thoughtfully. Now she said, "You know, there are some Yugoslavians staying at the chalet. They're what they call Royalists, and they don't like Tito. They say that if Europe is not returned to the same governments they had before, the world will be Communist sooner or later, and even America will not be able to stop it. Oh, I am sure they will try, but they will bleed themselves white just like Marx, Engels, and Lenin said. Oh, yes," she smiled, "I have also studied Marxism and the Russian revolution. In general, the Swiss do not like the Russians. They are afraid of them."

"Well," I said, "Marxism, the Russian revolution, the future of Yugoslavia—things I never thought I'd be discussing on a mountain in Italy with a German-born Swiss citizen." We both laughed.

We walked on up the trail. Some places were quite steep. I wondered how anyone could get a car up here, but Erica said she had been up this trail several times in a Fiat, which went up without too much trouble, although it was steaming when it got up to the rest area at the top. She said the Germans had used horses or oxen to get their equipment and supplies up when they were here. It was now nearly three hours since we had left the lodge. The sun was high in the sky, but a cool breeze made it comfortable to keep walking.

"We are almost there now," Erica said. "Do you have matches to light a fire?"

I told her I didn't smoke, and didn't carry matches.

"That is all right, the waiter at the chalet would make sure some were in the backpack." I asked her if she came here often, and she said, "Yes, I love it up here. No war, no people. I usually come up here by myself. One of the German soldiers used to see me coming up the mountain and he would come down and we would talk. He did not like the war, either. He was a mountain boy from Bavaria, a very nice person, and I hope he will get home."

"You *were* in contact with the Germans then," I said.

"How could one *not* be in contact with the Germans? They were all around us. There were nice ones, bad ones, and some so dedicated to the war you could not make sense with them. I am sure you have the same in your army. Take your General Patton, for instance. He is a dedicated soldier, loves his country and is willing to die for it. He is probably often in conflict with your government, when they do not agree with him on foreign policy. Most of the Germans I talked to wanted nothing more than to go home. They felt the war was useless, and they wanted to go back and start rebuilding their lives. They had families and some did not even know if they were alive or dead. They were really nice people, caught up in something they could not control—just the same as the Americans and a lot of other peoples."

"You're right Erica," I said. "But let's not spoil a

beautiful day by talking about the war anymore. The hates must be forgotten, but I'm sure it'll take a long time on both sides."

The spot Erica had told me about was a little cottage, chalet style, about a hundred feet off the trail. If I had not known it was there, I would have walked past it and never noticed it. Inside was a table with benches, a big stone fireplace, a bedroom with a bed and a chest in it. I asked Erica if anyone lived here. She said, "No, not now, but at one time a woodsman did. The chalet now takes care of it for some of their favorite guests. My uncle told me about it when he knew I liked to walk up here, in case I was ever caught by a snowstorm or got tired. I come here often, just by myself. I think of my mother and of my father. I think of how easy my life has been because of my father's foresight. I could be just another refugee now if it hadn't been for that." She had a sadness in her eyes that I had not noticed before. I felt a sudden rush of warmth and compassion for her.

I set the backpack on the table. She opened it and started to unpack it. I had thought there would be a couple of sandwiches in it, and maybe some coffee or hot chocolate in a thermos. But it turned out to be venison in a container which could be placed in the fireplace, two bottles of a French wine whose name I could not pronounce, little onions and potatoes, French pastries, a tablecloth, napkins, a corkscrew, and the matches. There was even a bottle of brandy for after dinner. Erica asked if I would start the fire. There was wood outside the back door, already cut and split.

The view from behind the cottage was unbelievable.

You could see for miles—through the passes, the high, snow-covered mountains. I wondered how people could fight each other in the midst of such breath-taking beauty.

I carried the wood inside. Erica had already prepared the food for heating and all she needed was the fire. I put some chips into the fireplace and lit a match. They were very dry and caught fire immediately. In another five minutes she had a roaring fire going. We waited until it had burned down to coals, before we cooked. In the meantime, we opened one of the bottles of wine.

I wasn't very good with a corkscrew. I'd never opened too many corked bottles of wine back home. My grandfather made a lot of wine, but he put it in kegs and if you wanted a drink, you went down to the cellar and opened a pitcock into a pitcher. But I did get the bottle open without too much trouble, and when I turned to see what we would drink it from, there on the table were two wine glasses of the most delicate crystal I had ever seen.

"Where did the glasses come from?" I asked.

"The waiter put them in the backpack. He knows how I like to do things. He knows the food I like, and he knows the style I'm used to."

The wine was the smoothest and deepest I had ever tasted. It was one of the best French wines one could obtain in Italy, and it did warm a person. After we finished the bottle, the coals were glowing and Erica put the venison on. She arranged everything and hung it low over the coals, then came over to the couch where I was sitting and sat down alongside me. It had been a long time since I had thought of kissing a girl, and Erica looked very beautiful. I bent over to her and she leaned toward me, and we kissed. It was kissing like I had never experienced before. I tingled all over. I pulled her closer and she pressed her body to mine, both of us clinging together. Her mouth tasted sweet and fresh. We held each other and kissed for a long time before Erica finally stood up and said, "I think the food is ready. We had best eat now. It will soon be getting to the point where it will be difficult for us to go down the mountain, and I don't think it would be wise to stay up here all night." She turned and added quickly, "I have a feeling for you like I have never had for anyone before."

I said, "Yes." It was all I could say.

I opened the other bottle and poured out the richly colored wine while Erica served the food. I thought to myself, what a way to camp out. The army was never like this! The food was very good (I do not remember eating better), the wine was beginning to take effect, the fire in the fireplace was warm, and a beautiful girl was having lunch with me—a girl I felt I was falling in love with. What else could a soldier want, except maybe to go home?

We finished the lunch, and Erica put the glasses and china back into the backpack. I put the pack on my shoulders, and we began our descent. The temperature was dropping, and even with the wine and brandy and the good warm food, we stepped lively against the cold.

We arrived at the main chalet after about an hour and a half. The trip down was much quicker but uneventful. Erica said she would like to take a nap before dinner. There was to be a little celebration for the American soldiers that evening, since we would be leaving the next morning. I thought a nap was a good idea and I decided to do the same.

I had started up the stairway to my room when I heard a lot of singing coming from the bar. The singing was in English, so I knew who was doing it—my comrades from the outfit. I decided to peek in to see who was sober and who was not. As I suspected, old Stutzman and Black were feeling no pain. Schidt, the first sergeant, was trying to get them to leave and take a nap so they would be in decent shape for the party. Stutzman always listened to me, but Black was a hard-nose. I walked up to Stutzman and said, "Mike, I think you've had enough for this afternoon. Why don't you listen to Schidt and go take a nap?"

He said he would; after all, the food and beer were going to be free that night, and, "I just don't want to miss any of that free stuff."

I turned to Black and asked him the same thing. His answer: "Go pound sand up your ass. I don't like you, I don't like Schidt, and I'll do as I damn well please. Who the hell're you trying to please, these god-damn Krauts here? Or is it that little Kraut girl you been running around with? How is she? Can I have a little piece of that too?"

Before he got the "too" out, I hit him in the mouth. He fell backward, and for a minute I thought I'd killed him.

Schidt jumped in and grabbed me.

"Don't hit the son-of-a-bitch again, he ain't worth it!"

I told Schidt okay. I had my composure back. Black was getting up. He looked at me and then left the room and went up the stairway. I wondered, does that girl mean that much to me that I'd knock someone on his ass for making a remark about her? Or was it my upbringing, having been taught to respect all people, but especially women. I had to think about that. I left the bar and went up to my room, lay down on the bed, and fell asleep. I was really tired after a day of skiing and walking up that mountain.

The affair that night was not a very friendly one. The Americans tended to stay by themselves and sing dirty songs, drink beer, and gorge on the delicious food that was put out by the chalet. The Germans, Swiss, and Austrians tried to be friendly to them, but to no avail.

I spent as much time with Erica as I could. This was the last time—or at least it would be a long time—before I would see her again. No denying it, I really had a thing for this girl.

The party broke up at about 2300 hours, when the lieutenant advised us to hit the hay since we had a long trip back to base early in the morning.

We left at 0600 hours and arrived at base about eight hours later. I could not get Erica out of my mind during the entire time.

Chapter 4

We arrived at the top cable-car station, and I got out. It was warm in the sun. The air was thin, but I didn't mind it too much as long as I wasn't moving too fast. It was a beautiful view: The village lying down below; the valleys, some rocky and some green with grass and trees. I had always been fascinated by the aspen, which is very much like the birch we have in the East, yet different. From the top I could see groves and groves of aspen, and I feasted my eyes on the whole scene.

I took the next cable car down, again all by myself. I walked toward the lodge, thinking I might run into some of the new arrivals, but I didn't see any and so I headed down to the Ale Hoffbrau House. Although it was only ten o'clock, there were several people lifting big frosty mugs of beer. They looked good, so I ordered one. It really tasted great after that trip on the cable car. I did not recognize any of the men sitting around, so I guessed they must be from different companies. I walked up to a table of three fellows and asked if I could join them. I sat down and introduced myself, said I was from Company L, and asked them what company they had been in. They all laughed and said "Company L, First Platoon. Ike, we'd have recognized you anywhere! You haven't changed in thirty years." They introduced themselves: Al, Gardner, and Reds.

I couldn't believe how old they had become. Reds didn't have his red hair anymore. In fact, he had very little hair. After Al identified himself, I noticed some mannerisms that I remembered very well. I could not believe Gardner. He was fat, white-haired, and had a stringy beard. He had always been the fastidious one. Even in the muddy foxholes he was always a fashion plate.

Reds had been our platoon's mule driver, bringing food and ammunition up, taking back the wounded and dead. He was a Mormon, and had had some choice words for those mules so he wouldn't have to use actual curses.

Gardner had been our platoon guide, later our platoon sergeant, and a good one. He never asked any man to do anything he would not do himself. Al was a funny guy, one of the originals. He had fought in Kisko and been wounded up there. He could have been—and should have been—a sergeant, but always refused it.

We talked some about what we were doing now. Gardner was a mountain guide in Oregon, his home state, and only worked during the hunting and fishing seasons. It was one thing he had always talked about during the war. I asked him, "If you're that active, how come you're so out of shape?" He answered, "You want to try me? I may look that way, but I can get around pretty good. It's just that I have a lot of down time and I always liked beer and good food, so I eat and drink as I please, and work when I have to."

Reds cut in. "He's not like the rest of us, having our noses to the grindstone every day of the year and ending up with nothing in the end anyway." He continued, "I have a little ranch in Utah, where I raise cattle for the market. I've got some horses—and oh yes, four of those blasted mules, same type we used in Italy. I got to like 'em and I keep 'em for pets, but I'd hate to put 'em to work."

But it was Al who'd had the most eventful life since the war. He said that he'd returned to his old job at a clothing factory when he'd been discharged from the army, and nearly went crazy there, so he took off for Ohio and ended up working in an auto assembly plant. It was steady for a while, he said, and he even got married. But he found he couldn't take married life, and divorced—only to meet another woman, a young widow with three kids, and marry her. "That lasted about two years," he said, grinning over the memory. "By the time we got divorced, I was living in Tennessee, working as a lumberjack, and wouldn't you know, I met someone, fell in love again, and got married." That one lasted all of six months; one day he came home and found his new wife in bed with a bigger lumberjack. "So I got me another divorce and split for Florida. A great place to live." Al was working as a ship's hand on a pleasure boat and *not* looking for a fourth wife. "I'll stay with the fish. Let you guys worry about the ladies." We all had a good laugh with Al over his story. Three wives and three divorces. So far, he was ahead of everyone.

Reds started talking about the first time he and I ever saw each other. He was bringing four pack mules up a hill, and I'd asked him if he had them trained like circus elephants, to be able to walk in such a straight line, as if one held the other's tail.

"That's it," I said. "Les, Stutzman, and I had just got in that day. Stutzman and I'd been assigned to the first squad, and Les had been assigned to the second. Right. And Levin was our squad leader, and Sulli was squad leader of the second. Levin told us to dig in where we could find space, so we did. Worked all day on that foxhole, because we were told that tanks had been rumbling around close by. And that's when I saw you coming up the hill. I believe to this day it was the funniest sight I've ever seen. I can see it now, you leading those four mules, packed down with C rations, water, and ammunition."

There was a lot about the scene that hadn't been very funny, though. For one thing, Reds had to step his mules around the bodies of both GIs and Germans that were lying around. Then, when he reached a fox-hole just below ours, he stopped to ask a big guy there what was going down on the next trip. Bodies, of course. The big guy turned out to be First Sergeant Blue, the company top kick. He told Reds that he could take two bodies on each mule, and then he ordered Les and Stutzman and me to get down there and wrap the bodies in blankets. "Let their feet stick out," he said, "so they can tell at the bottom of the hill if they're our men or Germans." Then Blue turned and walked away. He didn't even look back. Reds explained to us that one of these bodies was Blue's kid brother.

That was my first encounter with Reds—wrapping and loading eight bodies onto those mules. It wasn't a pleasant job. The bodies were well preserved because it was so cold up there in the mountains, but you had to look at their faces . . . these were just little kids. The oldest couldn't have been more than nineteen, and just thinking back three or four years ago these kids weren't even old enough to go out with girls. Now they were dead. "God, may they never be forgotten," I prayed. "They did their best. They died in a righteous cause. But they should never ever be forgotten, as long as man inhabits the earth."

Reds asked us to help him down the hill with the load: "Just steady it so the packs don't fall off or lean too far one way. It'll take us about fifteen minutes to go down the hill to the medical aid station."

When we reached the aid station there were about twenty-five other bodies there, covered, lying on litters, awaiting transportation back to Castel Fiorentino for final processing and burial. Some of the uniforms were unfamiliar to me. It was explained to me they were Brazilian, that a Brazilian company was up here with us. We were advised not to let our M-1 rifles alone at any time, since the Brazilians were issued the old Springfields and would steal our rifles and leave theirs.

I said to Reds, "I've never seen so many dead bodies in my life."

"You should have been here yesterday," he said. "After the fight was over, we brought down over three hundred just from that ridge where Company L is dug in. The fight started at dawn and was over in about an hour. The Germans pulled out their infantry just as soon as they had their heavy equipment off the mountain—they never leave any equipment behind if they can help it."

Reds said it was important that we take this mountain. Several other outfits had tried before us, including another American one, a South African one, a British one, and the Polish Free Forces, but without success.

"They didn't think we'd take it either, but they thought it would be good practice for us for when we reached the Alps, the main reason we were brought over to this theater of operations to begin with. Well, we fooled them. We stayed in there 'til the Germans hollered Uncle this time. With this mountain in our hands, we can move along the whole American front and a great part of the British front without the Germans knowing about it. When they had this mountain we couldn't move an ant across the road that they didn't know about. This could break out the whole front, and the Po Valley is only eight miles north of here. We could be in the Alps by March or April, and if we can keep the Germans from digging in there, maybe we'll be in Austria and even Germany by June or July. Now *there* is where the going is going to get tough! Hitler has an elite corps, and they're sure to fight to the last man around his eagle's nest at Berchtesgaden. Those're some of the most rugged mountains in the world. I've never seen them, but you can talk to Willie, he used to ski up around there and knows the area well, and he says they're tough."

We loaded three of the animals with boxes of C rations and one with hand grenades and went back up the hill. I remembered what Reds had told us about our M-1 rifles, and as soon as we got to the top of the hill I went to my foxhole, expecting to find an old Springfield in its place. But my M-1 was still there, so

I picked it up and walked over to where Reds had started to load the bodies again. Stutzman and Les were doing the same thing. I heard a voice saying, "Just this once I watched them, but the next time I won't do it! If you haven't learned your lesson by now, fight with a Springfield." The speaker was a very neatly dressed fellow with a two weeks' beard, who announced he was our platoon guide. "Just call me Gardner," he said.

I asked Reds why he didn't wear stripes, and he told me Germans use them for targets. "How does he keep so clean up here when the rest look like they've been sleeping with hogs?"

Reds said, "He uses his shaving water to wash his shirts instead of shaving. Says he can't stand a dirty shirt." This was my introduction to Sergeant Gardner, and one damn good man he was, too.

Sergeant Blue said we couldn't see well enough to make another trip that night, so Reds was to take three of the mules back to the aid station and keep one for us. He told us to go back and eat something, then get into our foxholes and keep very quiet, so they could hear any German patrols that might come in. If there was any shooting, we were to keep our heads down. There were designated people who would take care of the patrols, and if we stuck our heads up these gunners would shoot at us, thinking we were Germans.

We didn't get much sleep that night, what with the mortars, artillery, and small-arms fire coming in. There was no real danger—unless a shell hit your hole—but the noise was enough to wake the dead.

In the morning, Levin came over to our foxhole. We had dug it down about four and a half feet, and then dug back under the ground so we could lay flat when we were sleeping or resting. He said it was a good hole, but to make sure we had our feet underground and heads out in case a shell hit nearby and caved the hole in.

Chapter 5

Levin had told us about the battle that was fought two days before. The mountain had had to be taken, because as long as the Germans had it they could survey our movements for thirty miles in any direction. He said the Germans had had a lot of artillery and tanks with 88s protecting the mountain, and our losses had been very heavy. In some cases, officers in charge had issued orders to pull back, but the men just kept going. Company L had been especially hard hit. The Germans had had heavy weapons sitting just around the bend in the trail, and when our company had advanced, it was right into their fire. He said he knew of thirty-four killed from the company, fourteen of them from the first platoon. The bodies we had taken down to the aid station were the kids who had hit that bend.

The clouds had finally opened up enough so that we could call in an air strike, and they plastered the place with bombs and machine gun fire so the Germans finally had to withdraw. They left a lot of dead there, too. There were very few prisoners, only wounded ones that could not be hauled away. Most of the German equipment was also gone. The Germans fought hard until they had all of the equipment removed, and only then did they pull out their infantry. The tanks and artillery that they pulled off the mountain were what was plastering us now. Germans don't like to lose equipment, and the German mountain troopers know what they're doing. They're very well trained, and most of them have lived in the mountains all their lives. But they also know they can't fight without that equipment, so they keep fighting until it is safely away and ready for another battle.

Levin also told us that as soon as the other regiments in the division had caught up with us we would be moving again. This should be in two or three days, so we had to get our equipment ready, clean our rifles and make sure we had a full complement of ammunition and rations, because sometimes supplies were slow in catching up with us.

He was right. On the second day we were told that we were moving out in one hour. We got into platoon formation behind a rise, and were given the command to march. We started out to the right. After about two miles, we were told to drop our packs, except for a blanket and our combat equipment. Squad leaders were called back to the platoon leader who informed them what our objective was. We were spread out in squad formation, scouts out, and began our little walk through a grove of trees. Squad leaders kept calling to keep under cover. We wanted to get as close as we could to the ridge immediately in front of us before we were spotted.

One hell of a racket broke loose to our right. It was a wailing sound, the likes of which I had never heard before, and as we looked in that direction, we saw three men blowing into a bag and making the damnedest sounds. Levin told us they were Scottish and they always went into battle with their bagpipes playing. We were the American anchor and that the British would be on our right during this attack.

We crossed a road and were ordered to lie in the ditch on the enemy side of the road, in front of a house which was set back about two hundred feet from the road. Schidt stepped out and, in German, hollered toward the people inside to come out with their hands up and they would not be shot. Very shortly after, a white flag began to wave at the door, and out stepped the most miserable little character I have ever seen. His coat was too big, he had on glasses that looked like the bottoms of milk bottles, and he had a suitcase with him. Behind him came some other Germans, all in ill-fitting clothes, all looking like they could stand a good meal, and all scared. Schidt said something else and they dropped their weapons and took off their helmets. Levin said, "Always remember: A German soldier does not consider himself disarmed until his helmet is off. They've been known to throw grenades, or they might have a small pistol."

All in all forty Germans came out of that little house. I don't know where they all were — they must have been standing on each other's shoulders. Schidt ordered Levin to take his squad and search the house, which we did. All we found was an old Italian man and woman, frightened to death. They were sent back, along with the Germans to be questioned and processed.

The ridge was just behind the house, and the whole platoon was ordered up to take any more Germans there and to establish an outpost. Schidt had said we'd get an artillery barrage before going up, but it never came. The colonel's orders were to go up and dig in before it got dark, and to expect a counterattack from the Germans.

We went up the ridge, and there was not a German in sight. We had just started to dig in when the damnedest barrage I had ever seen started coming in. There were large trees on top of the ridge, and shells were exploding from them, showering us from above. The shells were coming from the rear. Someone said we were so far out in front that we had passed German mortars, and these were what we were receiving. Some of the old hands said they were not German mortars, that they were heavier and must be 4.2s. The shelling went on for about five minutes, though it seemed more like twenty-four hours. There was nothing to do but lie there and hope and pray we didn't get hit.

When it finally stopped, we counted our dead and wounded. There were five killed, including a champion jumper, a second lieutenant attached to division who did not have to be here; two from the second squad; one from the third; and one from the first squad. We dug in like beavers, rocks and dirt flying everywhere, and within an hour had a fairly defensible outpost.

We found later that what had come in was indeed 4.2 mortars, chemical mortars. But since there was no gas for them, they had been converted to fragmentation mortars. They were supposed to be in on the barrage before we went up the ridge, but apparently no one had been notified not to shell, so they proceeded as previously ordered. Needless to say, anyone wearing a chemical warfare insignia caught hell when we were off the line and went back to his camp with a sore ass and a few cuts and bruises.

The other platoons of the company came up and dug in on adjacent rises; the British, on our right, started their fires for teatime. We let them know we did not appreciate this, but they paid little attention to us. Fortunately, the Germans were busy moving back behind the next ridge and setting up there in case we continued our attack.

We didn't get much of a chance to see what our surroundings were, because by the time we'd prepared our position, it was dark, and we had to set up for the night's defense. We would have cold C rations, no fires, and no one was to sleep that night. Reds was bringing up supplies and grenades. He had found another mule, so he would also be bringing up some rations. During the night he would bring up water, so we were to conserve what water we had. Just before dark, I saw a German walking across the road about half a mile away. I thought, *What the hell am I here for?* and aimed my M-1 and fired. I saw the German go down, but he crawled to a ditch before I could fire again. Well, I thought, at least I wounded one of the bastards who were keeping me from going home.

Chapter 6

During the night there was a lot of small-arms firing from our lines. Our guys were keyed up and on their toes. We had been told the Germans almost always counterattacked, and that they would probably run some heavy combat patrols during the night. Our engineers had not had a chance to set up traps and wires, and we felt just a little naked. The firing was a good sign, because it meant that everyone was on his toes.

I don't know whether the Germans ran any patrols that night, but none came through. The firing might have kept them away, they might have thought they had been spotted. Or maybe they didn't run any because they were too busy setting up their defenses against what they thought would be a continuing attack from us.

Sunrise promised a beautiful day for February in the mountains of Italy. By this time we were all getting a little tired. We thought the command would let us alternate sleeping a little this morning — that is, let one man stay awake while the other in the foxhole slept — but they had different ideas. We were allowed to heat water for coffee and our C rations for breakfast on a Coleman stove, if we kept it in the bottom of the foxhole. This helped a lot. We all had several packages of coffee, and the hot drink seemed to loosen us up a bit. During the night some poor bastards had got the honor of digging a thirty-foot latrine trench, so we had what passed for the comforts of civilization. Then the order came down to dig our holes deeper, camouflage the dirt, and prepare for a long stay. When we left, another division would replace us. They would hold these positions, and we were to be transferred to another front for a fresh attack that should take us into the Po Valley. It would be our honor to make the breakthrough—a reward for taking the mountain that no one else could take.

We asked Studebaker, our platoon leader, when we would be pulling out. His answer: "When we receive orders."

Later in the day, we received our replacements for the men we had lost during the shelling. Our squad got three men. One was a Kentuckian who had been in the army six weeks. Another was a fellow of thirty-six from Chicago, in bad physical shape, who had been drafted three months ago, right after his mother had died. He had bad feet, high blood pressure, a bad stomach, and a host of other troubles. The third was from the coast artillery, a unit which had been disbanded. He had been stationed in Canada on the Wellington Locks for four years and had had it made—until now.

It was, all in all, a very quiet day. Our mortars and artillery were lining up their targets. We did the digging we were ordered to and camouflaged our holes, ate our fill of good old C rations, and someone even found some wine on a trip back of the lines. It was good and helped us to relax. We all had a little sleep, took off our boots, and spent a comparatively comfortable day. We would at least be better prepared than we had been last night.

Colonel Track, our battalion commander, came around in the afternoon to see how prepared we were in case the Germans decided to pay us a visit in the night. He was quite satisfied with our efforts. Track was not a man who only gave us hell if he found something wrong; he also gave us a little praise and thanked us for a job well done when the occasion called for it. He was a West Point man, but not at all typical. Most of the other West Point men had a bad habit of giving everyone in sight hell—no medals, no praise. The old hands told us about one West Pointer who even raised hell with the men because they didn't have their boots clean while on the line.

During the night, small groups alternated sleeping two hours and being on guard two hours. This gave everyone a chance to get some rest and be a little more alert in the event we were attacked. It began to drizzle at about 0300 hours. It soon got muddy and cold, and we had to stamp our feet to keep them from getting too cold.

I was asleep when dawn broke, and was awakened by the pounding of shells coming into our position. Stutzman was ducking his head everytime he heard the whine of a shell coming in. I got up and looked out. The shelling seemed to be concentrating on our rise. I looked down the slope where the new men had dug in and saw a line stretched across two trees with a blanket and two jackets hanging on the line. They had got wet during the drizzle, and the new men were drying them out! They must have been visible for five miles up on this ridge. I called down to them, "Hey you dumb bastards, get that line down and get the hell back into your hole! Can't you see you're drawing fire?"

The Germans kept up the shelling all day. They caught a lieutenant in the latrine trench, a new man, and he just disappeared. Another shell hit about three feet from a hole down the line, and two men were wounded. We called the medics, who came running immediately. One man was carried off on a litter, and the other was rolled up in a blanket. The medic said he had died of shock. His wound was not bad enough to have killed him—he just died of fright. He was a kid of nineteen, well educated, taken right out of college. I knew that his father was a millionaire from Massachusetts. Money didn't help much on the front line.

Toward evening the shelling began to slow down. The Germans would fire eight or ten rounds every half hour just to keep us off balance, but we knew they had us zeroed in and would keep up the firing all night. It looked like we would all be awake tonight again—they were liable to send in an infantry charge under one of these shellings. Our artillery hadn't located any viable targets as yet because the Germans still had their artillery behind that next ridge. There was a village located at the base of the ridge, and we were sure those houses were full of German infantry just waiting to attack. So our artillery was concentrating on the village.

The shelling kept up, eight or ten rounds every half hour. They were now firing along the whole line, so at least we were not getting the full treatment. But between the artillery and the closeness in the holes, everyone was getting a little edgy. Arguments broke out.

The night grew colder, everyone quieted down, and soon all you could hear was the stamping of feet or a cough now and then. Studebaker came around every hour or so to keep us informed and to make sure we were all alert. Sometimes Levin was with him and sometimes he was by himself. I did not envy him his job; we had some trigger-happy and nervous guys who would shoot first at a figure moving in the dark and ask questions later.

When dawn finally did appear, the order was given to let one man sleep and the other stay on watch. I took the first watch, since I knew I was too keyed up to sleep anyway. Stutzman crawled down into the hole and was asleep in a minute.

Then at about 0600 hours all hell broke loose. The Germans poured everything they must have had on us, and kept it up for half an hour. They were getting some hits, too—you could hear the screams down the line. So far, our squad had been lucky and hadn't taken a hit. They must have been throwing in forty or fifty rounds a minute. I started wondering why they seemed to want this ridge so bad. They didn't have the kind of supplies to keep pounding us like this for long, and it definitely seemed like the prelude to an infantry charge. I awoke Stutzman, who was sleeping like a baby, and told him I thought the Germans would be coming pretty soon and that he should get ready.

While we sat on our rise taking the artillery pounding, our engineers had been busy every night. Between the rises they had mined the passes, wired them, and dug tank traps. If the Germans were coming at us through those passes, they would get quite a surprise. We had our machine guns trained down on them as well as the mortars, and I'm sure the artillery was zeroed in to wide spots in the passes.

I was looking down on the road below us about a half mile away when suddenly I saw three panzers pull off the road into groves of small trees—each one accompanied by at least two squads of German infantry. I called out for Studebaker or Levin, and they both came crawling up. Studebaker issued orders that the riflemen were not to fire until they knew they had a target, that the machine guns and mortars would open up as soon as the attack began. He headed down to our BAR team and told them to open up when the machine guns opened fire. The guys were now nervous and shaking in anticipation. For some of us— including me—this was the first battle, and we didn't know what to expect.

Meanwhile, more German infantry was spotted coming off the road and heading for the groves. This was beginning to look like a regimental attack, with mobile artillery (88s, no less), and it could get a little hairy around here very soon. Over to our right I could hear machine guns start firing, and the dull thud of mortar shells being dispatched, but still no artillery. We had an artillery observer several holes away from us, and I could hear him giving instructions to his pieces behind us. I hoped they could clear the ridge we were sitting on; the valley was deep in front of us and the shells had to be fired very low over our position.

Two more tanks with supporting infantry pulled off the road below, that made five 88s right in front of us. Just one of these guns can do a lot of damage, and now we knew there were at least five there. I wished our artillery would open up, and I hoped and prayed our officers knew what the hell they were doing. I was sure the infantry was climbing up the ridge at that very moment and that the 88s would soon open up to cover their movements.

We sat and we waited. This was the old army game, hurry up and wait. It all depended on those damn German troops. I hoped they were not mountain troops but city boys, but I knew I was wrong. They would be the best the Germans could muster. They had mountain infantry divisions galore, while we had one.

We waited. It seemed the British on our right were catching hell with all the firing going on over there. Machine guns and mortars going full blast, and then rifles starting to pop. Was it possible the Germans were trying to make their breakthrough there? If so, they'd have a sad task ahead of them. These British fight like devils — ask no quarter and give no quarter. Maybe it was a feint to lull us back to sleep, and then the Germans would hit us hard. The 88s had not opened up yet. The artillery hitting us and the British was coming from behind the ridge in front of us and was not 88s, but heavy stuff: 155s or maybe 205s. It started to come in a lot heavier and still our artillery did not answer. I didn't know of any tanks of our own back down on the road. If they had come in during the night, we would have heard them — and anyway, they were no match for the panzers; they were only mounted with 76s which were ineffective unless they were right on the panzers.

The artillery coming in was getting heavier, but we still couldn't see the infantry. For a least three hundred yards ahead of us was open field. The Germans would have to come across that to get to our position, and the only protection they would have across that field would be some rocks and a few tree stumps. Our machine guns, mortars, and even the riflemen should have a field day once they hit that open area. We waited. The firing was ferocious from the British line. They were definitely being hit by infantry—you could hear the grenades now. I thought we should at least give the British some fire with mortars if they were that close. I looked down on the road below and saw Germans all over. They were crossing it to a position in front of ours. I thought, if they're hitting the British like they are, and more troops are crossing that road down there to our front, the attack on the British is a feint.

I looked over to the left where the passes were in front of our second platoon and Company K front. They were now taking heavy shelling. I saw movement—not troops, but movement. I thought that it probably was troops, and maybe some panzers moving through the undergrowth and groves. I began to see what the Germans had in mind: They'd keep attacking the British position, and at the same time move into a large pass with panzers and infantry—the panzers for support, and the infantry would come up into that open field, maybe forty or fifty yards in front of us. After all, the Germans had been in this area for a long time and had plenty of opportunity to plan what they would do if they were knocked off any of these ridges. They probably had plans for every ridge, mountain, and valley between here and Berlin.

I heard the artillery observer giving orders, so I knew he had spotted movement, too. I was sure there was another observer down the line giving his unit instructions, and that when the time came they would open up along the line . . . and the Germans would finally know how it feels to get a few rounds.

All at once the German barrage increased, heavy stuff, and I was sure now the 88s were firing. Man, it felt like the whole ridge was bouncing. And it looked like it was on fire. They were pouring in everything. When this barrage began to lift, the Germans would cross that open field and we had better be ready, because it wouldn't take long for the infantry to be at our throats.

I kept my head up but low; almost all of us were buried in the bottom of our foxholes. I figured if I was going to get it I wanted to see it coming—not be buried before I was dead. I kept my eyes on the pass and that open field. I could see the movement well now; they had to be getting near our mine fields. I was sure they didn't have time to cut a path through, since some of those mines had been laid last night. I saw two panzers moving up close, where the groves were sparse, and they were firing. I wondered where the other three were. Could they be keeping them in reserve? Or were they back down in the heavier part of the grove, waiting to fire on us when their heavy artillery let up to let their infantry through? I saw puffs of smoke in our mine fields and knew some poor German bastards were not with the living anymore. More puffs of smoke. They were deliberately walking into that mine field to make a path! I wondered if they were Polish, Czechs, Italians or what; I knew the Germans wouldn't drive their elite troops into a mine field on purpose. The artillery was still coming in heavy, and those 88s were firing, so I knew we had a few minutes before we would open up with small arms. How did our machine gunners and mortar men feel just sitting there, waiting . . . waiting?

Two of the panzers were out of the grove now and heading into the mine field. I could also see a third panzer sitting at the edge of the grove firing his 88, and I could make out the men moving toward us. They were climbing up to the open field about four hundred yards to the front left of us. The German artillery was beginning to lift, but those 88s were coming in from all angles now. There must have been more than five panzers, the way the 88s were slamming into us.

Studebaker called out, "All right, everyone, get your heads out of the ground. They'll be here in a couple of minutes."

Our mortars opened up across the whole field in front of us and directly on the German troops climbing toward the open field. All at once, five P-47s came out of nowhere and dived down on the grove. They were dropping bombs all over that grove. They seemed to be after the panzers, but they were killing plenty of infantry, too. The 88s let up on us and backed into the grove out of sight of the P-47s, who in turn were making a second run across the grove. The ground shook when the bombs exploded, and I was glad I was up on the ridge. Meanwhile, the mortars kept falling on the Germans. There were several platoons of Germans in the open field now, and more joining them. They were going down at a fast clip and our machine guns had not even opened up yet. I thought about the commander of this impending disaster. Was it his plan, or had he been ordered to do it? If this had been a night attack it would have been successful, for we would never have been able to spot the panzers moving in. We would have heard them, but we could not have seen them. As it turned out, a lot of good German infantrymen died that day because of the stubbornness of a German general. I wondered why I should give a damn. If we killed them here we would not have to kill them up the road, and we'd save a lot of Allied lives.

I heard the bolts on the machine guns clang and they started firing. The Germans were now only 250 yards away and coming like bats out of hell, running all over the field. Some were in squad formation, but mostly they were just running helter skelter. The machine guns cut into them like a reaping machine, but still they kept coming. They were climbing onto the field from the pass by the hundreds now. The planes were strafing—concentrating more on the grove—but the mortars were pouring it into the pass and on the field, I don't think the Germans had any place to go but forward.

Some were getting through the machine-gun fire now, and we received the order to open fire with our rifles, making sure we had a target. The German artillery had all but stopped firing, and it had become a small-arms battle, the heaviest piece firing now being an 81 mortar. Our artillery had not fired one shot, and I still wondered what they were waiting for. It seemed to me that they could have been firing into the grove, into the village, and even on top of that ridge. There had to be observers up there, and maybe even the division officers. Nothing would have made me feel better, after seeing all these infantrymen die, than to see a German general get it in the ass—and a few colonels and majors, too.

I drew a bead on an advancing German and fired. He just fell over and did not move again. Others who had gotten through the machine-gun fire were now falling all over the place. At this rate none would reach our positions. I wondered, *Why the hell don't they go back, or do something? They're just dying out there for nothing. No German commander except a crazy one would put his men through this. We're just too much for them!*

The P-47s left just as soon as another squadron flew in. They dropped their bombs on the groves and strafed. Two of the planes were behind the enemy ridge and came over it toward us, firing all the way. Bullets hit all around us, and we scampered for our holes fast. I didn't like that strafing, but it gave me a small taste of what the Germans were going through, and made it even more of a mystery that they continued to fight.

Finally, some of the Germans closest to us threw down their arms and held their hands aloft, shouting something to us which we could not hear above the noise of the gunfire. The signs were there, though; they were surrendering. Levin jumped out of his hole and waved them up, at the same time telling us, the riflemen, to hold our fire. We were to concentrate on groups farther on down the slope; possibly we could bring in more prisoners.

A group of ten came in with their hands on their heads. Levin called out to McHugh and Worth, two of our newest replacements, to help him get them behind the lines and search them. Once they were back behind a rise there were plenty of hands to do the job.

Meanwhile, two more groups were coming in with their hands up. Most of the Germans were now running helter skelter down the slope, heading for the groves, going back toward the mine fields, fleeing in disarray—something you didn't see the Germans doing very often, at least not up to this point in the war. The machine guns kept firing, and the mortars kept up their pounding until not one live German was in sight. Then the heavy weapons were given the order to cease fire, and our artillery began. Every gun we had within twenty miles must have opened fire, plastering the groves, the village, the top of the ridge. Two more flights of P-47s came in over the groves, and flew on to strafe the village. The Germans were getting back what they had given us tenfold. It looked like the whole ridge was on fire, and the village was fast disappearing. For about a half hour the planes kept dropping their bombs on the groves and the ridge above it. Later, B25s came in and bombed behind the ridge; they must have discovered a big German concentration to bring those planes into this battle.

I was sure the fight was over. It had accomplished nothing but killing men, destroying a lot of equipment, and making one set of generals happy and another set sad. But what else was war?

Studebaker came around to see if we were all right.

We asked him what the casualties were, and he said we had lost five men from the platoon, plus eight wounded so severely that they had to be evacuated. The first squad had only one man killed, a fellow named Scheider from Brooklyn. He had been a replacement, and no one knew too much about him. There were no wounded at all in our squad, so only one replacement would be needed the next time they sent a new batch up. All in all, we took seventy-four Germans prisoner, killed at least three hundred that we could see—and only the Lord knows how many others down in the grove, over in the mine field, and on the slopes leading up to the field. The Germans had found out we could fight.

Chapter 7

The artillery on both sides had finally subsided. I looked at my watch: the attack had started about 0600 hours and it was now almost 1200 hours. I wondered how many of the Germans lying out in front of us were just wounded, not dead. I didn't have to wonder very long. Studebaker and Levin came over and asked me if I would be willing to run a patrol around 1700 hours down among the Germans. If any were alive, the litter bearers would go down and bring them back. The wounded would be sent to our hospitals until they were well enough to be sent to a prisoner-of-war camp (probably in North Africa or even the United States) until the war was over. I thought that was pretty good treatment, and asked Studebaker if the Germans treated our wounded as well. He said they did in some cases, but they didn't get the chance to do this very often now, since they were mostly retreating, while we were advancing.

The British troops had got the worst of the battle on our side. Apparently, the Germans had wanted to take the road that the British were on, in order to get some panzers around behind us. But they'd put up their customary valiant fight, and the Germans ended paying dearly for attempting their plan. After we'd talked to some of them, I started forgiving these incredible soldiers their teatime fires.

I had a funny feeling we were still not done with the Germans at this position, that we would see our boys tonight again. I was also interested in what happened down in that grove. The Germans would pick up their wounded, but they had to leave equipment and panzers there. I was sure that between the planes and the artillery, we must have gotten some of them. I realized there must have been more than the five I had seen. Both the British and us had taken an 88 pounding. There must have been at least ten panzers—and the way our planes were pasting those groves, some must have been lost. Maybe we'd run a patrol down there later tonight and see what was going on.

Since I would be going out on patrol later that afternoon, I had time to get some rest. Stutzman said he would keep alert, but more trouble was not likely during the daylight hours. I snuggled up in my blanket at the bottom of my foxhole and went to sleep.

Stutzman woke me up at 1630 hours. While I was asleep they had brought up lots of hand grenades, M-1 ammunition, C rations, and water. We had so much water now we decided to shave, something we had not done for over a week. I thought I would take a sponge bath, too.

Studebaker showed me the route to take to the field where we were to check for wounded Germans. If any of the dead or wounded had had any maps or papers that looked official we were to bring those back. We were not under any circumstances to go below the rim of the pass, because there were mines close by. There would be four men besides myself—Worth, McHugh, Rodrigues, and Homer. Rodrigues was a real smartass and Studebaker gave him to understand that I was in command of this patrol, even though he was an old hand from the training days in Colorado. Studebaker told him he had a couple of counts against him already, and if he fucked up this patrol he would gladly have him court-martialed when we got off the line. Rodrigues said he would behave.

We headed over to our second platoon, who knew we were coming. We found the beginning of the pass and heard a lot of *good lucks* as we started down. They all promised they'd be watching us and ready to give us covering fire if we needed it.

There was a well-worn path going down the pass, but I told the fellows not to use it—to walk on the grass alongside. There had been Germans there that morning and they could have planted antipersonnel mines. Rodrigues said, "You're nuts, you been reading too many army books. They'd have you walking a foot off the ground if they had their way." He continued to walk on the path, so I told him, "This is the first and last time I'll tell you: Get your ass off that path and walk on the grass, or I put you on report."

He said, "If you get back," and stepped off the path onto the grass.

After we had walked about a hundred yards or so we could see dead Germans down in the mine fields and on the slopes ahead of us. We passed on, and after another seventy-five yards or so, I halted the patrol and walked up the rim so I had a clear sighting on the open field in front of our position. I will say we did a good job of camouflage: I could not pick up our lines by sight, yet I knew they were immediately to our right. I couldn't see a gun, a face, fresh dirt — nothing.

There were bodies all over the place. I didn't see any moving, nor did I hear anything and I was quite sure that they were all dead. I told the other fellows to walk down around them to see if any were alive. It quickly became apparent these Germans had been hit with machine-gun fire, rifle fire, and, judging from some jagged wounds, mortar fire, as well. We found some map cases and other official-looking papers, packed these up and finished our inspection of the bodies. They definitely were all dead.

I looked down the slope toward the groves and could see little fires burning. At first I thought I saw soldiers sitting around fires, but on closer observation I saw it was the end of fires burning vehicles. I saw the long snout of an 88 sticking out and the remains of what had been the trucks. The Germans had not left that grove on their withdrawal; they had left men and materials there preparing to counterattack at the first opportunity, I thought. They had lost at least a regiment's vehicles, plus I don't know how many panzers. I could only see one, but there must have been more. They had really been plastered by the planes. It seemed to me that we should run a patrol into that grove. I didn't think we would find anything alive in there, nor did I think the Germans would counterattack us again in this position. They had paid a heavy price and they knew it. It just would not be worth it to come back at us again, and besides, they were probably in trouble in their own ridge now after the plastering they took from us. They may have moved back again, thinking we were attacking and that their losses would be too great for what the ridge was worth. I thought maybe we should attack, perhaps tomorrow morning. We had the supplies now, and all we needed was a general's permission, possibly the Fifth Army's okay. I would suggest this when we got back to Studebaker; possibly he would take me to Captain Bear for a report on what I had seen. I wanted to see us on that next ridge right away before the Germans had a chance to recover. It would certainly save a lot of lives, both Allied and German.

I called out to the other four men in the patrol in a low voice to fall in at the ledge of the slope, and we'd start back. Rodrigues had four P-38s he had picked up, Homer had found a map case, and the other two hadn't found anything worthwhile. I told Rodrigues to give each of the other three men a P-38 and he said, "Screw you, buster, I can get a hundred dollars for each of these the next time we get back to Florence. You think I'd give any of these bastards any, anyway? What the hell do they know about fighting, anyhow!" I didn't think this was the place to have a fight with him, so we fell in and started up the side of the path. It was tough going. I hadn't realized it was such a high grade when we came down. When we got about fifty yards from where I thought our lines were I called out, "Patrol coming in."

I heard someone call down "Abraham," and I called back "Lincoln. Then we came up one at a time to be recognized.

We returned to our platoon headquarters. Studebaker told the other four guys to go back to their foxholes and get some sleep, just in case the Germans started something later that night. He told me to come in. He had a dugout with a roof on it, with three or four feet of earth thrown over it and then tree limbs for the camouflage. It had room for four or five people. Captain Bear was there, and the radio man, as well as Sergeant Gardner. They asked me to make my report. I tossed down all the map cases and other papers we had brought back, and they started to go through them. Captain Bear, who could read German, said these would have to go back to the regimental S-2. There were some things that he felt someone higher up than a company commander should know about. He said that from what he had seen, we had broken up a concerted effort by the Germans to make a mad dash around back of the mountain to cut off American troops and retake the mountain. This was why they had made the attack on us this morning. They had to get us off the ridge before they could make their move. It suddenly began to make sense to me why so many men were sacrificed for this ridge. As long as we were here the Germans could not get behind the American lines and consequently could not get behind or control the mountain.

It also began to make sense why *we* sacrificed so many men on the mountain. Whoever commanded those heights commanded the whole area and the troop movements for thirty miles in every direction. War at times did make sense—not very often, but at times.

I told them what I had seen in the groves, and they were not surprised. They knew from the explosions that something was going up besides bombs and shells.

They asked me if I had seen any men in the groves and I said no. Captain Bear said he was very happy with the patrol, that we had done a job that was messy and had found out more than we were sent down for. He made me a corporal on the spot. I asked him about the other fellows who had gone down with me. He said that I was in command and I would receive the honors; that is the system, and that's the way it has to be. Another army tradition that did not meet with my standards!

Since we had been on patrol, the five of us were given the privilege of sleeping all night. They said they would awaken us only if trouble seemed imminent. Luckily, there were no troubles, not even much artillery—just enough for us to know that the Germans were still there.

I awoke at dawn, and since it was quiet, I took a walk to the latrine trench and relieved myself. Funny how much better you can go when you're relaxed. Les was back there talking to Levin.

"I heard you made corporal last night," Les said.

"Not only that, that he's the assistant squad leader, too," Levin added. "Schidt is going to company headquarters and Gardner is going to be platoon sergeant. I'm supposed to become platoon guide, which means you'll be the squad leader, probably today."

"That's moving pretty fast—assistant one day and leader the next. I didn't know you could be promoted that quick," I said.

Levin said, "I've seen people wake in the morning a private and go to sleep a lieutenant. In fact, I've seen it twice in the last four weeks."

It was as Levin said. Before long, orders came down

that I had been promoted to staff sergeant, and I was now the leader of the first squad. I was two men short, and would receive replacements when we pulled off the line in the next several days. The scuttlebutt was true, we were to be pulled out and replaced by another unit. It would give us a chance to catch up on our sleep, get a bath, some clean clothes—and a trip or two to Leghorn or Florence. I always liked Lucca, and I was looking forward to seeing it again. Italy had some very beautiful places to see and a lot of art—which was something most of us did not know anything about, though some of us did appreciate it.

We spent a quiet day. Our planes were overhead most of the time, flying around observing. Every once in a while a plane would dive and we would hear his guns firing, usually behind the ridge in front of us, then he would pull up and just continue to watch. I suppose every time the plane dived, some Germans died. I would have liked to be able to feel sorry for them, but I couldn't help thinking that every German those planes killed is one we won't have to kill—or who would not be killing some Allied soldier.

Chapter 8

I was looking down on the village at the foot of the ridge we'd occupied. It was old, thousands of years old, with a castle high on a hill at its center and smaller houses at the base—a typical Italian mountain village. It must have held quite a history. I could imagine it being ruled by an overlord in the middle ages, then a king from a further place, and all the citizens laboring to pay their tithes and taxes. I wondered how many battles had been waged over the centuries in and around this town. And now it was being destroyed again because two armies, neither of which had—probably as usual—anything to do with the townspeople or this land at all had found it a convenient battlefield. The people who lived here were not noblemen, knights, or warriors; they were just people who were trying to keep alive. Many, I am sure, lay dead inside their bombed-out houses or along the rubble-strewn streets; and others had probably taken to the hills, living in caves like animals until these two armies decided to take their fight somewhere else and leave them to the job of living.

My thoughts about the village were not happy ones. I kept thinking, *Well, at least, my own people haven't had to go through something like this.* It wasn't much of a consolation. But I knew that Americans were the luckiest ones in this war.

I was pulled from my thoughts by Studebaker's runner, panting up from behind me as I stood surveying what had once been a busy little village. He said that the lieutenant wanted to see me immediately, very important. I couldn't believe it would be anything more than a briefing on details for pulling off the ridge tonight before the replacements showed up.

When I arrived at the dugout, Levin was there, Captain Bear, Studebaker, and the radio man. They had maps, and as I glanced at them I recognized the area as our own sector. Captain Bear greeted me with, "That promotion I gave you to corporal didn't last long, Sergeant. I wish you the best of luck." Then he continued: "The outfit that is replacing us on the line wants to know more about what's down in that grove of trees below the slope. I don't like to send the same man on two patrols in a row, but you've been down there, Ike. You know how to get there, and you've seen the fires burning from the damage that we did to them. The commander wants to know if the Germans are cleared out, or if they're building up again, possibly for another assault on this line. I'm half asking you if you'll go, and half ordering you to go."

"Well, the quickest way home is through the enemy lines. I'll go. How many men are going with me?"

"I thought we would send five riflemen, a three-man BAR team, and three men armed with Tommy guns and extra grenades in case you have to depart in a hurry."

"In other words, a 'squad heavily armed,' I believe the newspapers would call it."

The captain laughed and said, "Yes, I think that's what they would say."

I studied the map of the sector. The captain advised me that the engineers had planted new mines to replace the old, and marked that area on the map.

I would be leaving as soon as it was dark, and besides one man of Captain Bear's choosing, a Mike Snick, I would choose my man. Snick would act as my assistant patrol leader. The whole inspection shouldn't take more than a few hours, I figured.

For the BAR contingent of the patrol, I chose Les and his team. Stutzman, Carney, Worth, and Rodrigues were my riflemen, and for tommy-gunners, I chose Murray, Reds, and a guy everyone called Brooklyn. It was a well-balanced patrol.

We assembled behind the first platoon dugout at the given hour. Everyone was on edge, some eager to go and others apprehensive. The older ones knew what could happen, and the new men thought they could win some recognition from the patrol. Although I was a newer man, I had been on patrol before, and I just wanted to get started and get it over with. Everyone carried a full complement of ammo, plus five grenades, and the tommy gunners carried ten grenades in addition to six 20-round magazines. We had enough fire power to start a small war—but I was hoping we wouldn't have to, that it would be a routine patrol, and we would find that the Germans had pulled out. Then we could come back and get ready to pull off the line for a much needed rest and a few side trips.

It was not to be.

Chapter 9

It was so dark when we hit the trail that you couldn't see your hand in front of your face. Since I had been down this trail once before, I led the way, with Snick taking the last position in line. I had one tommy-gunner behind me, then the four riflemen, then two more tommy-gunners, with the BAR team bringing up the rear in front of Snick. This lineup would give us the best fire power in the event we had to use it. The engineers had cleared the trail of any personnel mines the Germans had left, so instead of walking on the side, we walked down the trail itself.

When we had gone about four hundred yards, I stopped the patrol and told them to take a break while I scouted the grove. I told Snick that if he heard any gunfire, *not* to come after me, but to take the patrol back up to our lines, and I would do the best I could to get out of the grove myself and back to our lines.

About seventy-five yards below the spot where I had left the patrol the trail turned to the right and followed the bottom of the draw. I kept to the left and hit the edge of the grove. I crouched down behind some bushes to catch my breath and have a look around. It was very dark but my eyes had become accustomed to it, and I could see some trees and bushes up ahead. At first I didn't see it, but then I caught sight of a glow through the bushes. I watched it for maybe five minutes, but couldn't make anything out. Then I saw another glow to the right of the first one, but I just couldn't figure out what they were.

I returned to the patrol cautiously, and when I was within twenty-five yards, I called out very quietly to Snick that I was coming in, not to shoot. The patrol was sitting by the side of the trail. They seemed to be keyed up and ready to go. Rodrigues asked if we were going back. He thought we'd seen enough. I asked him, "What have you seen?"

He answered, "You're the patrol leader. You're supposed to know everything."

I ignored his sarcasm, but filed it in the back of my mind. Someday he and I were going to tangle, and I was sure he would come out on the bottom. I very quietly told them what the plans were: They would follow me down to the edge of the grove, set up a fire zone to cover, and Reds and I would advance into the grove as far as we could to see what was going on.

We went down the trail, turned off to the left and approached the bushes. I put Snick in the middle of the patrol, two riflemen at his right, and a tommy-gunner at his extreme right. The BAR team was next to Snick on the left, then one rifleman, then another rifleman behind the line about ten yards.

I took Reds down about ten yards in front of this line, behind a bush, and told him the situation. I showed him the glows I had seen before, but now I could see three instead of two. Something was definitely going on. I asked Reds if he was nervous, and he said, "You're doggone right I am, but the sooner we get started the sooner we get back to that nice cold muddy stinking foxhole up there."

I started out at a crouch, with Reds about five yards behind me. I would go to a bush and get into a firing position, then Reds would pass me in a crouch and get to the next place behind a bush or tree where he could set up in a firing position.

One thing was missing, and I couldn't figure out what it was. Then it came to me. There were no bodies, no smell of the dead. That meant that either the planes were bombing nothing, or the bodies had been picked up by the Germans. Bodies were still lying on the plain in front of our position. As far as I could see, the last time I looked they had not been touched — and that was shortly before we left on this patrol. But down here there were no bodies. I cursed the dark. At least if it were lighter we would be able to see if the grass was worn down, see blood spots where they had been hit, fallen and died.

I had moved up behind a large tree about thirty yards from the glow. I motioned to Reds to sit tight, not to move. I peered around the tree at the glow, and it began to show a shape. All at once I could see what it was — a large heavy tent, erected over something — either a truck or a panzer . . . Sure, it was a panzer! The Germans were rebuilding the panzers that had been knocked out in the bombing and artillery fire during the attack.

I crept up on all fours, my belly flat to the ground, my carbine cradled in my arms. I just had to have a better look. I was only about five yards away from the first glow now, and I could hear Germans talking very low. I could see them moving from one tent to

74

another. There were four that I could make out now, so apparently they were working on four vehicles, probably all panzers.

I had to see more, but I also had to leave word with Reds. I crawled back to him, told him what was going on, and that I had to see more. The Germans didn't know we were down here, so as long as we didn't get caught, maybe I could pick up some more information that would be useful to the new troops coming in to replace us. Reds said he would go this trip and let me rest, but I said no, I knew the layout and he'd have to learn it. I would go, and if anything happened, if there was shooting or I called out, he was to take off for the patrol and tell Snick to get them back to our lines with the information he had. "Don't worry about me, I'll get back myself." We shook hands, and he took up a firing position as I crawled back toward the glows.

I returned to the spot I'd been, about five yards from the first glowing tent. I decided I wanted to see behind that canvas, so I crept up to it, and very carefully lifted the bottom about one inch from the ground. Six Germans were working on a Tiger. They had what appeared to be tape on their wrenches, which was why we had not heard them. They were eviscerating the panzer, taking everything usable from it and carrying it to another tent, where I figured they were rebuilding another one. The 88 on this panzer had been damaged beyond use, but they were taking the treads, armor plating, machine guns, and several of the men were working on the engine.

My hand automatically went toward my grenades, but I realized how foolhardy it would be to throw one.

I wouldn't have been able to get them all; I would have surely been killed myself, and possibly some of the patrol wouldn't get back either.

I decided to try to get behind the glows to see if there were any infantry units dug in. I couldn't believe they would just send engineers down here to repair panzers and not have them covered. There could be a company of infantry lying up above, watching for any intruders.

I had gone thirty or forty yards in a crouch, making my way from tree to tree, bush to bush, staying at each position for thirty or forty seconds to listen and observe as much as I could. I was lying behind a bush to get my bearings, when suddenly I heard voices nearby. They were very close to me, not more than fifteen or twenty feet away, straight ahead. They seemed to be arguing about something, and were fairly mad at each other. I can understand some German, and I tried to listen, thinking I could pick up something of value. I picked up the word *paper*, and *shit*, then *asshole*, and *stinking pig*, but I couldn't put them together. I was about to turn back, figuring I had gotten all the information I could. I still did not know how big the unit was, but I did know there definitely were infantrymen as well as engineers here. Just at that moment I heard a thud, and I could vaguely see someone moving to my left. I froze. A German soldier walked within five feet of me, stepped into a hole about twenty feet below me, pulled down his pants and squatted. I waited, thinking, *Isn't this bastard ever going to wipe and get back to his foxhole?*

I decided to start back to Reds and the rest of the patrol. To this day I do not know if I hit a trip wire or the Germans heard something, but a flare went up and lit the whole area. I looked in the direction of the patrol and could see some of them stand up and then dive for cover. If I could see them, I realized the Germans could see them, too.

They did.

They cut loose with burp guns, rifles, and small mortars. The squatting German saw me at about the same time, and I pulled the trigger on my carbine twice. He never knew what hit him. He not only died with his boots on, he died with his pants down. I crouched low and moved from tree to tree as fast as I thought was safe. Apparently, the other Germans had not seen me yet. I got back to Reds as the flare was burning out, told him we'd better get back to the patrol before they put up another flare. We raced up the hill, hit the trail, and ran headlong up to the spot where the patrol was supposed to be. I hoped they had taken off for our lines, but I suspected they had hit the dirt when the firing began and were still there. I was right. Reds and I both called out that it was us coming in, not to fire.

Snick was lying near the trail, bleeding from a hip wound, but he was still conscious. I told everyone to start up the trail, and to remember the password, Thomas Edison, when they were challenged.

With all the excitement—bullets flying and now and then a mortar going off—I could not see how many went up the trail. Reds and Stutzman carried Snick, whose arms were around their shoulders. I was there alone, so I decided to look around a bit to see if anyone had frozen and was still there. I found Murray, with half his head gone; Carney lying beside him holding his stomach, definitely dead; and I found one of Les's ammo carriers lying there dead, but didn't feel any blood on him. He must have been killed by the concussion of a mortar shell. I couldn't find anyone else, so I headed up the trail with bullets buzzing past me, expecting one in my back at any moment.

When I neared our lines I slowed up until I heard someone call out "Thomas!"

I answered real fast, "Edison!" I was told to advance and be recognized.

The lieutentant of the second platoon was there to greet me and tell me we did a great job. I heard him call on his walkie-talkie to go ahead. The whole line opened up—mortars, machine guns, artillery—right down into that grove where we had been fifteen minutes before. I asked the lieutenant, "Do they know what they're firing at? I haven't made a report yet."

He said Sergeant Snick told them what I had told Reds to tell them. "The whole line was zeroed in on that spot anyway, but we couldn't fire until we knew everyone was out of there—and from what I've heard about you, I knew you'd be the last man back up here."

The artillery was blasting away at the grove. I took a good look down there, thinking, *This should discourage them from coming into the grove again.* They'd have to give up all the equipment down there, and it would become just so much junk for some Italians to find and turn into something useful later on.

I reported back down to Lieutenant Studebaker's dugout. Captain Bear was there as well as the lieutenant. They said they had already debriefed the other members of the patrol and sent them back to their foxholes, and now they wanted my report.

I gave it to them, adding that it was probably my fault that the flare went up. "I don't know if I tripped a wire or the Germans heard something that made them suspicious." I told them that I believed the enemy was dug in at the right in the grove, and showed them on the map where I suspected the enemy to be. I asked for permission to go down later with litter bearers to bring back the bodies I'd left behind. I hadn't even gotten their dogtags nor their personal papers they might have been carrying. But Captain Bear said, "No, we'll be pulling out of here tomorrow night and the new outfit will be coming in. Graves Registration will be here soon and they'll take care of the bodies. You did all right. Anyone would have done the same under the circumstances. You identified them, and for the time being that's good enough. Their families will get a missing-in-action telegram until their bodies are recovered, and then they'll be notified they were killed in action. That's the best you or I can do."

I went back to my foxhole. Stutzman was already sleeping, taking up most of the space. I knew he was tired, and relieved to be back. It had been his first patrol fire fight and he had seen death. The best way to get this off your mind is to sleep it off. I crawled down into the hole, trying not to awaken him. I found a place I could sit up in and fell fast asleep.

Chapter 10

I was awakened before dawn by Lieutenant Studebaker's runner, calling me to a strategy session in his dugout. Squeezed into the place were the lieutenants of the three other platoons, as well as the captain.

Bear was to the point. Command had sent down orders in the night that they wanted to know more about what was going on in that grove, how much damage we'd inflicted on it. They wanted to run the Germans out of that position for good, and since the replacement outfit coming in hadn't much experience, they wanted us to do it. And Company L was picked to do the job.

He briefed us on the positions of Companies K and M, who would be moving in to take new positions as we moved into the grove. My platoon would lead off down the ridge, the third platoon would be held in reserve. The heavy-weapons platoon would follow mine.

We were given our positions—where to move our artillery and arms—and while we studied the maps and the captain's markers, he told us to have our men ready to move at 0800.

I returned to my foxhole, woke up Stutzman, and

briefly told him what was up. We moaned for a few minutes over our fate—no time off for a while, after all. No Florence, no Pisa, no tangy Italian wine until this damned grove had been taken care of.

At 0715 Company K's platoon moved into our area, and our platoon moved over behind our own second platoon and lay on the grass behind a rise. It could have been a glorious day. It was sunny, warm, quiet. No artillery was exploding from either side. I hadn't had much rest, what with last night's patrol and the early awakening this morning. I could have slept a week just lying there in the grass. The lieutenant shook me out of my dreams with, "Saddle up and be ready to move." I got my squad ready to go—what was left of it. I would again be my own scout, and I had designated Reds assistant squad leader. He would bring up the rear and could replace me in case I didn't make it.

At 0740 hours our artillery opened fire. They plastered the grove, and the big stuff opened up on the ridge and on the village itself. I had never seen anything like it before. That ridge was rocking, and it looked like the whole thing was on fire. If the Germans hadn't figured out that an attack was coming, they must be dead above the necks. After this barrage, I was sure there would be some Germans knocking at the gates of Heaven, asking to come in.

The barrage kept up until 0755 hours, when everything went quiet. No German artillery returned our fire. I was pretty sure they were waiting until the attack began to pour everything they had on us. I was hoping the planes would show up and do some bombing behind the ridge, and that we would open up again with our big stuff when we started to move. At least that should pin some of them down to the point where we could slip through and get behind some bushes and trees before they realized we had moved in on them.

At 0800 hours the artillery started again, the light stuff into the grove and the heavy stuff on the ridge. Lieutenant Studebaker gave the command to move, and I started down that trail for the third time. It looked different in the daytime. I saw rises, rocks, and ditches that I had not noticed before. I thought they would be good cover for our heavy-weapons platoon. The artillery kept landing on the grove as we moved down the trail. I reached the bend in the trail and turned off to the left, followed by my squad and then the second squad and the third.

Lieutenant Studebaker called me back and asked me about what lay ahead. I told him where I thought the tents were, and pointed up above where I suspected the infantry was dug in. We lay there for quite a while, just looking over the terrain. It actually looked new to me, too, for I had seen it up close only at night. I could not see the tents anywhere, but I knew they were there. No shots rang out, so either the infantry was not there today, or they were lying in their holes, waiting for the artillery to lift. I suspected the latter. I looked back and saw Captain Bear about fifty yards behind us. He was waving the third platoon over to the left of us. He had said he might use them for a flanking movement, and was apparently moving them into position in the event he decided to do so.

The artillery began to fire toward the rise where I had seen the infantry the night before. The 50-caliber machine guns of the heavy weapons platoon began firing, then came the command from the captain, "Move out!"

Our platoon started to move from bush to bush, tree to tree. As we moved out of our positions, the second platoon started to move to our right. I prayed the Germans did not send in mortar shells now, or we'd all be dead.

All at once, we received fire from a thicket ahead, burp guns and rifle fire. I realized the thicket was the well-camouflaged tent, and that the engineers were probably firing. The second was receiving fire from another thicket and was firing back. I realized that if the engineers were still here, the infantry had to be, too, and I called this back to Studebaker, who was urging the platoon to move on the thickets. Captain Bear was quite a ways back now, so Studebaker raised him on his walkie-talkie and told him my thoughts. The captain said he would commit the third platoon in the flanking movement to the left and that we were to keep up a steady fire-and-movement pattern as best we could. He also said he was ordering our heavy weapons to open up with 60s and the Company M platoon with 81s on the infantry position. He said, "By all means quiet the engineers as quickly as possible. Don't worry about taking prisoners unless they want to surrender peacefully. Just move the best you can, and stop before that rise where we think the infantry is. We'll take them with all three platoons when everyone's in position."

I could see the third platoon moving in Indian fashion to the left of us. There wasn't too much cover where they were moving, and I thought that if I could see them, the Germans on the rise above us could see them, too.

We were moving toward the thicket, firing as we went. The firing from there was beginning to wane now. Either the German engineers were pulling out or we had killed most of them. When we were within twenty-five yards of the thicket, I told my squad we would make one rush to it and finish the job.

I gave the signal. It was a long twenty-five yards, but we received very little fire, and it didn't seem to be coming from the thicket but from somewhere higher—probably from the infantry on the rise, though I knew they had to be firing blind since they couldn't see us.

We hit the thicket and tore into the tent, firing as we moved. It was unnecessary. There were four dead Germans lying on the ground and one on top of the panzer.

While we were busy taking the tent, the second squad was taking another. There were at least two more camouflaged tents, and we concentrated on them. The small-arms fire had all but ceased. My squad seemed to be in good spirits and ready to go again. They could see the power they had, and they knew they could do the job. It's a great feeling when you find out the enemy is not invincible. They were not the supermen that we were led to believe they were, just flesh and blood, dying just like we did—and wanting to live and go home just like we did.

The next thicket was about thirty to forty yards up ahead. I could not see Studebaker, so I ordered my squad to attack. They rose and rushed forward, reaching the thicket as one man. We fired into it, cut the canvas, and entered firing. There was no one there. The Germans had all fled, probably up to the rise to the infantry.

I immediately ordered the squad to spread out and find cover. I was sure we were now in the line of sight of the infantry, and that they would start firing at any moment. Studebaker came up and said the second platoon had taken the fourth thicket and were ready for the frontal attack we would make on the infantry position as soon as we got the order from Captain Bear. He said the second and third squads of the first platoon were deployed to our right and that the first squad would be in touch with the third platoon who was deployed on the left flank, also awaiting the captain's order. We were to be ready to kick off as soon as it came.

The artillery opened up on the village again, really pouring it in. Our machine guns and mortars were quiet now. We were so close to the village that every time a shell hit we could feel the vibration from it.

I saw a movement over to my left about twenty yards away. I was about to let go with a grenade, when I recognized a face from the third platoon. They were now in position for the attack. They would come in from the left while the first and second platoon made a frontal attack. The command from Captain Bear should come shortly. The artillery barrage was to keep as many German gun crews pinned down as possible.

Studebaker was about ten yards behind me. I could hear Captain Bear's voice on the walkie-talkie, but I could not make out what he was saying. Then our machine guns opened up, both the 30 and 50 caliber, and the mortars, both the 60s and the 81s, started throwing their messages of death.

I looked up at the rise where the German infantry was dug in, but could not see it for smoke and dust. Our mortars were landing smack dab where we'd figured their position. Germans had to be dying up there, but then, I thought, Germans have a funny way of surviving these things. They know how to dig fox-holes, how to cover them up so shells would practically bounce off them, and then they'd come out and fight like tigers.

The order came. We were to advance from bush to bush until we ran out of cover, then in no less than squad strength attack up the rise on the open ground and take the German infantry position, killing everyone unless they wanted to surrender, not taking any chances. It all boiled down to *kill or be killed.*

When we had advanced about sixty yards, we began to run out of cover. I told Al to set up his BAR and keep one man. With the other seven still left in my squad, I prepared to set out across about fifty or sixty yards in the open, up a slope of about thirty degrees. Our machine guns and mortars were still laying it on, and I told Al not to fire unless they stopped and he had a target.

The third platoon was to our left and above the rise. They weren't drawing any fire, and they were already out in the open! I couldn't believe it! They could be seen from everywhere. Maybe the Germans were concentrating on us in the frontal attack and not thinking they could be attacked from their right. Our artillery was still coming in on the village and the surrounding area hot and heavy.

With the BAR team set up I gave the order to move at a fast walk. We had plenty of grenades, but we had to get within throwing distance before we could use them. I had told my squad not to fire until the Germans did. There was a possibility they had not yet seen us, and we could get that much closer before the firing started. As we emerged from cover, the second and third squads came out of their cover also. I glanced over to the right and saw the second platoon coming out of the cover, too. That meant we had all three rifle platoons on the move and attacking, nothing in reserve. This doesn't happen too often, but there are times when it's necessary and I felt the captain was right in committing his whole rifle command.

We were within forty yards of the German position, and the mortars stopped. The machine guns were still firing, but I knew the Germans had to know we were coming now, even if they were in the bottom of their holes. Heads would be popping up soon and the firing would begin.

We were only twenty-five yards away now. The captain had ordered our heavy-weapons platoon to advance to the bottom of the rise and set up to cover us. That meant that we were only being covered by the 50 caliber and 81s of Company M's heavy-weapons platoon.

Twenty yards to go, and we were within grenade distance. I ordered everyone to throw one, then to get up and rush the distance, firing on the move. The 50 caliber stopped firing, and we were on our own.

We hit the German line at the same time the second and third squads did. These weren't foxholes—they were bunkers. The grenades we'd thrown had exploded with no damage to the enemy. Firing from the bunkers finally began. We were firing back as best we could, but we had a lot of men going down. I ordered my squad to toss grenades through any opening they could find, and it seemed to work. We cleared the first line, tore into the back of the bunkers, and killed Germans left and right.

The third platoon, who had attacked above us, were firing down into the back of the bunkers, and the Germans were being sprayed with fire from all sides now. The second platoon had gained the second line of bunkers, and the Germans were beginning to pull out. They never had a chance. No mercy was shown them.

One thing I was worried about now was the German platoon who'd be in a covering position. Wherever it was, they had not opened up. Since the village was right behind here, I figured their position was in the village.

We had reached the last of the bunkers, and my squad seemed to be intact. I ordered Al to bring his BAR up and place it covering the village. We were getting some mortar fire now from behind the village and the surrounding ridge, so I felt a counterattack was imminent. Studebaker told us to round up any wounded and prisoners who might still be in the bunkers and take them back to the edge of the cover, where a platoon of Company I who had come down for the purpose would take them off our hands. We took more than seventy Germans prisoners, about half of them wounded, and four of them officers, one a major. I did not lose a man, but the platoon had fairly heavy casualties: seven killed, nine wounded. However we probably broke up an operation that would have cost a lot more lives if it had been permitted to continue.

I had my squad get into the German bunkers since the mortar fire was getting heavier, and the other squads did the same. The third platoon, who had attacked down from the right, was now taking over the bunkers at that end of the line, and the second platoon was taking over the bunkers on the other side, leaving us in the middle. I had taken a pair of field glasses from a German officer, and, looking toward the village, I could see nothing moving. The village was very badly torn apart, but the old buildings had thick walls and deep cellars and Germans could have been hiding there very easily. Up on the ridge, things seemed quiet, but I knew those bastards were there watching us, getting ready either to attack us or be attacked.

My guess wasn't far off. Later, after Colonel Track had come up and consulted with Captain Bear, I learned that the interrogations of the prisoners had proved fruitful. They'd told them that there was at least a brigade of panzers somewhere behind the village, so well back and camouflaged that our planes and heavy artillery hadn't even touched them. Bear said that the colonel wanted us to run another operation back there, much as he hated the idea of us having to do it. "We've been promising you guys a break for a week now," he said, "but I'm sure no one would want to go off now only to come back and have to do the whole thing over again. Anyway, it does mean that we're not going off the line tonight under any circumstances."

The decision would still have to come down from Regiment Command, but it looked like pretty good odds that we weren't finished with our friends down there yet.

Colonel Track had brought along a demolition team to blow up the panzers in the grove once and for all. The ground rattled and shook when the explosions went off. Then, when it was all finished the colonel took his engineers back to our old lines while we dug into the German bunkers. The German mortars were still coming in, but at a slower pace. Our 81s were hitting the village behind their position, and the 60s were concentrating on the village itself.

At 1300 hours, Captain Bear called all the platoon leaders back to his bunker where he'd set up a forward command post. Most of us were sitting around opening C-rations and eating or just relaxing. One thing we all agreed about—the Germans sure knew how to make a place comfortable as well as protective. We figured that we would get orders to pull back to our lines when the platoon leaders came back, so we could get ready to pull out for that long-awaited rest. I just hoped we wouldn't have too many casualties when we pulled back. I was feeling good. My squad didn't even have one skinned finger among them.

Les was over behind a bunker, eating out of a can of C rations. He was now the assistant squad leader. His squad had only five men left. They had run right into M-34 fire. He told me that the platoon from Company I had picked up all the wounded after they had taken the prisoners back, and were now picking up the dead. He said they also picked up the three fellows we had lost on the patrol the other night, which made me feel better.

When Lieutenant Studebaker came back from the officers' meeting, he wasn't looking at all happy. He called the squad leaders back to his bunker and gave us the bad news. The final word had come down from Regiment Command, and we definitely would not be pulled off the line tonight. The brass were thinking of putting another company down here tonight and possibly kicking off from here, taking the ridge ahead of us so the whole division could move up. "And we still have to wait for the word from Colonel Track as to what our next move will be."

I went back to my squad and told the guys what the brass had in store for them. They were numb. They didn't say anything, just sat there and looked at me, but their eyes said, "Hey, you lying fucking bastard, why the hell don't you tell us the goddamn truth just once?"

It was 1600 hours. The men had made themselves as comfortable as possible. The bunkers' defenses now faced three sides. We were sure we were surrounded: the village in front, the ridge on our right, and the Lord knows what on the slope to our left.

I hadn't seen Levin or Gardner all afternoon. They had been with the lieutenant during the attack, but had since disappeared.

Chapter 11

We were getting ready for the damnedest fight we'd ever been in. If our hastily composed strategy worked, we could be out of these hills soon and on our way across the Po Valley, into the Alps. We expected a German attack tonight, and we should go after them in the morning. By 1800 hours, I had met with Studebaker again and got the word on the plans. Reds and the other mule skinners were already behind the line. They'd been coming and going with supplies for hours, and we were well stocked with water, rations and ammo. The mystery of where Levin and Gardner had gone was solved when I learned that they were manning bazookas on our left. Company M would be sending up more rockets later, and one platoon from M had dug in at the edge of the cover. Company I and Company K were with us, and it looked like we had all flanks covered. It meant that the whole damned battalion was ready for the German attack.

There had been mortar fire from the Germans all afternoon, but it was light, and from the pattern of fire, I was able to tell that they were just setting up for the night. Their attack wouldn't come until around midnight. One thing about the Germans, they were consistent with their strategies. I'd also learned from my recent experiences with them that they probably wouldn't be bringing in panzers if they attacked at night; for some reason, they never used machines after the sun went down.

The moon was about half full tonight. At least there would be some light before we had to use our flares. It was about 2000 hours when the guard on duty came down into the bunker to wake me up. I'd caught about two hours' sleep since my meeting with Studebaker and felt as if I'd been snoozing for a week. Ready for action. It was time for a last check-in at Studebaker's bunker, and as I made my way over there, I could hear the men from Company M who'd been digging in at the edge of cover yelling obscenities toward the Germans, and getting their curses returned with a few mortars. Fortunately, the Germans were far wide of the mark.

The orders were steady. Colonel Track and Captain Bear were in with Studebaker, and before I'd been able to ask if there were any changes in orders, the colonel told me that I'd be up for two medals, the Bronze and the Silver Stars. "If you hadn't handled that patrol so well, we'd still be back there on the old line," he said.

"Yeah, well," I chuckled, hearing the heavier German mortars, "maybe next time I'll keep my mouth shut." A shell exploded nearby, probably a hundred yards or so from the front of our line.

Before I ducked out, the colonel added that the men who had been on that patrol with me would all be up for medals, too. "Tell 'em," he said, "before the fighting begins again."

I brought supplies of K-Rations back for the squad;

they're lighter, easier to pack, and it looked like we'd be doing some moving around tonight. We sat tight in our bunker, listening to the shells explode. The German mortars had increased in the past hour. At about 2230 Reds hailed us and slipped into the bunker. His mule-skinning job was finished, and he'd be in on the fight. "Christ," he sighed, "those were some rough hauls. They're shooting at anything that moves out there. Damned near lost a mule."

"And that'd just about break your heart, wouldn't it?"

The other men started to rib Reds about his mules, until he shut them all up. "Hey, you oughtta see the new troops back there at our old line," he said. "Just finished moving in. Never saw so many scared people in the same place at one time! And you should see their uniforms. Still got the creases in 'em. Think I even saw a few neckties back there."

"What's a necktie, Daddy?" one of the men in the back asked.

Reds answered with his usual half-curse, then started spilling some of the scuttlebutt that he'd heard on his supply trips. A whole division was just a couple of miles behind our line, and as we moved up, company by company, battalion by battalion, this outfit would replace ours. But it wasn't a combat outfit—all they'd ever been used for was guard duty or spit-and-polish parades in Italy. Apparently, they'd been tried in battle several times—"dinky little street-fighting battles, not like this," Red said—and they couldn't fight; they'd take off and run, and their officers couldn't do a thing about it. "Lotta leg wounds in that division," Red said, "and you can bet they're not from

German bullets, either, but the U.S. officer-issued .45s!" That kind of thing happened; better to have one of your men up in hospital with a bullet in his leg than up for capital punishment for desertion.

By 2340 hours, the mortars were coming in more heavily, and the Germans had opened up with artillery on our old lines. I heard the explosion of some 88s, and thought, *Damn, they're going to use those tanks after all.* I breathed a silent thanks for Levin and Gardner and the others nearby with bazookas.

All at once two flares went up one to our left and one to our right, lighting up the whole area in front of the village, the slope where we thought the tanks would come through, if they did at all, and part of the ridge to the right of the village.

The sight was enough to make your blood run cold. It seemed that for several seconds nothing moved—the world just stopped turning and everything on it was frozen. Then more flares went up. I fired mine, and at the same time saw Germans in all directions. The closest ones were within seventy yards of us.

The line exploded, machine guns opened up, rifle fire, mortars, and more flares. The German mortars were still coming in on us, and their infantry was advancing, but dropping like flies.

More flares went up and still the Germans came. We were killing them further back now. The first ones had been sixty to seventy yards away; now the closest were eighty to ninety yards away—and still they kept coming.

It was like daylight with all the flares bursting. The German mortars were doing some damage down to the right of us. They had got past the bunkers and had hit the foxholes Company I had dug. I could hear guys screaming, and the cry, "Medic!"

Our whole platoon was firing. Gardner and Levin had brought along some grenade launchers and were using these very effectively.

The German soldiers were bunched together so closely that every time one of our mortars or a grenade was lobbed at them, three or four men would be out of action. Most European armies fight that way—with the idea of increasing the fire-power of their foot soldiers. The method does have its drawbacks, obviously. Americans are the opposite; foot soldiers scatter, stay more widely apart. Much better defensive formation.

There were dead and dying Germans everywhere now, but others kept on coming, pouring out like I'd never seen before. They sure wanted this position back—or else they wanted to make sure we didn't attack tomorrow morning. They must already have committed a regiment, it looked like their casualties were practically a hundred percent, yet they were still sending men in. Our riflemen were taking careful aim, only firing at sure targets, and we didn't miss. Just among the three of us in this bunker we had downed twenty-six German soldiers in the first few minutes of the attack.

Studebaker came rushing up to our bunker. He said he had just had a conversation with Captain Bear. The Germans had broken through the lines over to our right. They had killed a lot of men in Company K, and he had to send a couple of squads from the second platoon over to help them. We seemed to have contained the Germans, but part of the line was still being hit pretty heavily.

"Just keep firing," he said. Without another word he took off. And we just kept on firing. I couldn't get out of the bunker to see if the rest of the squad was okay, but I did call down the line. Reports came back that we were doing very well. Only one casualty was reported, and everyone had plenty of ammo and a good field of fire with plenty of targets.

I couldn't believe how many men the Germans wasted. The flares kept the battle well lit, and between our mortars, machine guns, and the riflemen, the Germans were definitely being rolled back. They had stopped pouring out of the village now and the only ones you could see to the right were trying to get back to the ridge and under cover. We were beginning to think the battle was over, when we heard a distant roar of engines to our left front. More flares went up, and sure enough over the rise in the slope the panzers came rumbling, big ugly Tigers, with their 88's held high. They were about 200 or 250 yards away.

I hollered over to Levin and Gardner that panzers were coming, and they hollered back that they'd seen them and had four bazookas ready to fire just as soon as they came into range.

When the panzers made their appearance, the infantry poured out of the village again. They seemed to be concentrating on our position. They had found it too tough on the right side, and now with the help of the panzers they were going to try a breakthrough on the left side of the line. Enemy mortars were shelling us like the end of the world was coming. The panzers were now within a hundred yards, and I wondered when Levin was going to open up. They were coming at us two abreast, their 88s poised for point-blank fire into the bunkers. If they fired now we'd all be dead.

Just as I was giving up hope that the bazookas would ever open up, four of them fired at the same time. The first two panzers stopped in their tracks, completely engulfed in flames. I never saw their crews leave — if they hadn't been killed by the blast, they were roasting alive. The next two panzers opened up with their 88s but, obstructed by the two burning ones, they fired high and hit 'way back of us.

More flares went up, and I saw several people leave the bunkers where Levin and Gardner were holding up. They had bazookas and were running forward, apparently to get a clear shot at the next two panzers. I saw them disappear behind a rise. I didn't know if they'd been hit or just crawled behind something. The next time I looked, they were within twenty-five yards of the two tanks. I was sure that if we could see them, so could the German infantry, but they held their ground, set up, and fired. Two more German Tigers went up in flames. I saw the four guys scramble back to their bunker. One seemed to be limping.

They'd knocked out four panzers and effectively blocked the slope so no more tanks could come over that route.

In the meantime, our machine guns, mortars, and rifles had been doing a job on the advancing infantry. When they saw that their tanks had been stopped, they began to lose their bellies for fighting. They knew as well as we did that the fight was over and they'd lost. They began pulling back, but we didn't relent. Everyone on the line was firing now, and the Germans were going down on the retreat. They were running all over the place, and many a German soldier died that night because he'd lost his leader. At least you could take most American soldiers and put them in the same situation and they can figure out how to keep alive. I suppose that's the difference between living in freedom and living under fascism.

Studebaker called up to us, "No more flares. The mortars'll keep the area lit up."

I could hear the same word being relayed along the line by the other platoon leaders.

It began to grow dark. Everyone was still alert, finger on the trigger, and would stay that way all night. No more sleep for us! Now we could begin to think about tomorrow, when our turn would come to leave the bunkers and advance on the Germans. They'd lost a lot of men this night and they had to be shaken, but they were good defenders and would fight to the death.

The German mortars began to let up now, but the burning panzers gave enough light for us to see if the Germans came again. Every once in a while the mortars lobbied flares, so a small chance remained that they would sneak up on us in another attack.

When he was reasonably sure things had quieted for the night, Studebaker called all the squad leaders back to his bunker. He was almost grinning. "I have good news to pass out to you guys for a change," he said. "We're not making the attack tomorrow. Colonel Track just notified the captain, that from what the brass saw tonight, it'll take more than our battered battalion to take the village and the ridge, so we'll be passed sometime in the morning by the first and second battalions. We're to stay where we are. They'll make the attack, and we're to back them up if things get too hot. Otherwise we just stay and rest."

Dawn was beginning to break when I hurried back to our bunker, to tell the squad the good news. The guys were still pretty shaken from the battle, tense and half expecting another attack from the Germans. As I told the news to the bunker, the fellows didn't show much emotion. One guy said, "So some other mud slinger has to take the beating tomorrow while we sit here and worry."

It wasn't long before the casualty reports started coming in. My squad was lucky again; no one killed, only one wounded. In fact, our whole platoon had very light casualties, just several wounded and none bad enough to be taken off the line. But the second platoon was in bad shape. They'd gone down to help Company K when the Germans hit there, and had taken heavy hits, fourteen killed and nine wounded. Company K and Company I were chewed up pretty badly, too. A couple of their squads had been wiped out. Many officers were lost, including the captain of Company K. But we had held the Germans.

I still could not figure out why they had fought so hard for this area. Their casualties were absurdly high—surely, more than half, and they had gained nothing. They usually don't take casualties like that for no purpose. There had to be a reason.

Chapter 12

It was dawn, and the scene in front of us was one of pure horror. Germans lay everywhere, piled on top of each other, strewn where they had fallen. Many had their trigger fingers set on their rifles ready to fire, and here and there a bayonetted rifle pointed toward the sky like an empty flagpole. I could see what our job would be when the other two battalions moved up: we'd be carrying dead Germans for days. Later, when the count was taken, we learned that there were over four hundred dead Germans lying in front of our area alone. In all they'd lost almost a whole regiment, plus the four panzers that Levin and Gardner had knocked out.

It was quiet, not a shell coming in or going out. The sun was just peeking over the ridge when I looked at my watch: 0530 hours. The other two battalions were massed in back of us, behind our old line.

There wasn't much for us to do now but keep our eyes open, in case the Germans did attack again. I wondered how many of the enemy soldiers out there were still alive. No one made a move in that direction. It seemed to me the Germans should make an effort to get a truce declared so their medics could come down and take the wounded away. But I realized that our side might not honor a truce at this time. After all, the battle was still in progress, and I don't think either side was ready to call it quits. Well, we had to fend for ourselves, and the Germans had to fend for themselves. It's a hell'uva comment on the brotherhood of man, but that's the way it is in war: You come first and to hell with everyone else. It's drilled into you from the day you land in the army, and after a while it becomes second nature to think that way.

I stayed on guard with one other man and let the rest of the squad take a well-deserved break. We had plenty of food and water, and it was so quiet you could hear a pin drop. Everyone seemed to relax, and with the relaxation came weariness. We hadn't had any sleep in well over twenty-four hours, and in that time had gone through what most men do not experience in a lifetime. We were tough men now, and could face anything we had to, including death. And I knew, looking into the faces of some of the men, death seemed to be welcome.

By 0700 hours I was beginning to get edgy. We hadn't seen any movement behind us to indicate that the two battalions were moving up. The sun was quite high now, the ridge was bathed in light, and the Germans no longer had the advantage of the sun at their backs. I couldn't figure out why our attack hadn't come, so I decided to go and ask Studebaker if he knew anything. I awakened one of the other fellows and asked him to stand guard while I went back to the platoon bunker.

Levin and Gardner were sleeping, and Studebaker was sitting in a corner eating C rations. He had a Coleman stove going with some hot water on it. He handed me a tin of hot coffee.

"Lieutenant," I said, "it's way after 0700 hours now and nothing's happening, not even a barrage. When is this miracle going to happen, when we become rear-echelon troops?"

He said, "You know as much about it as I do, and I doubt if even the Captain knows any more than us. Haven't seen the colonel around since the fighting. He's probably back at regimental headquarters now, getting the word. So just keep your Hoosier pants on, Ike. Go back to your bunker and get some sleep." I could see that he was exhausted, trying to stay up with the coffee. My own edginess, I realized as I made my way back to my bunker, came more from exhaustion than anything else.

Most of my squad was in the same condition. Too keyed up—too tired—to sleep. Not unusual after the kind of fight we'd just been through. I talked with the men. Some of them were suffering inside from having killed men—the same men whose bodies they could still see littering the field out there. They were re-pulsed both by the sight and its implication—next time, that might be them.

But most others took it in their stride: What comes, comes. Do the job, finish it, and get ready to do the next job, regardless of what happens. These were the unemotional pluggers you seldom hear about. They don't win medals or get their names in reports, but they're the backbone of the army, the ones who really win wars.

Toward noon, still nothing had happened. There was quiet on both sides, and we hadn't heard a shell go off for so long that we might have thought the war had ended and someone forgot to tell us.

There were more observation planes than usual flying today. The little two-seater Pipers were very low over the ridge and dipping down over the village and behind the ridge. They took photographs, looking for enemy artillery, foxholes, tanks. They were probably looking for the brigade of tanks that were supposed to be in reserve behind the village.

At 1400 hours, when Studebaker called the squad leaders in for a meeting, I found out I was right. They not only were looking for the panzers, but they'd spotted them, along with a big German infantry reserve and some other troops which had been identified at headquarters as Italian. The photo experts back at Command figured that they'd been there quite some time, hidden in the groves beyond the village. And they suspected that those units were low on fuel but high on ammo, or they'd have started to move them out last night.

"This is no longer a regimental movement," Studebaker went on, his brow knit and his tone dead sober. "The whole damn corps has become involved. And this isn't the kind of breakthrough into the Po Valley we'd thought. What's happening is that our forces are going to destroy every piece of German equipment and every soldier they can. And we're going to stay put in the rear, and if this plan succeeds, there won't be any Germans to fight in a last offensive when we get the word to move into the Po."

He gave us our orders to have our muleskinners bring up reserve food and ammo from company headquarters behind us, and then to return the mules back to company again. "They'll be picked up during the night by the othere battalions who'll use 'em in their attack. We should have plenty of supplies up here by dusk, enough for several days. In the meantime, prepare your men for a helluva lot of strange sounds tonight while the rest of the division gets ready for the attack. Motors of all description, tanks, trucks, et cetera. They'll be down on the road to our right rear, over toward the British area. It means that once more we won't get too much sleep. But we have to be on guard. The Germans may send in patrols to see what's going on. You're not to tell the men what's going on until it happens. I don't even know the time schedule myself, but at least we know enough to keep the men from pushing the panic button when things start to pop. So get back and start your preparations."

I went back to my bunker and told my squad to get all the rest they could, because tonight we were to expect enemy patrols. I told them there would be no attacks today or tonight, but that preparations would be made and they might hear some weird noises during the night.

At 1530 hours most of the fellows ate their fill, checked out their equipment, made themselves as comfortable as possible, and went to sleep. I told Reds I would awaken him when it was time to go get his animals, and then I fell asleep.

I awoke with a start. I had been dreaming about home. I was out plowing a field with a good team of horses, and my pop was spreading manure. We would be planting soon. The winter wheat was green and growing, and my mother had onions, radishes, and lettuce coming up already. She would soon be putting in the other seeds. It wasn't too often I dreamt of home. I thought now about my older brother, who had a family and used to work in a factory making cabinets, tables, and chairs, but was now turning out weapons crates and ammo boxes for the war effort. He didn't fancy the farm, and had left at his first opportunity. My sister was married to a farmer who had given up the farm for the war and was now building tanks for the army. He's tried to get into the service but they turned him down for a number of reasons.

I looked at my watch and saw it was 1830. I'd slept for three hours, but it felt like I had slept for twenty-four. The sun was sinking behind the ridge to our left, and it would soon be dark. I awakened Reds and told him he could go get his animals now. He stretched and said he felt like a new man, this was the first time he had had sleep like this in about three days. While we had been sitting in our bunkers up here getting some rest, he was out bringing up supplies. He was a good guy who never complained, just did his job and did it well. He was the assistant squad leader now, but the company hadn't sent up orders yet making him a sergeant. I was beginning to wonder if there might be some politics involved, since my orders had been cut the same day I was promoted.

Reds left, and it was still quiet. It was a funny thing: All day long we almost never heard a shell explode, and when we did it was in the distance. I had gotten so used to them going off near us that I actually missed them and was growing suspicious that something would pop on us at any moment. I awakened the rest of the squad, and told them to get themselves organized for a long night.

At one point, early on, Studebaker came up to the bunker to tell us he had been called back to company headquarters, and that Gardner would be in charge while he was gone.

It sounded good. If they were calling the platoon leaders back to the company, that meant they probably had the poop about the coming attack and we would soon be rear-echelon troops. He brought us his Coleman stove. That was a boon to us; we'd lost ours earlier, and this would be the first time we had hot coffee since we'd occupied these bunkers. We lit it carefully, kept it on a low flame to prevent the light from being spotted.

When Studebaker left, it was almost 2000 hours and had got quite dark. I told the squad to get on the alert and to choose a buddy, on two hours and off two hours, and we would keep this system all night long unless something happened. Stutzman and I were one team. I took the first watch. I probably wouldn't sleep much anymore. I'd be going from bunker to bunker all night to make sure everything was all right with the rest of the squad.

Levin had returned to the bunker he'd been in with the bazooka, just in case the Germans tried to come at us with panzers again. He brought the third cook with him to load his rockets. There was very little danger they would attack again with panzers—their path was pretty well blocked, and they knew we could stop them—but it didn't hurt to be on the alert. The Germans might be losing, but they weren't dumb.

Around 2100 hours Reds came back with the supplies. He also handed me a bag of cigarettes and candy. Very welcome to the guys who smoked, and I couldn't wait to get my hands on the chocolate. I asked him if he had brought any ice cream and cake. He said he'd see what he could do next trip down, then headed out, saying he'd be back within an hour.

He returned without the animals around 2200 hours. He, Stutzman, and I shared one bunker. When he crawled in first thing he said was, "You know, I'm hungry! I forgot to eat when I was down at the supply point. Isn't that the dumbest thing you've heard today? They probably had a hot meal down there, too. Oh, well, easy come, easy go."

I asked him if he'd seen anything going on down at the company headquarters and realized I didn't know where company headquarters were anymore. He said they had moved to the far rear of the grove, where the first panzer had been blown up—in fact, they were using the panzer for a wall, and the rest of it was logs with earth piled high around. He had seen what looked like all the officers of the company there, and Colonel Track among them.

We were speculating on the long night still ahead of us when Studebaker returned and called the squad leaders to his bunker again. We didn't learn much more, except some reassuring details. The division would be moving 36 tanks with 90 mm guns in around midnight. The first and second battalions would start to move up to the groves behind us about then, as well, and the artillery would be in place. It wouldn't start firing until around dawn, he said. There would be artillery from our division and from the Corps. "So keep the guard up," he said, "and for god's sake, don't fire unless you're damned sure who you're firing at—we don't want to shoot each other."

It was sometime past midnight when Studebaker brought two men up to our bunkers. One was a Lieutenant Crow, and the other, a Sergeant Wisnewski. They were the observers for the first battalion, which would be passing through us when the attack began. The lieutenant decided to stay in our bunker until his company picked him up, and the sergeant went down the line. They were both from Company C.

Lieutenant Crow was a Navajo, from Arizona. His father was a rancher, and Crow himself had grown up with luxuries few of his people had. He'd gone to college on the ROTC program and had graduated with his commission, just in time to be shipped overseas for the invasion in North Africa. He'd seen a lot of fighting all over Africa, and then into Sicily, and up the Rapido River in Italy, where he'd been wounded. He ended up with this outfit after he'd been released from the hospital. Crow was a serious but personable guy, as set on getting home as I was. He was intent on getting back to his people, to teach advanced farming and ranching techniques. There was something at once warm and courageous about him. We hit it off right away, and I remember, we promised to get in touch if we both got out of this war alive.

It was around 0200 hours when we heard troops behind us digging in. There was still no noise from the road, but I supposed the tanks would be moving into position at the last moment. I wished those guys behind us would be a little more quiet — I was afraid the Germans could hear them too.

The German artillery had become a little heavier now, but they seemed to be firing more to the rear of our old lines, than into the far edge of the grove where our troops were digging in.

Very suddenly small arms fire broke out to our right. A flare went up. About thirty or forty Germans were approaching Company K and Company I. Company K opened up on them and killed at least a dozen before the rest scampered out of sight under the protection of the ridge undergrowth.

Another flare went up to the left of us, in front of Company L, third platoon, lighting up the German recon patrol we'd been waiting for. There were only six men, and they were lying on the ground, crawling forward, about fifty yards from the nearest third platoon bunkers. Our platoon opened fire, and above the gunfire I heard someone cry out in German for the patrol to surrender, to come in with their hands up. Three of them did, but the other three had had it, they were dead.

The prisoners were immediately taken to company headquarters for interrogation.

It grew quiet again. I thought that perhaps the Germans had sent out that combat patrol to take our attention off the recon patrol so they would have a chance to get through. They sure must be heartless bastards to sacrifice men in a feint. Or were they just desperate? I felt for the first and second battalions who would be going in this morning. Those Germans were going to put up one helluva scrap before they quit.

At 0300 hours the sound of motors could be heard very faintly behind our lines. In another hour the artillery would start firing. Since that first experience when we'd got fire from our own artillery, I was more alert to the possibility of such a mistake. We'd keep pretty low in our bunkers when the artillery did open up. It felt a lot worse to get hit by one of your own guns than by German artillery.

Lieutenant Crow said he couldn't understand the Germans sending out only one recon patrol, especially when they wasted a dozen men to cover the movement. He was afraid others might have got behind us and were wandering around back there, spotting everything we were doing. "I want to go back and talk to your lieutenant. He may not have experienced this type of German action before. I have many times." He continued, "You don't think he'll resent it do you?" I assured him that he wouldn't. When Crow was gone, I began to listen more intently. I could not hear any digging behind us now, which would indicate that our troops were in position. A faint sound of engines seemed to be coming from directly behind us, not to the right rear as we were told. Then I heard something else, and it froze my blood: a whispered "*Ja*," right behind my bunker. I was afaid to move. I could hear scraping, like someone crawling. It had to be another German patrol, but what the hell would I do about it? I couldn't throw a grenade; it was too close to the other bunkers. I couldn't shoot behind the bunker; the other guys would think they were being fired on and start firing back.

My hand slipped to my belt where I carried the bowie knife my brother-in-law had made for me. I'd never used it. In fact, everyone thought it was a joke that I even carried it. I kept it shined up and sharp, but I hadn't ever thought I'd have to use it. The idea of it made me sick.

I handed my carbine to Stutzman and motioned him not to ask any questions, then slipped out of the bunker. I quietly looked around. What I was looking for couldn't be more than a few feet away. I listened and heard the scraping noise again, but this time it was coming from two different places. A two man patrol—but that just didn't seem feasible. There must be more.

I heard the scraping again; it was coming toward me. I lay very still. Every muscle in my body was tensed to spring. Scrape, scrape, scrape. Something touched me. I sprang and came down on the German's back, plunging my knife. He gasped once, then lay still.

I heard another movement, then a voice whispered, "Ike, this is Crow. I just killed another one. And there's a third. My knife is on him now. I think it was only three men, we should keep one alive for interrogation."

I relaxed, wishing this lieutenant was in our squad. We disarmed the German and took him into our bunker. He was just a boy, probably no more than sixteen. And he was scared to death, sure we were going to kill him. In the little German I could speak, I told him we wouldn't kill him, that we would take him back to our headquarters where they would ask him some questions. And that they would send him to a prisoner-of-war camp until the war ended. Then he could go home. He nodded, but was still terrified. We started to take him back to Studebaker, but before we could leave the bunker, Gardner came in. He said that he and Studebaker had heard the noise and suspected what was going on. Studebaker had sent him out to see what the situation was. He would take the German back himself. They wanted everyone to stay in the bunkers now because the artillery would open up very shortly. That was okay with us; we would rather stay in the bunkers than be running over the ridge, especially since that artillery would be opening up at any time now.

There were signs of dawn now. In the distance were streaks of light just above the horizon. Lieutenant Crow and I checked out the dead Germans to make damn sure they were dead. Later, when the other battalions were locked in combat, we would have time to move them away.

Chapter 13

It was quiet now. Not a shell was going out nor coming in. It is an eerie feeling when you're used to being shelled, or hearing your own going out.

I could imagine what was going on right now with our artillery. Everything was loaded ready to go; the guys just standing by awaiting orders to start firing. Then they'd be breaking their backs for the next few hours, firing as fast as they could for the one-hour barrage before the infantry made its attack. Then firing on order from their observers, who would be with the infantry and would call for fire when the infantry ran into something too big for small arms. Or they would get orders for a walking barrage—to keep firing in front of the infantry as they advanced.

Then, shortly after 0400 hours, we heard the big guns from corps opening up, it was not very long before the shells were passing over our heads and landing on the ridge, in the village, and back of the village. The 155s and the 105s were next to open up. These were division artillery battalions and were used in close range to the infantry. Their shells were falling on the village and on the ridge. Some seemed to pass behind the ridge. We could hear them explode and see the flashes. The last to open up were our 75s.

Their shells were falling right in front of us. They were for close support, and they were hitting the undergrowth at the foot of the ridge and on the near end of the village straight ahead of us. The ground shook with each burst. Some of these shells were falling within a few hundred yards of us. We kept down pretty close in our bunkers. Lieutenant Crow sat down at the back of the bunker, opened a can of C rations, and lit the Coleman stove. He said, "I'd better eat something now. Only the Lord knows when I'll eat again." He asked if we had any sugar for the coffee. I told him he'd have to go to the officers' mess for sugar. They didn't serve it to the common soldier. He laughed. "I knew there was an advantage being an officer, but I never knew just what it was before."

The barrage kept up. It looked like the whole ridge and the village were on fire, I couldn't see how anyone could possibly live through a bombardment like that. The mountain was shaking, dirt was falling down on us in our bunkers. I couldn't imagine what the Germans were going through, but if it was as bad as it looked, I would have come down off that ridge and surrendered the first chance I had. There were shells coming the other way now: Germans shelling our positions. But they were passing over us. They were firing at our artillery position.

Our mortars were still. They would keep them quiet until the line companies started to move, and then use them for close support.

Studebaker came up to our bunker to tell us the infantry behind us was getting ready to move. When they started throwing in smoke shells, they'd come through here. We were to just hold our positions until further orders. No advancing. He didn't have to tell us twice; we were willing to let someone else carry the ball for a while.

I looked at my watch. It was 0445 hours. Fifteen more minutes of the artillery fire. It starts to get to you after a while.

All at once, the 81s behind us opened up. They were throwing smoke shells into the area between us and the village and ridge. They were landing all along our line, and in a minute everything in front of us disappeared. I could see nothing but smoke. Lieutenant Crow crawled out of the bunker and called for Sergeant Wisnewski, who came lumbering out of his bunker. He told the sergeant to watch for the advancing troops and to keep them going and not to stop for anything until they reached the village and the foot of the ridge.

The smoke shells were still coming in. I could not see how anyone could possibly breathe in that mess. I was happy we didn't have to cross through it, but I felt guilty feeling that way.

The smoke shells were lifting now. They were firing them further up the ridge and into the village. I could see slightly across the open area ahead of us. This would give our guys a chance to see where they were going and still keep the Germans blinded.

German artillery was coming in heavily now. They were hitting the area in front of us, and some of the shells were landing close to our bunkers. Lieutenant Crow said to Wisnewski, "Here they come. Let's go." I looked outside the bunker and saw the advancing troops. They were coming from behind us almost in a solid line as far as I could see. They were in platoon formation with scouts out, and they were coming fast.

Lieutenant Crow ran up to a captain; they spoke and then he motioned the troops on. It was his platoon from Company C. Apparently, the first battalion was passing through us and the second battalion was further down the line, in front of Company K and Company I. I couldn't see the village or the ridge now. They were covered with smoke. The area ahead of us was fairly clear, and the troops were walking at a fast pace, walking around the dead Germans lying out there. Some of the men were taking a good look. Some just walked by and didn't give them a second glance. These were the veterans. They'd seen all the death they wanted to. But the newer fellows took a long look, and God only knows what went through their minds. It's not pleasant to see a dead man, even an enemy. I never got used to it, and I don't think I ever would if I were to be on earth for a thousand years.

Another company came through, over to our right. They were heading for the foot of the ridge. I wondered how many companies they were sending into the village to clean out the Germans. I was sure they were well dug in, in the cellars of those old houses, in the towers that were still standing.

I began to hear lots of engines down on the road to our right. Our tanks had started to move. I used my field glasses in that direction, but it was too hazy to see anything. Our artillery, although we couldn't see it too well, was concentrating on the ridge now. The smoke shells were still falling on the ridge and toward the back of the village. If I looked real closely, I could see parts of the village through the haze.

I could hear small arms fire now—light machine

guns, BARS, and plain rifle fire. The small mortars hadn't opened up yet, and the 81s were only throwing out smoke shells, but the artillery was keeping up a steady barrage. The small arms fire intensified, and I knew this was not a fire-and-movement maneuver. Those guys in the village were engaging the enemy. I heard German burp guns and the *pop pop pop* of hand grenades going off. I knew both sides would take heavy casualties. And with that realization came a sick gut feeling that we would be in this thing before too long.

Toward the grove were about a dozen mules, loaded to the gills with ammo, mortar shells, hand grenades, and TNT. No food. Just ammo. Several heavy weapons platoons were there, too, setting their mortars up. I didn't see any machine guns. They were already moving up to support their rifle platoons.

The 81s were still pumping out smoke shells, but not as heavily as before. Soon they started changing over to fragmentation shells and were pumping them on the ridge. They seemed to be concentrating on the left side of the ridge near the village. The artillery kept up its pounding, and the German artillery was beginning to come in hot and heavy. A lot of their shells were landing very close to our bunkers. I told my squad to keep down as much as possible, that I would keep watch. I certainly was curious as to what was happening in the village. I would have liked to have felt the urge to join the fighting now. Even when it was someone else's turn to carry the ball. I wasn't satisfied.

A few hours later, with my field glasses trained on the village, I saw a couple of guys come crouching out, toward us. They were coming fast. I would have liked to have had a stop watch on them. They came running up, and I called out to them, "Where the hell are you going so fast?" It looked as if they were running away. They answered back that they couldn't stop now. They needed ammo up there and they had to get some mules up right away. They ran past me, and in short order, I saw them pass again with three mules, well spread out running like hell for the village. I hoped they'd all make it.

When the mules had taken off, the 60s opened up on the back of the village. I guessed that the runners had passed on orders for them to fire, and where to fire.

When Lieutenant Studebaker came around to our bunker again, he had some word on what was going on out there. He said he had been listening on his radio to the communications between Company C and the first battalion. They were really in it. It sounded almost like another Casino. The Germans were well dug in. They had pillboxes on every corner, and they were fighting from the cellars of the bombed-out houses. Our casualties were heavy, but we seemed to be getting a defense built up to the extent that our guys would have a line to fall back on in case of counterattack. Our troops were getting a lot of small arms fire from the ridge as well as from the village, and the German artillery was really pounding them. They were trying to get their wounded into some cellars and treat them the best they could, but there was no chance for evacuating them until after dark. They were going to send up a company from our medical battalion soon to set up some kind of a hospital and try to save as many of the wounded as they could, but without quick evacuation many would die. A useless waste of lives.

He said the tank attack down on the road was going well. We had a battalion of infantry behind the ridge, and the tanks were really giving it to the Germans. The battalion back there was well dug in and in constant communication with its regiment. Although they were taking casualties, they were inflicting a lot more damage themselves. "All in all, we're doing okay. The Germans seem to want to keep us from the left side of that ridge. I think that is where that armored brigade is. I have a sneaky feeling they're out of fuel and can't move them, which would explain why they hang onto that ridge as hard as they do. I'll let you know when that company of medics are ready to go through. We'll have to give them some covering fire, so be ready to open fire toward the back of the village." I felt a little better knowing what was going on up there. Another comfort was that there were two uncommitted battalions from the other regiment plus another entire uncommitted regiment out there. They would commit those troops first before they took an old tired outfit like ours and put us back in the line again.

When I looked behind us again, I saw a group of men coming out of the grove carrying lockers, full packs, stretchers and other medic's equipment. It was the advance of the company of medics. These fellows had no guns and they sometimes had to make the same advances the infantry made, but they didn't get the extra $10.00 a month that the infantryman received when he had earned his combat badge. I wondered why that was. It didn't seem entirely fair.

I gave the order to start the covering fire. As the medics passed us, I called out good luck to them, and, without acknowledgement, they passed out of sight and into the smoke. I hoped and prayed they all made it.

When the medics passed through it was 0820 hours. Our attack had been going on for about three hours. The days were getting longer now, and it would be daylight until about 1930. Certainly, by that time we should have the Germans on the run and everyone dug in for the night. I could not see how the Germans could hold out longer than that.

The smoke was lifting now, and we could see the village and the ridge quite clearly. The mortars behind us were lobbing their shells into the village and onto the left end of the ridge at a steady pace, directed by observers who were with the riflemen up ahead. The division artillery—75s, 105s, and 155s— were firing steadily toward the top of the ridge and the back of the village, but the large corps artillery was quiet now. When the last of the smoke had lifted, we could see the sun. Another beautiful day to fight a war, I thought. It even got a little warm, but it was cold down in the bunkers. They were damp, and the sun never was able to shine into them, so they never really dried out or warmed up. I shouldn't complain, I said to myself. After all I'm well protected. It's those poor guys up ahead who are in trouble. I'm just trying to keep warm.

Suddenly, something came over the rise from the village. I tightened the grip on my carbine, but as it came into plain sight I saw the team of three mules that had gone up with supplies a short time ago. They were coming toward us at a fast walk, and each was carrying something on its back. As they got closer, I could see that their loads were wounded men. They passed us, and the last I saw of them they were disappearing into the grove. It was encouraging to see at least some of our wounded were getting back. Maybe more would be coming soon.

I hadn't noticed before, but among the dead Germans in the open ahead of us were some American soldiers. They'd been wounded in the advance on the village. I saw two medics coming from the village, kneel over the wounded and start working on them. They ignored the shells and small arms as if they didn't exist and took care of those men. I thought of our own medic, DeSola, whom I had seen risk his life many times. I had heard that DeSola had been put in for the Silver Star for bravery back on the mountain. I think I'd have given every medic I'd ever run into the medal. They certainly deserved it. These were brave men. Once, I had asked DeSola if he worked in medicine before he came into service. He'd said no, he'd been a brewery worker, mostly a bottle capper and had never helped anyone even wrap a cut finger before. When I asked if he would go into medicine when he left the service he said he'd seen all the blood and death he wanted to see and would be glad to get back to the brewery. I knew how he felt.

The medics were still out there with the wounded when over the sound of the firing came the drone of motors. At first I thought they were tanks. Then I saw them. Formation after formation of planes, P-47s and B-26s, coming in from the east. They were flying just above the level of the highest ridge. Some formations of the P-38s were much higher, like birds of prey watching for their next meal. The B-26s let go of their loads behind the ridge. We could hear the explosions loud and clear. Something back there was taking one helluva pounding. Squadron after squadron of B-26s were coming in, dropping their loads and disappearing to the west and south of us. When they had disappeared, the P-47s dived down and dropped their bombs. They were hitting something big, maybe an ammo dump. The black smoke was rising higher than the ridge, and there were constant explosions.

After the 47s dropped their bombs, they came back and began to strafe. They hit the village, the ridge on the right of the village, and the lower ridge on the left side of the village. They must have been using some kind of incendiary bombs; it seemed the whole forest was on fire.

When the planes began to strafe, our second battalion passed through us. I watched them go. It seemed that two companies were heading for the village and one for the ridge. They were taking their heavy-weapons company with them, which meant they were moving and would need the covering fire of the large mortars and large machine guns. Either they were relieving the first battalion or they were pumping up the effort to move. Behind the men came the mules, eight of them loaded down with all kinds of ammo. These fellows were not going to be caught short. Not one shell fell on that open space while they moved in. The Germans must have been hiding from those strafing planes.

The men of the second battalion disappeared

behind the rise and into the village and the under-growth at the bottom of the ridge. The planes were still strafing. There were small fires all over the ridge now. The black smoke kept billowing. The explosions were still heavy, and the small arms fire had increased everywhere. I thought then that the attack was at its peak. I could hear renewed activity on our right down on the road. The tanks were moving, and they were firing as they moved. The infantry was moving with them. I was sure that this battle was drawing to a conclusion.

The planes disappeared now. Just a few piper cubs stayed up there to observe. I never did see the P-38s do anything except keep up high, watching that no German planes came into the fray while the other pilots were busy dropping bombs and strafing.

Chapter 14

Once the fighting had moved further up ahead of us, I crawled out of the bunker. The first thing I saw were the two Germans that Lieutenant Crow and I had killed. They were just like the prisoner we had taken. Young boys, no more than sixteen. I couldn't understand why they would send someone that young on a patrol. They must have been meant as a decoy, but had stumbled into our lines without knowing it.

Studebaker was outside his bunker, observing the front with his field glasses. He said he thought the planes must have hit an ammo dump and some tanks or trucks out there. Whatever it was, it hurt the Germans.

Our men were much higher on the ridge now, and the small arms fire had increased. A good fight was going on there. The planes had done a fair job of unnerving the Germans, but they were still capable of putting up a pretty good fight. The strafing had taken something out of them, and at the same time, it had given our guys a chance to move into better positions. The front line was still where the men with the rifles were, not where the planes bombed or where the artillery shelled. Just where that lonely rifleman with eight rounds stood. That was the front line.

Al was sitting outside his bunker now. I called to him to make sure he had a man on the BAR at all times. He replied that he was way ahead of me there. A man was in the bunker sitting with it. Men were coming out of the bunkers along the whole line. Some of the guys were taking their shoes off, drying out their socks. We tried to do this at least once a day, otherwise our feet would get sweat-soaked and at night could freeze up with trenchfoot. I've seen guys lose toes, and some even lost a foot just because they didn't dry their socks when they had a chance.

I heard Lieutenant Studebaker's commanding voice. "Ike, send Reds and two other men from your squad back here." Before I could turn around to tell Reds, he was on his way. I sent Russ and Stutzman trailing behind him. Reds came back after a few moments to tell me that the three of them were to report to company headquarters to skin mules and to bring up supplies for the other battalions up front. I told Reds I was sorry that I had got him and the other two guys into something like that, and he said, "You had nothing to do with it. Studebaker called specifically for me and it was God's will that the other two fellows were chosen. They'll be okay. I'll show them the ropes and keep an eye on them. We'll be okay." With that, he was gone. I felt bad about having chosen the two, but if they hadn't been chosen two other guys would have had to go. That was the awful thing about command, even for a squad leader. There were times when you had to ask your friends to stick their necks out, even though you might be ordering them to their deaths.

The tanks down on the road were moving now. I

could hear their engines faintly from toward the ridge. Their cannons seemed to be the only artillery firing. Anything else larger than a machine gun was a mortar, and most of these seemed to be 60s. If our side was moving, as the smoke from the ridge indicated, they would soon be at the summit and there would be nowhere for the Germans to go. The Germans were hard fighters, but they also knew when the fight was over. Regardless of the stories they were told, they knew they would receive adequate treatment from us and would be sent back to a prisoner-of-war camp somewhere in Africa or the United States to sit the war out.

It was 1110 hours. The attack was six hours old. Our side had made some real progress against a well dug in enemy. Lieutenant Studebaker came up and sat with me. He said the balance of the medical battalion had set up a station right behind our old line on the ridge behind us and would be receiving wounded as soon as they started sending them back. He also said that an evacuation medical battalion was setting up back on the road, and as soon as our wounded were patched up enough to be moved, they would be evacuated to base hospitals further back. He advised me to be on the alert for any walking wounded now. They would be coming in as fast as they could get out of the sight of the Germans. Reds and the other mule-skinners should be bringing in the more seriously wounded on their return trips, and as soon as possible we would probably be used as litter bearers ourselves. I didn't mind this, unlike some infantrymen I'd encountered who thought it was below their dignity. Behind us, the mules were coming in. I heard

Reds—who seldom swore—cursing away at a little gray mule, more jackass than mule, that was loaded down with ammo. It was kicking and jerking under its load, and as Reds passed me, he called out, "This goddamned jackass can't understand English! How do you say son-of-a-bitch in Italian, Ike?" He was laughing, but I believe he meant what he was saying. There were twelve mules in the convoy. As soon as they hit our line, they started to spread out, some heading for the village and some for the ridge. Our three men were heading for the village.

I called out to Reds, "If you get a chance, see if Lieutenant Crow is okay." Reds glanced over his shoulder and waved okay, then kept going. Another convoy of mules, about ten, came through later loaded down with mortar shells. They also spread out and headed for different areas as soon as they left our lines. I'm sure some of these guys had never been so close to a mule before, but they were doing a good job, and in most cases the mules were co-operating. Lieteunant Studebaker kept his glasses on the mules until they disappeared behind the rise. He said that as far as he could tell, they had all made it.

The small-arms fire was now so intense you could not hear the tanks down on the road. I could still hear the M-34s, so I knew the Germans were still fighting, but our machine guns were firing back, and the small mortars were landing near the top of the ridge now. There were puffs of smoke when they hit.

Lieutenant Studebaker had his radio with him, and a message came over for Captain Bear: Be ready to receive prisoners. The same message went to the commanders of the other companies. Company K was nearest the road, and they were the first to see them. The radio man called out, "There must be a million of them. Krauts all over the place! What the hell are we going to do with all those bastards anyhow?"

Colonel Track came on the radio and said to him, "Get your commanding officer on the phone. *Now.*" When the commander of Company K was on he told him to get a couple of platoons down on the road and relieve the troops of their prisoners. "Keep them coming down the road. They will be taken off your hands by troops from the other division that'll be relieving us. And just make damned sure these prisoners are disarmed and searched; because that other outfit'll rob them blind." Then he ordered the commander of Company I to get two platoons down by the road, too. "I understand they have at least a division of enemy coming in. They were in relief behind the line, and when they saw our tanks coming they just lay down their arms and surrendered!"

The fighting on the ridge was still going on, but the heaviest fire was coming from the village. The Germans weren't giving up that fight so easily. If anything, they had shown their willingness to fight harder there. They gave no sign of quitting.

Some of the walking wounded were coming back now, and when they reached our lines, some of them sat and rested a bit before going on back. They said that the Germans in the village were not ordinary German army men. They were harder, tougher guys who wouldn't surrender. Our troops had got about four or five blocks into the village, when the Germans in the cellars behind them started shooting. As our troops had advanced and entered the cellars and found no one, they dynamited some of the buildings. They had thrown grenades all over the place, and still the Germans were there. Most of them had automatic weapons—not just plain rifles—and whatever the automatic weapons were, they were good, much better and more accurate than our tommy guns. They said our hospital was set up in the very last cellar at this end of the village, and the Germans had made a couple of raids on it until we had almost a whole company of infantry ordered to guard it.

These guys were mean; the men coming off the line didn't think they would surrender. They would have to be killed or run out. Among them were the black uniforms of the SS troops. Now we could see what we were up against, and why the Germans hadn't pulled out and run to the next ridge. The SS bastards were keeping their army there and would continue to keep them there fighting until they were all killed. I had wondered how all those troops down on the road had been captured. Now it was clear. They'd seen their chance to get out of this war and out from under those maniacal SS orders. This war was lost for the Germans. Yes, they would go on fighting and dying, but they knew they could never win. And those SS bastards were pledged to fight to the last man, and when they took that oath they meant it. They were hated by their enemy, and they were hated by their own people. The only thing they could do was to fight to the last man.

I thought about the Alps, and the idea sent shivers up and down my spine. We would have to fight for every inch of ground. A morbid thought. *No one will ever go home, we'll all die here because one man had decreed it.* And what made it so ironic was the fact that this bastard was not even German, but he was leading the German nation down to destruction for his own ambitions. I had never felt real hatred before, but at that moment I hated. I hated that man with such a passion. I could have tortured him to death and laughed while I was doing it. I'm sure I was not the only one who felt that way, may our God forgive us.

The mules were beginning to bring back their loads, one man to the back of a mule. I saw Reds and the other two coming. Reds said to me in passing, "I'll be back shortly with another load of ammo, then I'll have time to tell you a few things."

Levin came up to our bunker and said they had called for a platoon from our company to take back prisoners. He said they were getting Italian prisoners now, a lot of them. "It looks like we've captured all their reserves, and the only Germans left are those in the village and those on the ridge." We had taken thirteen to fourteen thousand prisoners. That's a big chunk out of anyone's army. The Germans had to be hurting badly after this battle. I don't think they forgot it for a long time. I asked Levin if they were mountain troops that we were capturing, and he said they weren't; they were young kids and old men from the streets of the big cities. He'd heard that some had only been in the army for six weeks.

I said, "Hmmmn, almost as bad a situation as ours." We both laughed at that.

He said he had a brother-in-law who had been in the army for four years and was never more than a hundred fifty miles from home in all that time. "I dread to go home, I'll have to listen to him tell how hard he had it, standing in line for cigarettes and mess, and sleeping on those hard army beds, you know the kind, the ones they have in those buildings they call barracks." We both laughed again. When you're an infantryman in the mud at some front four thousand miles from home, lots of things that wouldn't be funny anywhere else were funny up here.

Levin was a Jew. His father had gone to America as a small boy, then had been orphaned shortly after he arrived. He had gone to work as an apprentice for a furrier, and still worked for the same furrier now. He had married at 17, and Levin had nine brothers and four sisters. Levin was not an Orthodox Jew, and though he never declared himself a member of the traditional faith, he hoped to see the Jews have a national homeland after this war was over. If they were to establish a country of their own, he planned to spend a few years in it helping in any way he could. He felt this was his obligation.

A heavy-weapons company came through our position and disappeared over the rise into the village. They were going to put pressure on the back of the village now and try to get this battle over. At the far right of the ridge, nearest the road, the firing near the summit had ceased. I figured that our troops had reached that point, and with our troops from the other regiment behind it, there was nothing for the Germans there to do but to surrender.

More of the walking wounded were stopping to rest when they reached our bunkers. They kept us fairly well informed about the battle. Our troops were making progress in the village, but after they would pass, the SS would come out of the cellars and shoot them in the backs, then disappear back into the cellars. Our commanders would send back patrols to wipe them out, but each time they entered the cellars, they couldn't find any enemy; they would completely disappear.

Chapter 15

I was in Studebaker's bunker, trying to find out if anything new had come in on the radio. My squad was getting anxious, and I have to admit, so was I. Studebaker had just said that we should be getting off this ridge and back in a rest area as soon as this battle was over when a message came over the radio from Captain Bear. They'd located an engineering outfit with bulldozers which were on their way up now. They wanted a couple of men riding with each of the drivers as they entered the village. Our platoon was to furnish them. They had twelve caterpillars, so we would need at least twenty-four men. They would be coming down the path from our old position and would pull up at the far end of the grove. The mission was to enter the village and cover up those cellars, bury the Germans alive if they didn't want to come out. He needed the men to toss grenades down into the cellars to keep the Germans pinned down long enough for the big cats to bulldoze them shut. The prime duty, though, was to protect the cat drivers.

It was almost 1500 hours. We still had five or six hours of light, and we could certainly do the job in that time, or it couldn't be done. The lieutenant turned to me and said, "Take everyone from your squad but the BAR team. Leave them in your bunkers on guard duty. I want Gardner to stay here with me, so in case anything happens he can come up and warn you fellows." When I got back to my bunkers, and told the men what we'd be doing, they didn't show too much enthusiasm. But neither did they show much disappointment. We loaded up with grenades, and each took two extra bandoleers, filled our canteens, packed a couple of boxes of K-rations, and took off back to the edge of the grove to await the bulldozers. Soon we heard engines behind us, and we could see them lumbering over the slope. The operators had their blades up high, using them as a shield. Levin was standing out in front of the other fellows, with a walkie-talkie. He mounted the first cat, and I was his assistant. He asked me if I wanted a tommy gun, and I told him no; the carbine and all my grenades would be all I would need.

We crossed the open area without any trouble, although there was some shooting from the ridge. The driver kept that big blade up; about the only way they could knock out these things would be with an artillery shell, and then it would have to be almost a direct hit. It was a helluva lot better riding instead of walking into battle.

As we approached the village, we headed for a wall that looked pretty sturdy. The other cats came into view, and found places where they could be out of sight of the Germans. We were getting small-arms fire from somewhere. Levin kept looking at the ridge to the right and finally, he lifted his walkie-talkie and called for Studebaker. He asked for some mortar fire on the ridge while we made our plans and awaited our guide.

I said to Levin, "I think we should scout around and find that hospital, so we know what we are *not* to cover up." He said he thought that was a good idea, and I said I'd go. I thought it was odd that no one had met us with instructions. I had thought the plans were already made and that as soon as we approached, we would begin covering up cellars.

I jumped off the cat and took off along a wall, toward the main street of the village. I figured the hospital would be along there somewhere. It was very noisy, with small-arms fire. Up ahead, I could hear 81s landing, but I didn't see any GIs. I scooted around the corner of the wall into the main street and still couldn't see anyone. Then I heard bullets hitting all around me. I dove for a pile of rubble against the wall and curled up like a worm. I couldn't see who was firing at me, but from the angle of fire, it had come from behind me. Then I saw him. I just saw an arm come out with a funny looking piece, something I'd never seen before, and he was about to fire again. He was behind me, in the first doorway into the village. He was only about twenty feet from one of the cats, but they didn't seem to see him. I waited until he put his head out to aim his piece. Then I let go with the carbine. The German came tumbling out and hit the street. He was dead before he hit the ground. I had hit him with both shots, just about two inches apart, right in the middle of his forehead.

Someone said, "Good shot soldier," and I spun around expecting to see another German. There was Lieutenant Crow, and a little farther back, Sergeant Wisnewski. They hit the dirt up ahead of me in a sheltered spot and told me to join them. They'd been sent back to meet us, but had been pinned down by this one lousy sniper and couldn't get to the edge of the village. Crow said they couldn't mark the hospital with the SS troops in here; they'd just keep dropping artillery on it until there was nothing left. These bastards don't give a damn about anyone. I've never seen such savages in my life. They respected nothing but that son-of-a-bitch in Berlin. Crow went on to say that we could see their panzers from our front lines up ahead, they couldn't move them. But our artillery was firing on them, and they were sitting there just being blown apart by our tanks. But they would not surrender. "Here in the village, they're practically cut off. There's no way out, but still they fight. What the hell kind of men throw their lives away when they know the game is over and there's nothing to do but surrender or die? Why no one'll even remember they were here." I couldn't answer the lieutenant's questions. No one else could give him an answer, not even the Germans who were dying here.

I told the Lieutenant the man in charge was about thirty or forty feet away with a cat. I thought we should get back to him so we could make our plans. We wanted this battle over before dark. We crouched low and ran around the corner to the cat I'd been on. The mortars Levin had asked for were coming in now, but they didn't seem to be doing too much good. The small-arms fire was still coming our way. He said the mortar shells were hitting the trees and bursting, and with the Germans having covers over their foxholes, they were not affected by them. We would just have to chance it and go into the village under fire. The cat operators didn't like this idea. Their captain came up and he was told what the situation was. He told us that his men were not combat engineers; they were used to building roads and airfields, but never under fire. He said he didn't know what they would do if they were fired on. I told him that they seemed pretty steady now, and he said he was willing to give it a try.

Lieutenant Crow stuck his head over the wall and pointed out the doorway to the hospital. It was about a hundred fifty feet into the village, under what had been a very large house at one time. He said there were probably seventy or eighty wounded men down there plus some medics and a whole company of infantry surrounding the area. There was also a platoon of men inside the hospital. The captain looked over the situation with his field glasses, and said there was plenty of rubble to fill the cellars with and that the cats could do it, but they would need an advance man to point out exactly what they were to fill in. Levin said he would send one advance man ahead of each of the cats, with grenades. The advance man would throw three or four grenades down each cellar, then the cat could start filling in. Lieutenant Crow and Sergeant Wisnewski led us off. I was the advance man in front of our cat; Levin rode shotgun with the driver. I was just as satisfied doing that. I'd rather be down on the ground where I could dive into something if a sniper opened up.

We moved down past the hospital doors, and then I found the cellar entrance. I crept up to it and pulled the pin on two grenades and dropped them in. The explosion was ear-splitting. I motioned the cat operator to begin his grizzly work. He dropped his blade and scooped in small stones and loose earth for several minutes, then found some larger stones to pile on top until the cellar was completely filled in. I looked over the area to see if there might be another entrance, but could find none. These cellars were probably built during the middle ages, when the village was actually only a fort, so they were built with defense in mind, and had only one entrance.

Two of the other cats were filling in cellars behind us. Sergeant Wisnewski went back to instruct the advance men what to look for. We were receiving sniper fire from somewhere, but I couldn't tell where it was coming from. I thought it could possibly be coming from the ridge, but I could see no activity up there. There was a lot of small-arms fire in that direction, but it seemed to be directed mostly the other way, which led me to believe that our troops were fast approaching from the right of the ridge and that the fight on the ridge was about over. All that was left then was this damned village and those panzers behind it. I was sure that our tanks would take care of the armor back there, but here it was strictly man-to-man, with the help of these cats which would bring this fight to its conclusion.

The cat Reds was riding pulled up close to ours and he called over to me, "I'd rather have a mule!" Hell, even now he had room for a one-liner!

We kept moving forward, throwing grenades into the cellar entrances and filling them in with rubble. I'm sure we buried quite a few Germans, how many, only the Lord knows. We were still getting sniper fire, but couldn't pinpoint it, because it was coming from all directions. There were some cellars the cats couldn't get to; they were back off the main street, in narrow alleys. The only thing we could do there was to throw grenades down and hope. Every once in a while I would hear Levin's tommy gun let go, and sometimes I would hear a scream. Levin was a good man to have riding shotgun. Nothing escaped his attention. All he had to see was a little movement and he fired away. He hit at least five or six Germans that day. If I didn't hear any firing from any of the other cats, it was because Levin had done the job before they arrived.

There were four cats working now, and I couldn't see how we could work many more. We came to some houses which didn't have too much damage to them. I thought for sure that there would be Germans here. I tightened the grip on my carbine, pulled the pin on a grenade, and stepped into one of the houses. I couldn't see or hear anything out of the ordinary. After a fast search, I found the cellar entrance and threw three grenades into it. I returned to the cat and told them, but added that I didn't see how they could get the cat to that cellar entrance, since the house was still mostly standing. The operator told Levin to get off the cat and told everyone to stand back. He pulled the big bulldozer up to the front of the house, threw it into low gear, and proceeded to enter the house. The walls came tumbling down. It hit again and again. After hitting it about six or seven times, there was no house, just a pile of rubble that looked just like most of the rest of the village. He proceeded to the cellar entrance and filled it in, then called down to us, "Where to next?"

Levin re-mounted the cat, and I advanced to the next cellar. I was about to throw down the grenades when I heard a voice speaking in broken English: "Please do not cover us, we would like to come out and surrender but we are afraid you will kill us."

I shouted back, "How many of you are there?"

The voice came back. "There are seven of us. We

do not wish to fight anymore. We wish to surrender."

"Throw down your arms and come up, one at a time." I called out to Levin to come in, that I had seven Germans wanting to surrender and I might need help. Lieutenant Crow came running up to the cellar as the Germans started coming out. We searched each one as he appeared and lined them up against a wall that was still standing. We found only a small pistol on one of them. He begged us to let him keep it. He wanted to kill himself. We took it, and I told him in my broken German that if he wanted to kill himself he should have done it in the cellar. We didn't allow it in our army.

"What the hell are we going to do with them, now that we've captured them," I asked Lieutenant Crow.

He said, "You have several men back there on the cats that aren't in use. Send them back with a couple of those men."

But Levin said to wait. He would radio Studebaker and see what he thought we should do. After a little conversation, he said, "Just wait here a few minutes. Gardner and Willie will come up here and get them." Because they were SS men, Division G-2 was very interested in questioning them.

It was just a few minutes before Gardner and Willie came panting over the rise into the village. A German machine gunner was spitting bullets at Willie as he crossed the open area, and he was really lifting them and putting them down. They finally reached a wall and dove behind it. We were standing by our cat, and they called out to us to take cover, we were being fired at. We just laughed, and told them they should come up to the front more often; that was the trouble with rear echelon troops, they weren't used to being under fire. We didn't get any laughs from those two, just dirty looks. Willie had been wounded twice and Gardner once, so they knew the score very well.

They came crouching up to us, looked the prisoners over and asked if they had been thoroughly searched. We told them they had. They had had nothing on them at all except some German cigarettes and several lighters which we had taken from them. I handed Gardner a rag that held the stuff, and the pistol.

"Didn't they have any *weapons*?" Gardner asked.

I told him they had lain down their arms before they came out of that cellar, and that I had no intentions of going down there to recover them. "We'll cover the hole and that'll be that." They could have booby-trapped the place before they left. If I was going to get killed, I was going to get killed fighting Germans, not blown to hell by a booby trap in a hole in the ground.

While Willie was speaking with the prisoners, the small-arms fire from the ridge above the village became very intense. They were not firing at us. They seemed to be firing in the opposite direction. Lieutenant Crow said he thought our troops were coming down the ridge, and the Germans up there were putting up their last stand. He told me to alert the troops back with the other cats and see if I could find the commander of the infantry company near the hospital, to alert him as to what was happening.

Gardner and Willie decided this was a good time to start back with their prisoners. I was worried that they wouldn't make it back, especially if those troops on the ridge were SS. They would shoot the prisoners as soon as they showed out in the open. But if they were busy with something else, maybe our guys could get them across that open area before they were seen. Willie explained to the prisoners what the plan was. They would run as fast as they could, but they were to keep their hands behind their heads, else someone in our bunkers might mistake them as attacking and would blow them to hell.

Gardner said to Willie, "Let's go," and they broke into a run and were running like hell when they passed over that rise.

Lieutenant Crow was shooting now, and so was Sergeant Wisnewski. Crow said they were not SS, they were German army running all over hell. "Be damn careful where you fire. Our guys are up there somewhere, too. We don't want to fight the war with them."

Everyone was firing now. All the guys on the cats, and some of the company that were guarding the hospital. We almost forgot what we'd been sent up here for, until I saw several fellows from the guard company keel over and lay very still. I knew they couldn't have been hit from the ridge. The snipers, sensing what we were doing had seen their opportunity to come out of their holes and start hitting us.

Levin opened up with his tommy gun and started throwing grenades, they were that close. Lieutenant Crow turned his attention back to the village also, and soon we had quite a firing line, and we were hitting some of those snipers. We could see them falling, and they definitely were coming out of the cellars.

Levin told the operator of his cat to put his blade up to use as a shield and move up. The operator hesitated, but Levin told him to do it now, or he'd shove him off the cat and move it himself. The blade came up and the cat started to move. Levin told the engineering captain to do the same with all the other cats.

Crow, Wisnewski and I fell in behind the first cat. We had moved only about twenty or thirty feet when we came to the first cellar. I saw several Germans pile down it. I let go at them but don't know if I hit any of them or not. It did not matter. In just minutes the cellar was filled.

The other cats were moving in now. It looked like the engineers were parading for the general, all lined up, each with two other men aboard firing as they went. The infantry company was behind us now. They had set up a defense line and were firing up on the ridge at anything that was moving.

We kept moving, and covering up cellars. The cats were spreading out now, knocking down walls, covering up cellars, killing SS and generally moving up where the first battalion had a firing line. We could see our tanks now, and our infantry troops lining up prisoners.

There were many Americans lying dead in the streets and behind walls, too. The medics had picked up most of the wounded, but they left the dead where they fell. Among the dead I saw quite a few medics. That thought about them not getting that extra ten dollars went through my mind again.

Some of our troops had reached the far end of the village and were fanning out into the groves where the enemy panzers were sitting. We were still receiving sniper fire. We had filled in fifty or sixty cellars by now, but we had quite a few to go. Up on the ridge to the right, I could see yellow smoke. It meant that Americans had overrun the ridge.

The company around the hospital stopped firing and started moving up the ridge on the left side of the village. I don't think there were very many Germans left up there, but it still had to be searched and cleared. If any Germans were up there, they could play havoc with us and cause a lot of casualties.

The sniper fire from the rear had practically ceased now, but we were getting it from both sides and from the front of us. More of our troops were breaking through the far end of the village now, and the Germans' organized resistance had all but ceased.

Our tanks weren't firing anymore, so apparently the panzer crews were out, and the armored infantry was also surrendering. I couldn't understand why these last snipers still kept up their lost cause. They could do no good for their fatherland any longer, but as long as they fired, we kept covering up cellars and knocking down walls. Pretty soon there would be nothing left of this village. I'd seen villages destroyed before, but never so completely as we destroyed that village.

We were getting close to the front line now, and Lieutenant Crow said we should stop and take cover until he found out what the score was. The sniper fire was very sparse now; it practically had stopped. We kept well down behind the cats, with just one man on lookout. There couldn't be more than a dozen or two more cellars, and we would have them all covered. I wondered how many Germans we'd buried alive.

Men started coming down from the ridge. It began

to look like old home week in the streets of the village. They were bringing with them quite a few prisoners, all German army, no SS troops. The only action still in progress was down below the far end of the village now, where the panzers were, and that seemed to be almost over. I gave the area a good look with my field glasses. I could see hundreds of prisoners. It almost looked like we had fought the whole German army here, and that there were no more Germans to fight. But I knew we would have to fight all the way to Berlin.

An eerie silence fell over the area suddenly. It was a weird feeling: all at once, here we were, after days of fighting. Maybe we would definitely get that rest behind the lines this time for sure. I began planning what I would do with my free time, first a bath, then clean clothes, then about three days of sleep. Then I should be rested enough to take a trip or two into Florence, and I didn't want to miss Lucca. And of course, I would only be a few miles from Pisa, so I must go and see that famous leaning tower. I wasn't much of a drinker, but I did hope our beer ration would catch up with us. A beer would taste very good right now.

Lieutenant Crow came back and interrupted my thoughts. He said our job here was finished, and we could return to our bunkers. He also said he had seen the commander of the first battalion, and he had sent his heartiest thanks and would be writing a recommendation to our battalion commander, and to the engineering commander.

We were happy to get out of there and didn't waste any time turning those cats around and scooting back to our bunkers. I never thought anything ever looked better than those bunkers as we reached the rise outside the village and saw them in the distance.

When we returned, we jumped off the cats and waved to the operators, and they took off to their road building. We just sat and looked at the village. It was all over. Our troops were setting up defense lines up on that ridge now; then they would be pulled off, to be replaced with the other division. And we could go back for that rest. I hoped we would get at least two weeks back there, but I also knew they were getting ready for the big push that would take us down into the Po Valley and on to the Alps. We had to receive our replacements and train them. We knew as mountain troops we fought differently than the flatland divisions, but the basic training these replacements would have received would be strictly flatland. We fought very much in platoon groups most of the time, we didn't even know sometimes where the other platoons of our company were. Of course, we did know how to fight in company and battalion groups, as the battle we were just in proved, and I'm sure once we hit the Po Valley we would fight that way again. But basically we fought as small units.

We didn't go into our bunkers now; there was no sound of gunfire anywhere. Some of the other units were coming back, most of them bringing prisoners with them. Every once in a while a unit would bring in SS troopers, and they were well guarded. Many of the prisoners were very well dressed, in uniforms I hadn't seen before. These were from the panzers, tankers—the elite. They lived well and died well; they were the cream of the crop, and they were good.

The only reason they hadn't been moving back there was because they were out of fuel. There had been 96 vehicles back there, panzers of all sizes, and if they could have maneuvered, the outcome of the battle might have been very different. As it was, we dealt the Germans a blow that they never recovered from.

Chapter 16

Later that night, Lieutenant Studebaker called out for a squad leaders' meeting. The four of us went back to his bunker to be informed, finally, that we would be pulling off the mountain starting tomorrow morning. They had already pulled back one regiment; another regiment was setting up defenses up on the ridge we'd just taken, and our other battalions would be pulled back early tomorrow morning and taken off the line. The first and second battalions would withdraw first and the third would be last. After we pulled out they would bring up an armored division to put in reserve here, and the troops of the other division would move up and replace the regiment up on the ridge. By noon, the whole division should be moving back to the rest area, which he said would be somewhere near Pisa. "As far as the battle we were just in, we hurt the enemy badly. We took fourteen thousand prisoners, including four thousand Italians. And we got sixty-one panzers and other armored vehicles and sixty-six artillery pieces. We took a great amount of information which we will use when we hit the Po Valley and beyond."

The reasons the Germans had fought so hard here were that their panzers had no fuel but they had plenty of ammo, and, second, they thought we were trying to break into the Po Valley. "They feel, once we break into the valley, their war in Italy is lost and they'll head straight for the Alps. There they plan to fight for every inch of ground." He paused, then smiled one of his rare smiles. "Well, gentlemen, that's about all I have to say to you now. Be prepared to move fast when the order comes. We'll cross back over the ridge back there and down to the road. Oh. And I don't want anyone going ape and getting drunk now. I know there's plenty to drink up here, but just have the men take it easy. We'll get our chance. Okay, move out and have a good rest tonight. We are well guarded for a change."

I went back and gave the fellows the good news. They took it like they always took news. I did notice that they all started packing things, though. They would be ready to move when the order came. Our barracks bags would catch up to us when we arrived at the rest camp. I could put underwear on that fit me for a change; that may not thrill anyone, but it was just one of the pleasures of life that an infantryman looked forward to. I also had a pair of low-cut boots that we were allowed to wear. They were very comfortable and light. These mountain boots became very heavy after a time, especially when they never had a chance to dry out. Can you imagine, I thought, going to sleep with your boots off? Maybe if we stayed in Lucca at a hotel they would have sheets we could crawl between. Such luxury! I had to get it off my mind. I wrapped up in a blanket, took my boots off, and went to sleep.

Early the next morning, at the break of day, I awoke. I couldn't believe it, I had slept the whole night through without being disturbed once!

Stutzman and Reds were curled up on the other end of the bunker. Reds had taken his boots off, but Stutzman had not. He also slept with his rifle folded in his arms and grenades nearby. The enemy was not going to catch *him* napping!

I lit the Coleman stove and put on some water to heat. When I stirred in the coffee, Reds awakened. He stretched and put his boots on. Stutzman just slept on. I opened a K-ration, and had a quarter pound of American cheese with crackers for breakfast. It tasted good. Reds heated his water and made his coffee. He also opened a K-ration. He had eggs and bacon with crackers. I looked out the bunker entrance. It was going to be a nice sunny day. We would be going downhill, so it would probably warm up and we could at least enjoy our trip back. It was getting into March now and before long the rains would start and we would be wet and miserable most of the time, but for now we could get the creaks out of our bones and loosen up.

When I finished my breakfast, I crawled outside the bunker. The first battalion was moving back now. I saw Lieutenant Crow, I called out to him, asked if there were any snipers left in the village. He said, "Not one shot all night. We must have covered them all up, or killed them with grenades." He said he had slept a lot during the night just taking his turn as officer in charge, but that the night was very quiet. He said he had to go now, but would see me back at the rest camp. Maybe we would get a chance to go somewhere together; but I thought, *Fat chance, you're an officer and I'm only a sergeant.* The army frowns on officers and enlisted men fraternizing. I said we would see, and he was off.

There was a lot of movement now. Troops from the other division were moving up to the ridge and the village; troops from the armored division were moving into our area with their jeeps and half tracks and armored cars. They were a cocky bunch; they were good and they knew it. Their tanks seemed to be staying on the road, or near it; I supposed they didn't want to come back here where, if it rained, there would be a lot of mud.

We gave up our bunker and meandered back toward the grove. We just sat back there, some guys snoozing, some telling jokes, some clowning around. I thought this was a good chance to clean my carbine. I couldn't remember the last time I had cleaned it. When I looked down the barrel, I wondered how a bullet could have passed through it; it was filthy. I asked Reds where his mules were now, and he told me they would be the first ones trucked out; they were probably already in the rest camp, eating and just taking life easy.

Lieutenant Studebaker was back with us. He had his radio with him, to receive the order to move out. The whole platoon was here now. I counted them. Twenty-three men. That left nineteen line men out of thirty six, and we had had replacements once since I had joined this outfit. That's a lot of casualties in anyone's language, but the enemy had lost at least a hundred to our one, a good average.

The armored boys had brought their kitchens with

them, and they were setting them up in the open area between the bunkers and the village. The fires were already going, and the troops were lining up to have their breakfast. A captain came back and told Lieutenant Studebaker they had plenty of rations and they would be very happy to feed us too. The lieutenant said fine and told us to get our mess kits and line up. It was funny, half our guys didn't know what the hell they had done with their mess kits. I found mine; it was in my backpack, way down at the bottom. I couldn't remember the last time I had used it, but I'd hung onto it thinking that I'd eat regular again sometime in the future.

We lined up at the kitchen and a sergeant threw in about ten pieces of bacon, and on top of that a piece of steak big enough to last three days. He said they had to use it up; their rations had caught up with them and they had no place to refrigerate them, so they had to use it. I also got about two pounds of scrambled eggs. We hadn't had food like this for a long long time. When we stepped up to the coffee, the smell was enough to drive a man crazy. It was real coffee, brewed to perfection; at least, we thought so.

I had so much food, I wasn't sure I could eat half of it. I found a spot next to Reds, who dove in like a hungry pack rat. Between mouthfuls of food, he said, "They said we could have seconds if we wanted." I couldn't believe this guy; he was wolfing down his food so he could go back for seconds. Well, I don't blame him. Who knows when we'd eat like this again. You learn in the infantry that you don't waste anything, because tomorrow there may be none. I could hardly get off the ground I was so full, but there was Reds on his second serving. "Are you going back for thirds?"

He said, "Well, no, but I sure could use another one of those steaks."

I couldn't believe it, but he did go back and get a third one, bigger than the first two. That day, Company L ate well, and I suppose all the other companies ate the same down the line. As far as I could see, they had set kitchens up and troops were milling around.

After we ate, we went back down to the grove and, like big fat sleek animals dropped off to sleep. Life certainly was pleasant, I thought. Here we were living in the lap of luxury. You know, I'd never noticed it before, but some of the guys snored like hell. Funny I hadn't heard it before, but maybe that was because they never slept long enough at one time to snore.

It was around 1200 hours. I awoke with a start. Someone was calling out, "Saddle up! Third battalion is moving out." Company I moved down the line, then Company K, and finally our turn came. It was good to see all these troops going up the path. It gave a fellow a sort of pride to be part of it. Colonel Track was standing outside a jeep smiling; Lieutenant Studebaker gave him a salute and the colonel returned it.

We walked up the path to our old line. The mines had all been cleared now by our engineers, so we didn't have to be too careful where we walked. We passed over the foxholes we had dug. I wondered who would fill them in, or if they would ever be filled in. We went down past the farmhouse and saw the old Italian farmer and his wife. They were waving at us, but at the same time I think they were glad to see us go. They could start to live a normal life again. Down on the road we took a right turn and followed the column. It was a much happier bunch of guys now than when we had come this way before.

We walked for the better part of an hour until we came to a small village. There were trucks waiting for us there; some were division trucks, and some belonged to a quartermaster battalion that had been brought up to take us back to the rest area. We climbed aboard and the trucks took off.

After about two and a half hours we pulled up to a field with tents set up, and unloaded. There were guides to take us to our area, and after walking for about fifteen minutes, we saw a sign for Company L, first platoon. Each squad had two tents, and since we were the first squad, we went into the first two. It seemed like a palace in ours. Cots. We didn't have to sleep on the ground. And extra blankets. We unloaded and sat on the cots, four men in each tent. We didn't know what to do with ourselves.

I took a couple of blankets and spread them down on a cot. I was tired. I'd thought after that night's sleep I had, I'd never be tired again, but I was. We had walked five or six miles and ridden two or three hours, with just one stop, so we'd come quite a distance. No one knew for sure just exactly where we were, but someone in the tent said he had seen a sign just before we turned into the field that had said Pisa was thirteen kilometers in one direction and Livorno, six in the other. We had skirted Florence about an hour before we reached the rest area, so I was able to pinpoint about where we were on the map of Italy I'd found. We were near a small village named Stagno.

I was about to lay down to take a nap when someone called out, "Mess call! Bring your kits and line up!" I'd forgotten about food. They really didn't expect us to eat again after that terrific breakfast, did they? But then, I *was* getting hungry. I awakened everyone in the squad, and they grabbed their kits and headed for the mess hall—or, I should say kitchen, since the tables they had set up for us were in the open. At least we could sit down at a table and eat. That was a change in our lives right there. We were really living now—cots to sleep on, tents over our heads, and places to sit and eat. Man, this was living!

After another feast on thick steaks, and a lot of wine and beer, I looked at my watch and was surprised to see that it was 1930 hours. It was just starting to get dark. I also knew with all the beer and wine, there would be a lot of noise in the camp tonight, but I went back and lay down on my cot. Reds was there, too. He asked me if I wanted his beer or wine; he didn't drink at all. I said no, but to hang onto it, some of the other guys would be thirsty tomorrow for some hair of the dog.

The next thing I heard was mess call again. Willie was going up and down the street calling out. I said to myself, hell, we just ate, what're they doing, serving a late-night snack now, too? But then I noticed there was light in the tent. It was 0730 hours. I had slept for twelve hours straight. I must have been worn to a frazzle—either that or the letdown of responsibility was so great that I'd really relaxed, maybe for the first time in weeks.

I was fully clothed, except my boots, which I didn't even remember taking off. I pulled them on, grabbed my mess kit, and headed down to the kitchen. What do you think they were serving for breakfast? Steak and scrambled eggs! They gave me a steak that was bigger than the one I had had the night before. Reds, Stutzman, and Russ came and sat at the same table with me. Stutzman looked worse than he usually looked, and I asked, "What the hell happened to you?"

He said he had been in the other tent drinking beer with the guys there; they had consumed their whole ration, then the wine, and he guessed he got a little drunk. "I think it was the wine that made me sick, though. But I'll be all right as soon as I get this steak and maybe another one into me. Food always straightens me out right away."

I asked Russ if he'd been drinking, too, and he said he had, but he still had the wine left. He was saving that for tonight.

The supply sergeant came in and announced that we were to pick up our beer ration before returning to our tents. All I could say was, "Oh, no, not again."

After we ate, they gave us twelve more cans of beer, but no wine. It looked like another day of relaxing before anything would happen. Well, the command had to get their feet on the ground, too, and some of these officers hadn't looked too clean cut this morning either.

Shortly before 1200 hours, Gardner came around to tell us we would be taken to the bath house after we ate. We could bathe and get clean clothes. He told the non-coms to take the stripes off our sleeves or we would never see them again. I just remembered that I was a staff sergeant and hadn't yet worn any stripes; in fact I didn't *have* any stripes yet. "I'll give you my old ones, Ike," Gardner said. "I saved one pair. You can buy more at the canteen, if they ever open one, and I'll see the supply sergeant. He may have some around too." He also said there would be a division review sometime next week, and before we left for the parade, the regiment was having a formation, at which time medals would be presented.

It took about twenty minutes to get to the bath area. On the way we passed quite a few Italian civilians, among them some pretty nice looking girls. You would have thought some of the guys had never seen a woman before, the way they hollered at them. I think the women were used to this; they didn't bat an eye and they didn't turn around to look, either.

The bath area was just a big tent with steam coming out all over, and there were all kinds of signs: *Put all personal items and your boots in the net bag being furnished you. Make sure you write your name on the tag on the net bag. Put all articles of clothing in bins marked sweaters, shirts, pants, underpants, undershirts, socks. When you enter the first chamber soap yourself down completely and enter the second chamber.*

We took our one-minute showers, got our clean clothes, and hopped back into the trucks. Back at our tent area, Lieutenent Studebaker called a formation as soon as we jumped out of the trucks. It was the first formation we had had since we arrived. He had a list in his hand, and he started to call out the names. As he did, Levin and Gardner passed down the line and handed each of the men his badge. So now we had something to wear on our shirts. The lieutenant also announced that we would receive our replacements tomorrow morning and he wanted to see all squad leaders to double check how many men we would need to fill their ranks. Before he dismissed us, he told us that the rest of the day was ours, but we were not to go too far from camp, and we were not to get so damned drunk that the MPs had to bring us back.

I warned my squad that he meant it and I didn't want to go back on the line with some of them in a stockade somewhere. I asked them to behave like the gentlemen I knew they were. There were a lot of laughs after that remark. One of the men said, "Only congress can make a gentleman."

Chapter 17

We were actually on the outskirts of Livorno. It was only a short distance to the city itself, probably three or four miles. I had never been there, but I didn't want to spend the whole afternoon in a bar. I wanted to look around. And the guys from the squad had a bar in mind. I asked Reds, who didn't drink, if he had any plans. He said he hadn't even thought about leaving camp, but if I wanted to go somewhere to sight-see, he would go along. We both had a little money. There aren't many places you can spend it on the front lines. We hadn't been paid yet—in fact we hadn't been paid for two months—but we still had money. Les ended up joining us, too.

We started to walk toward the city, when a jeep came along. It was Captain Bear. He asked us where we were going, and we told him. He told us to pile in, he was going there too. He said he had to go to a staff meeting at Regiment Command and that the colonel was having it in the city at a restaurant, to get the officers to relax a bit. He didn't know when he was coming back, but if we wanted to check back at the restaurant at about 1900 hours, we could ride back with him if the meeting was over.

Livorno was actually the first city we had been in in

Italy. Oh, we had been to Florence, and I had been in Lucca, but for just a few moments.

Livorno's houses were built in rows, with the balconies and with girls sitting or standing on practically each one. It was clean at this end of the city, but it became dirtier the further in we went. It's a seaport, and there were quite a few ships at the docks and others setting out in the bay waiting to come in to be unloaded. There were a lot of sailors walking around. I'd heard there were a lot of fights between soldiers and sailors. I hoped no one would pick on us. I had seen Les in action, and Reds was pretty good-sized, and if he could handle an opponent the way he handled those mules, he would be a good guy to have on your side in case of trouble. I do not like to fight; I had had only one fight while in high school. A guy kept mussing my hair and one day he just got to me and I beat the living hell out of him. He never picked on me again, nor anyone else while I was around. My mother had written me he had been killed in the Pacific somewhere. The memory of our fight was painful, I never wanted to fight again. Fighting Germans was one thing. Fisticuffs with your own was quite another.

There really isn't too much to see in Livorno. Some museums—the art in them we did not understand. There were some old churches dating back to the 1400s. But the rest was strictly restaurants and bars. Bars all over the place, especially near the docks. They looked like they had been there for a long time, I suppose they were there for the convenience of the sailors when they came ashore.

We found what looked like a good restaurant and

decided to eat. It was just 1700 hours, so we had two hours before we had to meet the captain. We entered the place and were met by a maitre d', who said he spoke English. He seated us at a table and lit a candle, then gave us a menu which we couldn't read, but we could make out the prices on it. They were high, but we had enough money to afford anything they had on the menu. The maitre d' ordered for us, then brought a bottle of wine and poured each of us a half glass, after a big deal opening the bottle. It was a good wine, and reminded me of the kind my mother used to make. She learned it from my grandfather who made barrels of it every year. They soon brought our spaghetti. I said, "My first spaghetti in Italy, it had better be good, or I'll never believe another story about this country." I tasted it. It was unbelievable, I had never tasted anything so good in my life. It was a lot different than what they called spaghetti at home. This was just out of this world.

When we finished eating, Reds had another glass of wine and Les and I finished the bottle. Reds was getting tipsy. He was asking all kinds of crazy questions and laughing without anyone saying anything. He was funny. I would remind him of this tomorrow to see if he remembered it.

We headed back to the restaurant where we were to meet the captain. He was waiting for us, and he looked like he was feeling no pain, either. So, I thought, the boys were boozing it up while they were planning our next move against the Germans.

When we got back to camp, the other members of our squad were already there, drunk and drinking more. We would receive another beer ration tomorrow, so they were putting away what they had left from their last ration. I looked under my cot. Where there were supposed to be twenty-three cans of beer, there were three. Someone had been helping himself. I was going to give them the beer anyway, but I told them that this wasn't the gentlemanly behavior I'd asked for. They all said it wouldn't happen again, but I knew it would. I told them that the least they could do was pick up the cans and throw them in the barrels outside.

Someone said, "Ah, we'll do that in the morning."

"Like hell you will! You will do it now. And, Buster, I mean *now*." It was the first time I'd ever raised my voice to one of my squad members. They weren't sure how to take it. But they all hopped to it. When the party was over, they crawled into their cots and fell asleep. I couldn't sleep myself. It was still early. I took a walk around the camp, stopped near the kitchen tent, and lit a cigarette. I was sitting there smoking when Lieutenant Studebaker came walking by. He saw me and came over. "I didn't know you smoked," he said.

"I don't really. But up on that first ridge, I had a few to calm me down. They don't do much else for me though."

He sat down beside me and lit up a cigarette too. We started talking about what we'd do after the war. I asked him if he was going to stay in the army.

"Hell, no. I'm only a reserve officer. Got my commission from a military school. No. I plan to go to school, probably study law and then go into my uncle's firm." Studebaker was about nineteen then. He wasn't entirely sure that that was what he wanted to do, and added, "Of course, we may all be dead soon, and we won't have to worry about our future, isn't that so?"

"I don't feel that way. I think I'll come out of this war. I don't think I was put here to die in some God-forsaken spot."

"That's a good way to feel. It gives a person something to hope for. A goal. If anything does happen, at least you know to the end that you have that goal to reach."

As the evening wore on, he loosened up more than I'd ever seen him, and started telling me about himself. Studebaker had been kicked around between his uncle and aunt since he'd been seven years old. That was when his parents had been divorced. He hadn't seen his mother for five or six years now, he wasn't sure where she was. She had been in Europe when the war started, but he hadn't heard from her since. His father was a naval officer in the Pacific and wrote him very nice letters. He was a captain then, in command of a cruiser.

Studebaker's uncle and aunt were very good to him, but they weren't his mother and father, and he reached a point where they couldn't handle him anymore. So he was put in the military school to be straightened out. "They did a fine job, but it took me a year to get used to their way of doing things. We had had a general from the First World War as our commandant, and he'd brought along with him all the discipline and punishment of the old army. He was there for one reason and that was to make men out of boys, and this he did." He became thoughtful for a moment, then: "He's died since I left school. It's

164

a pity he didn't get to see the fine job he'd done, the fine record we established just because of him. That, my friend, is accomplishing something. That is having a mission in life. That old man lived for us boys."

He field-stripped his cigarette, stamped the fire out, and said he was going to hit the hay. We'd get our replacements tomorrow morning, then have a couple more days off, then back to the drag again, learning to be soldiers, before they sent us back to the front again.

The next morning, after breakfast, a formation was called. A lot of nice clean-looking fellows, well shaved and shined up, were awaiting us. They were replacements. They eyed us and we eyed them. I wondered how long it would take to get these clean characters dirty so they would look like us. But I knew: one engagement.

Studebaker addressed the formation, assigning men from the replacement troops to squads. The first four peeled off and joined our squad. Two of them were quite big fellows and two were quite small. I wondered how one of the small guys had been able to get into the army.

After the formation was dismissed, and I got acquainted with the replacements in my squad, the shortest fellow said something I couldn't understand, and one of the others said something I couldn't understand, and one of the others said they called him the Greek. He couldn't speak English, but could understand it. So we would call him the Greek. I asked him if that was okay with him, and he said, "Okay," about the only word he ever said to us as long as he was with us.

The next fellow was Fienberg. The third man was Miller. He said that was what he was always called, except back home. If you said Miller there, fifty people would look around. He was from the Pennsylvania Dutch country. The last said his name was Dollar, and that he'd been called a lot of things in his life, but it always came back to Dollar.

Gardner came around shortly after the replacements had been taken care of to announce that we'd be getting paid, and after that we were free to do as we pleased. He also said they were running an excursion to Pisa and Lucca after lunch. It'd probably leave about 1300 hours, and he wanted to see the whole platoon go, but, of course, it was strictly up to us. It sounded good to me. I was ready to go.

Reds, who was nursing a headache from his glass and a half of wine the night before said he'd go with me on the condition that I sew on my stripes. I laughed, and told him I would, but that he had to sew his stripes on, too; he was a sergeant now. The Greek was sitting there watching us, and when we'd produced the needles and thread, he took the shirts out of our hands and proceeded to sew them on. When he was finished, you couldn't even see the stitches. I looked at it and said, "My mother couldn't do a better job than that."

When I was a private, my pay was $19.50 a month, but with these stripes, I should be receiving more than twice the pay. When it came time for me to step up to the paymaster, he called out that I was to receive $130.84! What the hell would I do with all that money? When I stepped away from the pay table, I didn't even count the money, I was so shocked. I decided to go to the company clerk and have him get me a money order for $100 and have it sent to my mother. She'd put it in the bank for me. I should have a tidy sum when I left the army. It would pay for a lot of the schooling I had in mind.

The trucks left for Pisa very shortly after lunch. There were four or five guys from the platoon who weren't on the trucks. They had made what they called connections the night before and were to meet some girls today. There would go their pay. Tomorrow they'd be borrowing just to buy their cigarettes and candy.

The trucks rolled up the road, and it was not very long before we reached Pisa. We pulled into a large square and unloaded. The Leaning Tower was in front of us, and it really was leaning. It was leaning so much I couldn't figure out what kept it from falling. There were a lot of GIs here, not all from our division, but quite a few. The Lieutenant had a tour book and he was explaining as much as he could about the tower. He said, reading from a book, "There are also some very famous paintings here, a goodly portion of the old Italian masters being represented." It sounded pretty good to me, but some of the fellows were bored before we ever started the tour. Our guide finally showed up. He said the last group had taken longer than usual and that was why he was late. He showed us around. The first thing, of course, was the tower. It was funny walking around it. You had to walk something like you walked on board ship, and I felt a little foolish until I looked at someone else and saw him walking the same way. Some of the fellows had brought little stones up with them and they were dropping them off to see how far away from the base they'd fall. It was quite a distance.

We came out of the tower and our guide took us into the church, of which the tower is a part. There were the paintings. He gave us the history of most of them. Some, I recognized. I remembered seeing some of them in an old family Bible back home. Our guide told us that some of these paintings had been partially restored over the years, as they had been destroyed either by floods of the River Arno, or by enemy attacks when the city had been a city state and had had to defend itself against hosts of marauders.

After we left the church, we went into several museums. I believe that it was here in Pisa that I first became interested in art. Ironic, that it had taken a war to get me here among some of the most beautiful creations of mankind.

We loaded back on the trucks and took off for Lucca. Lucca is surrounded by walls and although most of the Italian cities have walls, too, there is something extraordinary about Lucca's. We entered the city over a bridge that could well have been over a moat at one time, then through the arch and into a large square with the inevitable cathedral facing onto it.

There weren't too many other GIs here so we would have the city all to ourselves. This was not an organized tour; we were on our own, but had to be back here at the trucks by 1930 hours. Reds, Les and I started in the cathedral first. A man in a dark brown robe came up to us and spoke in English. He said he was a Franciscan monk, and would be happy to explain anything he could for us. We asked him about the paintings, and he said although there were some by the old masters, many were by local artists who had never become well known outside this region of Italy. We told him it didn't make any difference to us, they were all beautiful. He appreciated this and said we must be real lovers of art to appreciate something beautiful but not famous. We told him we knew very little of art, that these were some of the first paintings we'd ever really seen. Eventually, we asked him about the wall around the city. He told us that it hadn't been touched in hundreds of years except to replace a loose stone here and there once in a while. It had been built to last a long time, and indeed it would, long after we had left the earth.

It was like a gift, talking with this learned gentleman whose main job here was the restoration of paintings. When we walked out of the cathedral, we crossed the square and went down a narrow street, to a smaller square. I'd learned from the monk that the word for square was piazza. Here was an outside restaurant, and some of the other fellows were sitting at tables drinking wine. I saw Russ, drinking wine. We hadn't eaten for quite a while so I suggested we eat here. Both Reds and Les agreed, so we found a table. An attractive waitress came out and took our order. She was also speaking English. I asked her if everyone spoke English here, and she laughed and said it was taught in school. Many students took it, hoping to go to America after the war. I asked her how the Italians could fight us and then break their necks to get to our country, and she said that the Italian people weren't fighting the Americans; only the Fascists were doing that—Mussolini's crowd, she called them.

After we ate (Reds stayed away from the wine this time), we walked some more, and found some steps up to the top of the wall. The wall is easily as high as any building in the city except the cathedral and a few other churches. On top of the wall were the battlements, where many armies in the past had stood and fought their enemies. I wondered how many men had died up here. I'm sure none were remembered now. We walked quite a ways around the wall. At each corner was a block house, usually quite large, where troops had rested when they weren't in battle. Each one would hold probably about seventy or eighty men. There was a lot of armor hanging on the walls, along with swords and spikes and several piles of cannonballs. On the walls were mounted the cannons. They were just heavy iron cylinders with fuseholes and powderholes. Primitive, but effective.

Returning to the truck later, we passed the restaurant where we had eaten. The waitress was still on duty serving more GIs and laughing up a storm with them.

Gardner and Levin were sitting near the trucks on a bench, they seemed very tired. I said to them, "What the hell were you doing to look so tired?"

Gardner answered, "This Jew got me mixed up with some babe this afternoon and she wouldn't let me go. I spent three hours in bed with her. That's why I'm tired."

Levin said, "You're the one who made the eyes at that other babe. She couldn't speak English, but she could do everything else in English and quite a few other languages, too." I asked them if they had been to the pro station, and they just laughed, "Did you ever try to march with a dose of clap? If you did you wouldn't have to ask that question. There's nothing in this world that hurts more. Take it from the voice of experience."

The other men were showing up now, and after a few minutes we loaded up. We were tired, and although it only took us about forty minutes to return to camp, some of the fellows fell asleep. Many were looking forward to getting away tomorrow again and possibly making a tour in another direction. We didn't know what was in store starting tomorrow; we were going to get back to serious training, starting about 0800 hours in the morning and from here on in the training was going to be tough and mean. When we hit the line the next time, we would be in the Alps.

Chapter 18

Willie came down the company street at 0600 hours the next morning, and with his German accent called out for a company formation in 10 minutes. The next order of business would be a two-mile jog. My squad was the first to get to the formation, and I was proud of that. It showed they were alert and ready to go, even though they didn't realize what they were doing, standing there half asleep.

Captain Bear walked out of the headquarters tent when the formation had been called to attention. Sergeant Schidt called for a report from each platoon leader, and then Bear took over, instructing the platoon leaders we would jog two miles on a marked course, then return to our camp, pick up our mess kits, eat our breakfast, and report back for a company formation. He also announced there would be no sick call this morning until the company had been dismissed for the day. With that, he ordered, "Left face, route step, forward march!"

We took off and marched for about two hundred yards when the Captain ordered, "Forward at a slow jog, march!" After another several hundred yards, he ordered us to increase cadence. We were already going at a very good jog when we speeded up again. We were ripping off the yards now. Some of the guys were beginning to feel it, but none showed any sign of dropping out. I was praying that the cadence wouldn't pick up any more. I didn't see many smiles. I figured the breakfasts would disappear fast this morning and there would be plenty of room for seconds. In fact, I could see myself eating one of those great big steaks we'd been fed the first couple of days.

We kept the same cadence and soon were back at our camp, in front of the company headquarters. We had thirty-five minutes to eat our breakfast and be back out here with full field equipment and arms, ready for a fast march of ten or twelve miles. We all ran back to our tents, grabbed our mess kits, and headed for the kitchen. They got the line fed with about ten minutes to go before we had to fall in again. We hurried back to our tents, packed up our backpacks, and fell in. We were ready to start our basic training all over again.

We marched out toward the northeast, for about an hour and a half, stopping only once for a ten-minute break. We were entering the rolling country, and some of these hills were much higher and steeper than they looked from camp. The captain decided we would jog the last two or three hundred yards, and by the time he called a halt, most of us felt we'd had plenty of exercise for the day, but the training hadn't even started yet. I checked out my squad, especially the new men. I know the older men could take this kind of punishment, but I did not know how well the new men would stand up. I was sure they'd come around, but for the first or second time, this kind of treatment can be trying. They seemed to be holding up very well, especially the Greek. He was a wiry fellow and seemed to have more stamina than two others together.

Training started with the rifle grenade. Sergeant Gardner demonstrated the grenade launcher with a live blank. He was very good with this weapon, having used it during the night attack by the Germans. But today he seemed irked at his own performance. His grenades were falling short of target at first, and it wasn't until he'd fired a few that he got back to form. Still, even when he was off, he was better than most. Five yards of a target is a great shot with a grenade launcher, and he was always closer than that.

Then, after more than an hour of the next exercise—close-order drill and the manual of arms—our mess truck came lumbering up the path. They set up a serving line, built a fire, and proceeded to prepare our dinner for us. Until I saw that truck I hadn't given much thought to eating, but I suddenly realized I was hungry and could probably eat half a cow. But no such luck. We had Spam, the most hated food in the United States Army. After we'd eaten, we took it easy until the officers were ready for us again. We didn't know what they had in mind, but we expected the worst. And it was not long in coming.

The order came for us to fall into company formation. We would drill for the next hour in platoon drill. We performed every maneuver a platoon can go through. We were carrying our full packs, and after the hour was up we looked pretty good. I was surprised how well we looked.

After a ten-minute break, a company front formation was ordered again. We marched to our position.

Ours was the first platoon, and all the other platoons fell in line with us. The captain announced that this was all today. He wanted to start us out easy and work up to the harder parts of our training in the days to come. We would, however, march back to camp.

We started off marching, but after the last break, he had us at a fast jog. It was too much for some of the newer men, and they started dropping out. None of mine did, and I was proud of that. We kept this pace until we were in camp and about fifty yards from our company street, past some of the other units, who just stood and stared at us like maybe our captain had flipped his cork. When we got back to our tents, we hit those cots, old men and the new men. No one said anything, and we didn't hear another sound until Willie came down the street and announced mess call at 1800 hours.

When I returned from mess, I really didn't feel like going to bed yet, so I decided to sit outside for a while. Reds soon joined me. Then Miller came out, said he had tried to sleep, but couldn't. We sat there talking. All three of us had a feel for the earth, and we all were farmers. Miller said they raised mostly corn and tobacco on his farm. A lot of the old Pennsylvania people were selling to the Amish now, he said, and going off to the city. The Amish, it seemed, could take a piece of rock and make something grow from it, Miller said. I had a lot of Amish friends in Indiana; they were good farmers. One of my Amish friends had joined the army and was in the Pacific, but I suppose he wasn't considered one of them any more. I said, "Come to think of it his name was Miller, too."

Miller laughed. "I think half of the Amish are

named Miller."

It turned out that both Miller's people and mine traced our ancestry to the southern part of Germany. Red's people were German, too, but he didn't know where they'd come from or when. He could trace them only as far back as Illinois and the founder of the Mormons, Joseph Smith. They'd gone west with Brigham Young and had been part of the founding fathers of Utah and Salt Lake City. He said he didn't believe in fighting and killing, either, same as the Amish, but if you're forced into a corner, he thought it was his God-given right to keep himself alive. That was why he'd enlisted in the army, and since he knew how to ski and climb mountains they put him in this outfit. He had worked with mules at home, but they were different than the army's. They weren't so stubborn and mean, as these were. "Don't forget, our mules got a nice barn and good feed back home. Sometimes these Italian mules never see the inside of a building or ever eat anything but grass. That'd make any creature mean."

Russ came out of his tent all shaved and cleaned up. I asked him where he was going and he said he was going with some of the other fellows to Stagno, they had some girls lined up for tonight. I thought he was crazy, but he was our youngest man and he had to sow some wild oats yet. I told him that regardless of what he does, just remember tomorrow. "The captain said he took it easy on us today. Tomorrow he's really going to start getting tough."

I looked at my watch. It was almost 2100 hours, I was just about to hit the hay, when the mess sergeant came walking along. He said he was on his way down to the kitchen to have a cup of coffee, and asked us to join him. We grabbed our cups and followed him. Some of the kitchen help were still working, cleaning up for the night, and I noticed they were fixing themselves a snack. I told the mess sergeant I could eat a little something, so he asked one of the fellows down there to fix up a nice salad for us. I mentioned that he'd never served a salad to us before, and he replied that we'd get one tomorrow. He'd just today received the makings.

We had the salad, and the coffee, and went back to our tents. We hit the hay and didn't awaken until the next morning, with the familiar cry of "Get up! Company formation!" It was Willie again. Who else?

Chapter 19

The next three days of our training were very much like our first day of training, but harder. Each day the training was turned more to fire and movement. movement.

In this time we had our regimental review and received our medals. Then, the division review. We would be the second regiment to pass in that review, and after it was over, we returned to our own areas and had the rest of the day to ourselves.

Some of the guys decided they would go see the girls they'd met. Reds and I cleaned up our equipment. We knew that one of these days we'd be ordered back to that front line again and might not get the chance again to do it at our leisure. We did want to take another trip before we returned to the front. To Florence. Les said he wanted to go with us. We spent the afternoon cleaning our gear and guns, had a few beers, then decided to take a walk out toward Stagno, hoping we could find a place that served pasta. We did find a place that made its own pasta, and ate very well, then walked around a bit before we returned to camp. There Lieutenant Studebaker came up with some bad news. He'd just left the company headquarters tent; with him were Gardner and Levin. "Are all your men in camp?"

"No. Three of them had taken off shortly after we returned from the review. I think I know where they could be found, though, if it's important."

The Lieutenant said, "No, it's not that important, but we are going back up early tomorrow morning, and I wanted everyone to get as much rest as possible. We don't know where we're going, or what we'll do, but it's our last chance to sleep off the ground for a while." We looked at each other. We'd known this was coming, but we hadn't known when. This was it. We would go back up, this time, go all the way to the Alps, before we'd have another chance to get a complete night's sleep or to relax like we'd been doing for almost two weeks.

That's war. That's life.

The guys who had been out came in about 2330 hours. They were drunk, laughing, and in general making a lot of noise. I had kept myself awake purposely to tell them they were to pack and be ready to move at a moment's notice. I didn't think they were capable of getting anything ready. I stayed with them until they had their barracks bags packed, then I watched them until they packed their backpacks. I checked their ammo belts to see that they were full. Then Reds and I checked their rifles to make sure they didn't have any live ammo in them. We didn't need any accidents back here now. After they'd packed and closed their barracks bags, they hit the hay. Before we left the tent they were sleeping like babies.

I didn't even take my clothes off, just my boots. I

knew I'd have some work to do to get those guys up and ready to go when the time came. I fell asleep, and it seemed that after only a minute or two someone was shaking me awake. It was Willie. He said to get the squad up now and get them ready to go. We'd have breakfast first, then load up and pull out. They wanted it kept as quiet as possible, and didn't want any more civilians to know than they could help. The Germans did have their paid agents.

I crawled out of that beautiful cot for the last time, stretched, lit a candle, and woke Reds. Then I slipped to the other tent to awaken the men.

The snoring inside was deafening. It sounded as if I was on the front again and the machine guns had opened up! I shook the first man. He mumbled something about the time, and I said, "Who cares? Hit the deck! Breakfast in ten minutes, then we are heading for the front."

"You're kidding!"

I assured him I wasn't, and he jumped up and started dressing.

The second and third were two of last night's drunks. They came up fairly good, I was surprised.

The next was Dollar. He came up right away, hopped out of his cot, and started dressing.

I dreaded the last one. DeAngelo. He was a bastard when he was drunk. I'd almost come to blows with him up on the front lines when I'd caught him drunk in a foxhole. When I shook him now, he struck out with his fists. I wasn't expecting it, and he knocked me ass over appetite across a couple of cots and out the tent flap, then hollered after me, "Get out of here you fuckin' German son-of-a-bitch! I'll get up when I feel like it, and go tell that fuckin' lieutenant the same thing. You're not a squad leader, you're just an ass-kissin' bastard. That's why you got all those medals! Now get out of here and go fuck yourself."

Well, my temper burst like a flare. A couple of the guys started to grab me, and Reds came running. I shook him off and went after that no-good bastard. I pulled him out of his cot, hit him, and sent him through the tent flap, out into the company street. I grabbed him again and hit him so hard I thought I might have killed him. He hit the dirt and didn't move again.

Lieutenant Studebaker came running up, wanting to know what happened. Before I could open my mouth, the other five guys in that tent all opened up to the lieutenant and defended me. Studebaker just said, "Get him up and get him to breakfast. If he tries anything else, I'll leave him behind for a court-martial. He's been asking for it for a long time."

I stayed away from DeAngelo during breakfast and had nothing to do with him until we formed up in the company street to march to the trucks waiting to take us toward the front. I knew the man would be sorry for what he'd done, when he sobered up, but right then I couldn't find it in my heart to forgive him. And I didn't even like myself. One thing I'd been taught all of my life was not to hold a grudge, and always to be willing to forgive someone. But right now I couldn't find that forgiveness, for DeAngelo.

Chapter 20

Early in the afternoon, we passed through Florence. I would have given almost anything to leave the truck and spend about a week there. Maybe someday, I'll get back here again, I told myself. And the next time I won't be passing through on a troop truck. Florence was truly the home and the beginning of the restoration of Europe after the dark ages. From here came the masters, and the whole world benefitted from their art. I would return, I knew I would. And in the meantime, I would have time to read up on the city.

From Florence we headed north, toward the front. The foothills around Florence began to turn into small mountains, and the small mountains began to turn into larger mountains. About an hour north of Florence, the trucks stopped, and we got out to stretch our legs. By this time, we were getting quite tired riding. The six by six truck is not the most comfortable ride in the world, especially when you're crossing roads that could do with some repairs. We'd taken the road out of Florence heading for Bologna, so we were heading somewhere below that city. Before we'd left the line for our rest we were only about eight miles south of Bologna. I hadn't read of any new offensives while we were back in the rest camp, so I assumed we would end up in the approximate same area we had left. We'd left the camp before the sun came up, and it looked to me by the number of trucks that there was no more than one battalion of us. That is the way the army usually traveled, in small units. Too many German agents around who would report larger movements. They would bring up a battalion now, another tonight, and maybe one each day until the whole division was back on the line.

After another hour the trucks turned off the main road and started up a mountain road. Shortly, we came to the same village where we'd loaded on the trucks when we left the line. The trucks stopped and we were ordered off with all our equipment. It was now 1400 hours, still a lot of day left. Our kitchen was in the convoy and was setting up. We would mess in about half an hour.

Most of the fellows just sat down. They'd begun to realize that they might have a nice long walk ahead of them tonight, back up to our comfortable old foxholes. I saw one soldier bargaining with a woman for a loaf of bread. We'd had explicit orders not to trade with the villagers, but there he was, haggling away. I looked again. It was DeAngelo! I walked up to him, took the bread out of his hands, and bid the old woman good day. Then I turned to him and said, "Look, you son-of-a-bitch, we have orders not to trade with these people. Why the hell do you always have to do what you're told not to?"

He looked at me. His face was getting red, his hands flexing. He was thinking about making a fist, but he just stood there. I called Reds over and told him to keep an eye on this bastard, then turned back to DeAngelo. "I won't turn you in this time. But the next goddamned time I catch you spitting on the sidewalk, I'm going to report you."

I heard someone behind me say, "You don't have to report him to the lieutenant. I saw the whole thing."

I turned and there stood Lieutenant Studebaker. He was mad. His face was even redder than DeAngelo's. I told him to forget it this time, that I'd keep my eye on him myself. The Lieutenant agreed, but reluctantly.

The rest of the squad were sitting on the ground, or just lying around relaxing. The new men didn't know what to think. This was the second incident with DeAngelo today, and I could see the question on their faces. They wondered if this went on every day. The old men knew what the situation was. They'd seen it for a long time. Several of them who had been with the original bunch to come overseas together said he used to pull the same thing back in the States, and had several court-martials to his credit. In a way, I felt sorry for him. Here he had left this country to go to America, and here he was right back, now fighting for his newly adopted land. I had an uncle who had come from Germany shortly before the First World War. He could hardly speak English, they tell me, but he was drafted and had to return to Europe to fight his own people. He was killed in France and lies buried there now.

When we left, at about 1730 hours, it was on foot. We had about six or seven miles in front of us.

The weather was getting nice now and I hoped it would hold up. But I knew that there was always one thing the foot soldier could depend on — bad weather.

Rain, mud, snow, and ice.

The order came to form up in platoon formation, no more company formations. We were back in the mountains, and we were to become mountain units again. Heavy weapons joined each rifle platoon, with their machine guns and mortars. We could hear the artillery now, very faint, but it was the same sound we would hear for a long time. It would be with us as long as the war was.

We walked for another hour, then took a ten-minute break. It was still daylight, so the fellows were allowed to smoke. Everyone seemed to be in good spirits. We were laughing and telling jokes. I heard a lot about what some of the other guys had done in Livorno and Lucca. It seems there were plenty of girls to go around, or else these guys were lying like hell. I suspected it was a little of both. Walking again, we passed some 205s poised and ready to go, their crews ever on alert. There was some calling back and forth as we passed them, about making sure their shells passed over us when we reached the line.

After another hour, I estimated we had walked, in all, about eight miles. We were close to the front lines, and the artillery was coming from behind us now. There was no small-arms fire, but once in a while an artillery shell would pass over us, just enough, I suppose, to keep the Germans from thinking we'd forgotten them. So far, we hadn't received any German fire. Maybe they were getting short of ammo, and keeping things cool until we actually made an attack.

Soon, Lieutenant Studebaker told us we would bivouac up ahead about five hundred yards. We were to dig deep enough so that we could get our bodies off the surface, but didn't have to dig foxholes. There was very little artillery back here, and we'd be moving again at break of day. We built no fires and kept our smoking to a minimum. I was happy I wasn't addicted to cigarettes.

After we had dug in Sergeant Gardner came around to see that we had all been properly holed, and to see exactly where everyone was in case we would have to get out in a hurry.

It was still a little light, so the guys sat around talking, very low, joking and smoking their last cigarettes for the night. Some opened K rations and mixed their coffee in cold water. Then, one by one we drifted off to our holes, wrapped up in our blankets or shelter half, and dropped off to sleep.

It was still dark when Sergeant Gardner shook me and told me to get the squad ready to move. I asked him how far we had to go. He said it was still about three miles, and that we wouldn't be going up to the front yet; we would be in reserve. That sounded okay to me. But there was something about being in reserve. Usually, the reserve battalion was the one that made the first attack.

We were all ready to go in about five minutes. Everyone was a little easier to awaken this morning. No hangovers. Even DeAngelo seemed in a better mood this morning. Maybe he would straighten out and be a good soldier, after all. I knew he could be. He could be very cunning and alert when he wanted to, and he was a good scout. Most of the guys opened a K ration and had some breakfast. We were getting low on water, and I wondered if they would find us some before we arrived in our reserve area, or if we would have to carry it up after we arrived. Dawn was breaking now, and we were ordered down on the road in the same platoon formation as we had marched in yesterday.

When we arrived at the road, the mules were there, tied to a picket line. Studebaker told each squad leader to pick a mule for supplies. Since Reds was the assistant squad leader now, I had to choose someone else for mule-skinner. The Greek came up to me, and with a very few words in English and a lot of motion, told me that he knew mules, and would like to be the mule-skinner for our squad. I was a little doubtful at first, but he convinced me that he had worked mules all his life. He even liked mules. He *wanted* this job. I looked at Reds, who was standing back with a silly grin on his face, and said to him, "Should we try him?"

Reds said, "Why not? He probably knows more about mules than anyone, including myself." So the Greek became our new mule-skinner. He looked the stock over and picked a small jenny. She didn't look like she could carry her own weight. Reds laughed. "Why the hell he didn't pick a big one, I don't know. But he must have his reasons." I could just see us pulling and pushing to get this damned jenny-ass over a hill. But the man said he knew mules, so we decided to let him do what he wanted.

The roads were getting higher now. It was almost constantly up hill. We were going through passes and could not see very far ahead. It was beginning to look like our kind of fighting country again, us down here and the Germans up there.

It was fairly quiet now. Every few minutes we would

hear artillery. Maybe we would be lucky. Maybe the Germans had all pulled out and gone home, and all we'd have to do is walk across the Po Valley and the Germans would surrender. *Ha, that'll be the day*, I thought.

A shell hit above us. There was no danger; it was that far away, but it shook me back to reality. There were Germans there somewhere.

We reached a point where the cliffs rose straight up. There was just enough room for a road to pass through. A little further on, the cliffs gave way to a ravine with a stream running through it. We left the road and headed down a path toward the stream. It was a beautiful little brook, running fast like mountain streams do and very cold. We found a flat space behind a cliff and started to dig in. This was the reserve area.

There wasn't much to see. The road above. And down in the other direction, the stream. It ran down, and through a wide ravine, as far as the eye could see, into what looked like flat land. That flat land was the Po Valley, and we found out that between us and the valley there were at least a hundred thousand Germans. And they didn't want us to get there.

We dug our foxholes, but we couldn't dig too deep because we hit water. They were about three feet deep, but we made them big enough that two men could be quite comfortable. To keep the water from seeping up on us when we were sleeping, we put our shelter halves on the bottom of the foxholes when we slept, then took them up during the day and let them dry out. It was fairly comfortable sleeping. We had plenty of water now. We could use our Coleman stoves. We had to post guards up on the road, and at the other end of our camp, but each man had to stand only one hour each day, except at night when we would post two men at each post for two-hour shifts. Our other two platoons dug in below us, further down the stream, but where the other companies were, I didn't know. Nor did I know where our other two battalions were. We hadn't seen them passing on the road above us, so I assumed that they had replaced the other division troops who were marching back in small groups. We were told that they would go back and be in corps reserve when the big offensive started. This would mean that they would follow us throughout the campaign and pick up stragglers. We didn't see the armored division troops we'd left in reserve when we pulled off the line. They were probably being assembled for an attack somewhere along the line, but they definitely were not in our sector.

We had been in position for four days, and were really enjoying life. The artillery from our side had increased somewhat since the first day, but it wasn't offensive fire. It sounded more like they would fire only when they had a definite target. They'd be quiet for a long time, then would fire two or three rounds, then open up and fire fifteen or twenty rounds.

On the morning of the fifth day, Lieutenant Studebaker called the platoon together to tell us what was happening. The other two battalions of our regiment were on ridges on both sides of our ravine. The other companies of our battalion were dug in up on the cliffs above the road and to our rear. When the offensive opened, our battalion, our company in the point, our platoon on point for Company L would start down the ravine, following the stream for about three miles. Not more than a mile downstream the ravine opened into a wide plain, about a mile wide, with ridges on both sides. It was suspected that there were Germans on these ridges. We were to proceed as far as possible until we drew fire. The command believed we would get very close to the three-mile mark. After we had drawn the first fire, the two other regiments of our division were to attack the ridges on both sides of the ravine, and the third battalion was to proceed to a ridge about a mile further down, and attack it. After we took that ridge, we were to dig in and await the other two regiments. The command estimated this whole operation should take no more than six hours, and that by nightfall our regiment should have advanced four miles and dug in for a counter-offensive. We would be told five minutes before we moved, and we were on alert from here on in.

"I don't expect any requests for permission to leave the area, therefore I'll tell you now that I don't expect to give any," Studebaker barked. Someone asked if he were assigned to a patrol, would he have permission to leave, and the lieutenant said, "If I chose *you* for a patrol, of course. Just be sure you bring back cigarettes, you clown." Everyone laughed, even the lieutenant. It helped ease us over the shock that we would soon be on the offensive.

The Greek had taken the jenny back several times to a supply point about half a mile down the road. They seemed to be made for each other. That little mule could take just as big a load as the largest mule around, and she was as sure-footed as a mountain goat. The Greek knew what he was talking about when it came to mules. The two together would keep us well supplied. We began to think the mule could understand Greek. He gave her commands in Greek and she responded. Maybe that had been the trouble with our mules; they hadn't understood English. They usually brought back cigarettes and candy, sometimes gum so the fellows had plenty to smoke, plenty of candy bars, and gum went into their packs for trading purposes later on, up the line. There were a lot of card games going, and once in a while you could find a galloping domino game. Though gambling was frowned upon by the army, no one said anything. In fact, one night I passed the lieutenant's tent, and heard everyone in there raising and calling. I don't believe they were planning any battle strategy.

The fifth day passed; the sixth day dawned. It was the 11 April, 1945, a beautiful day. As far as we knew, it would be just another day to relax and enjoy life. The mule went back to the supply point and brought up some more C rations, plus the cigarettes and candy. Some of the fellows were down at the stream washing their socks and laying them out on the sand to dry. A lot of the fellows down there were shaving.

The lieutenant came over and told me he'd just received orders for an officers' call. He expected some news. This was the first officers' call we'd had for several days. I knew it couldn't last forever, this easy living, but I sure did hate to give it up.

When Studebaker came back from the officers' call, he called the platoon together. He told us we would move either tomorrow or the next day. The weather people had predicted a rainstorm for tomorrow, but if it didn't materialize by dawn, we'd go then. So now we knew. We were about to become infantrymen again. We were about to start earning our pay. I checked with the Greek, to see what he had for Jenny to carry. He still had some C rations. I told him to give them all out. He also had two cases of M-1 ammo, a case of grenades, and two empty five-gallon water cans. He filled the water cans from the stream, and the mule would carry them plus the ammo and grenades. Then I inspected the men, to make sure they had everything they were supposed to. Last, I reported to Sergeant Gardner that my squad was ready to move out.

Chapter 21

During the night it started raining, a soft rain, the kind that lasts a long time. When we awoke at daylight to a gloomy miserable day, it was cold and wet in the foxhole. Stutzman and I climbed out of our foxhole, and with our shelter halves and a few sticks made a tent cover. We got the Coleman stove going, but that was a job; it has got wet, too. After we had drunk down a cup of coffee we felt better.

Some of the other fellows were crawling out of their holes now, stiff, miserable and mean. This was a good day for some fights to break out. I hoped no one would find a place dry enough to play cards, or I'd be spending the day breaking up fights.

The lieutenant called the squad leaders over to his foxhole. We sat under a canvas, the three infantry leaders, the heavy-weapons squad leader, and Gardner and Levin. Studebaker told us what we already knew—that we were not attacking today. But we would definitely attack on the following morning, marching out at about 0600 hours. There would be no artillery barrage, since we didn't know exactly where the Germans were, but if we got into trouble, we would have artillery observers with us, plus the support of the Corps.

One of the squad leaders asked why we didn't know where the Germans were. Hadn't the other division run any patrols? Studebaker confirmed our worst suspicion: No. They had not run one patrol during the time we were gone. "They just sat there and got drunk and ate and slept."

Someone else remarked that they probably didn't have officers who knew what they were doing. and Studebaker countered that the senior officers were indeed well trained. Many of them had been in combat. But it was the junior officers who were more interested in protecting their men from fight than they were in winning a war, and unless someone wanted to court-martial half a division, including its officers, there wasn't anything anyone could do.

Still, there was more to it than that, and we all knew it. But once in a while the air had to be cleared; things had to be got off the old chest. I think this was the main reason the lieutenant had called us in this morning. It was a lousy day, we were all wet and miserable, and we might as well get our bitching out now so we'd be ready to go tomorrow.

The afternoon passed slowly and uneventfully. Some of the men had saved a can or two of their beer rations, and I even saw a little wine here and there. It was, of course, against regulations, to have any booze out here, but no one would say anything about it as long as someone didn't get so drunk he didn't know what he was doing.

I saw DeAngelo sitting by himself. Not even Black, the other scout who shared a foxhole with him, would have anything to do with him. I was tempted to go sit with him myself, but thought better of it. Maybe the best thing to do with him was just to leave him alone, let him work out his own problems.

Reds and Stutzman were lying back with their helmets over their faces, under a shelter half. They were trying to snooze, but it must have been very uncomfortable with that slow rain coming down.

The kitchen came around, and we got one warm meal. We could thank the rain for that. We had to go up to the road, one squad at a time, get our food, and return to the foxholes. I took my squad down at 1700 hours. The rain had stopped by then, and the clouds had started to break up. It looked like we would have a clear day tomorrow, at least as far as the weather was concerned. I didn't know what else tomorrow would bring; maybe, the rest of my life.

Once the rain stopped, the ground dried off quickly, and the mood of the men improved. It was still quite light, and I heard someone suggest a card game. Without the wink of an eye, five guys were ready to play. They spread a dry blanket and before long had a red-hot poker game going. I watched them for a while, and was even thinking of getting into it, but decided to write a letter to my parents before it got too dark to see. I told them what we'd been doing—the rest camp and the visits to the cities, then added that we were starting the Po Valley offensive early tomorrow morning and not to worry, I probably wouldn't have much time to write for a while. When I finished the letter, I was ready to sleep. Stutzman was already sawing logs when I crawled into our foxhole and wrapped up in a blanket.

At 0400 hours Gardner awakened us, told us we had

ten minutes to get everything in our backpacks and be ready to go. The dawn was just breaking. The streaks on the eastern horizon were growing red, and it was only a matter of minutes before daybreak. A thin mist hung over the ground, and in the eerie quiet, I watched men up and down the line floating through it, up out of their foxholes. Company K troops were already coming down on our side of the stream stacking up behind us; and at the same time Company I troops were coming down the ridge on the other side of the stream. It looked like some kind of silent ballet, unreal and yet auspicious. An odd feeling crept over me as we waited for the word to move out—as if something awful were about to happen.

The silence was broken suddenly, not by gunfire, but by Lieutenant Studebaker's voice as he walked to the middle of our platoon encampment. What he said left each of us dumbfounded, aghast. He cleared his throat and read from a paper he held in his hand: " 'It is with deep regret that I must inform the troops of my command that the president of the United States of America, Franklin Delano Roosevelt, has died in Warm Springs, Georgia. Vice President Harry S. Truman has been sworn in as our thirty-third President. Signed, Mark Clark, commanding 15th Army Group, Cecerta, Italy. 13 April, 1945.' "

No one said a word. The men just stood there. Some took off their helmets. Some began to cry. Others had queer little smiles on their faces.

I really didn't know what to think. I hadn't agreed with many of the man's policies; but he was my president. He was my commander-in-chief, and he had been a good leader during this war. Still, I remembered many a farmer back home having wished him dead. I wondered how they felt now. I said a little prayer, as much for myself as for the fallen president.

It was 0450 hours, ten minutes to five. We did not have time to mourn Roosevelt's death. We got ourselves back into the spirit of soldiers and moved out, after the Germans. My squad, with DeAngelo and Black in front, led the way.

We were walking at a nice slow pace. I could look around and see what was going on. The ravine was beginning to widen, but not enough for the K Company boys to spread out and head for the ridge on the left. There was no enemy activity. Our artillery was dropping a shell now and then, but it was fairly quiet, so quiet you could hear the birds singing. It was the first time in Italy that I could remember when I had heard the birds sing.

When we had walked about a mile and a half, Studebaker called for a halt. Everyone hit the ground and looked in different directions. The machine gun squad set up the gun on its tripod, and one of the ammo carriers opened a case, ready to insert a belt. We all seemed to have the same thing on our minds. We took sips of water, and it tasted good. The sun was up now. It was going to be a very warm day.

Company K moved a little to our left while we were sitting. There still was not room for them to start moving up the ridge. I estimated that within another half mile, it would be wide enough for them. If one platoon could get up there and set up a defense, the rest of the company could move up.

The cliffs on the other side of the stream were still

fairly high and no attempt would be made for Company I to start moving there.

The ridge we were heading for was in sight now. It was larger than it had seemed when we first saw it, but it was still smaller than we were used to. There couldn't be too many more of these ridges before we reached that promised land, the Po Valley. Here and there you could see houses now. They looked like farmhouses. I saw five or six on our perimeter. They were favorite places for the Germans to hide their panzers. They were usually heavily built, with walls up to three feet thick, and the Germans could just drive in the back and stick their guns out the front, fire and move back. They were next to impossible to spot.

We broke position and started moving again for another half hour, covering about three quarters of a mile before we halted again. The ravine had widened here, and Company K was moved one platoon up. On the other side of the stream, the ravine had also widened enough for one platoon to position itself on the opposite side. Our platoon observed the front while the second platoon covered Company K's movement and the third platoon covered Company I's. Company M was spreading out on the floor of the ravine now with their heavy stuff. I could spot the bazooka squads loaded and ready to fire; they were our only protection against any possible panzers.

I watched the Company K platoon start up the ridge. Their scouts were out about forty yards ahead of them. Their number one scout was a good man; it was a pleasure to watch him work. He carried a tommy gun instead of a rifle, and walked very slowly, stopping every so often to look around and then moving another twenty or thirty yards. He finally disappeared into a small grove. When he emerged, he would be near or on the top of the ridge and able to see in all directions. As soon as he reached the top, he hit the ground and crawled behind a rock, and I could no longer see him. The rest of the platoon disappeared into the grove, then reappeared above the trees, and crawled on their bellies the rest of the way to the top. When they were in position, first one platoon and then another started up the ridge.

On the other side of the stream, the Company I platoon was having a little more difficulty getting up on their ridge. They were climbing half the time, and there were no trees up there. When the scouts reached the high point, they stopped and motioned the balance of the platoon up. It took them sometime to get four squads up there.

As soon as I and K were positioned, we started moving again. We were just about a mile from the ridge ahead, when six tanks came suddenly into view from between the ridge Company K was on, and us. We all tightened, thinking at first they were German, but Studebaker called up, "They're American. They'll give us mobile artillery from here to the ridge." They spread out and stopped, while we kept moving. Everyone was a bit edgy. I don't know if it was the sight of the tanks, or the approach to the ridge where we expected to receive fire, but you could see it in the men's faces. They were neither smiling nor frowning; they all wore stiff, shit-eating grins.

Up on the ridge to the left Company K was receiving some mortar fire. Not much, but two of the tanks moved over closer to the ridge. I could see the commander of the tank force in the third tank giving orders now, and all of the tanks started moving at a very slow pace, keeping up with the infantry troops. I wasn't sure whether I liked those tanks being with us or not; sometimes they drew fire, but on the other hand it was quick artillery if you needed it. Our second platoon pulled up even with the first, and Lieutenant Studebaker told me to bring in my out scouts on the left, and to bring my front scouts back about fifty yards.

We came to a small ridge, almost unnoticeable unless you were actually on it, and stopped. We took up firing positions. Our ridge was about half a mile ahead. It looked peaceful enough, but we were prepared for anything. It seemed there was a much larger ridge behind it. From our position, I could not tell how far away it might be.

The tanks had pulled up even with the troops. It was beginning to look like we would attack at any moment.

Brooklyn, the machine-gunner, had his gun set up and ready to go; back behind us, Company M had set up their heavy mortars and machine guns. Company K, up on the left ridge, had stopped advancing; and Company I, on the right, had long been in firing position on their ridge. The one platoon of Company I still in the ravine came up and lined with us.

This was hell, lying here not knowing what was going to happen next. Two observation planes were flying low over the ridge now; they were drawing no fire. I began to doubt there were any Germans there at all, and suspected that they were concentrated on the larger ridge behind it, just waiting for us. I turned around to see what Studebaker was doing. Levin was edging toward him, returning from the captain. He said something to Studebaker, and they started talking, but no orders were issued.

We had lain here now almost half an hour, when horses with riders came down the ravine from the rear. There were eight riders, and they were well spread out. They stopped at company headquarters, conferred with Captain Bear, then took off in our direction. They rode past us at a slow gallop and headed toward the ridge. When they were about halfway to the ridge, two of them cut out and headed right for it. They drew up. They stopped when they reached its base, then turned and galloped back to join the other riders and return to company headquarters. They stopped there and talked to Captain Bear, then took off back up the ravine.

I'd seen our mounted recon in action, and although they had not drawn any fire this time, they were daring and did their damnedest to do just that. Either the Germans were damn smart awaiting the infantry, or there were no Germans on that ridge. Yet, Company K was still drawing mortar fire up on their ridge. Not much, but it was there. I was about to scan the area with my field glasses when Studebaker called to me to return to his position.

"You'll take your squad—with your extra machine gun—and go all the way to the top of that ridge. If you hit any enemy fire, we'll come running. But stay where you are until we get there. Don't try to return. Just stay put."

We started out, fifteen men well spread out, about twenty yards apart. We had enough firepower to hold out for a while if we did run into the enemy—if we could find a place we could get below, or behind.

This was the kind of situation where DeAngelo became a soldier. He was at his best, and he was showing it, leading off as the first scout. We reached the bottom of the ridge in about ten minutes; surprisingly, there was a road running along it, which we hadn't been able to see from the ravine. It looked well traveled. There were tank tracks and large truck tracks, and they weren't very old; they'd been made since the rain the day before. Either the Germans had just pulled out or just arrived. I had a feeling we were in for a fight.

We were about halfway up the ridge when we started to receive a heavy mortar barrage. They were pouring it on. I looked to the top and saw a German. He had to be the observer. The mortars must be hidden behind the ridge. I hit the ground and took careful aim, squeezed the trigger, and the German soldier drooped, just laid his head down and didn't move again. When I fired, everyone let go, and I had a helluva time stopping them. I called out, "Don't shoot unless you think you've got a target! Just keep moving up the ridge!"

We crawled now. The movement was torturous, but we were making progress. I kept watching for another observer. The mortars were still coming in, following us up the ridge. I spotted another one, just as Stutzman saw him; we both fired and he just laid down and died. I figured our fellows would be coming now, or at least that we'd get some artillery fire on the back of this ridge. But nothing happened. I turned around to see if they were coming. I couldn't see anyone; I looked over to the left to see if Company K was moving up: Nothing. I couldn't even see them. There was some movement over to our right rear, where Company I was on their ridge, but they weren't advancing, either. I began to think we'd been sent out here to test the German strength and no one cared a damn if we lived through it or not. Some of the guys had taken some small hits—nothing serious yet—but if this kept up much longer, we'd all be just memories.

We were only thirty or forty feet from the top of this ridge. Maybe, if we got to the top, we could see some of the mortars and silence them; maybe that was what the troops behind us were waiting for.

We kept crawling. We shot two more observers, but still didn't receive any small-arms fire. Was this some kind of a delaying action on the Germans' part?

We seemed to be through the worst of the mortar fire now. They were still firing their mortars in the same spot they had been when we were coming in. Most likely we'd killed all the observers, and the mortarmen were shooting blind. If we could get all the way up so we could look down, I believed we could pick a lot of them off—if they didn't have too many riflemen down there protecting them.

We edged to the top and saw them—five mortars within sight. I ordered everyone to start shooting and not to stop until all the mortarmen were dead. Brooklyn brought his machine gun up and Al brought up his BAR team. We all started firing, and after a minute—though it seemed more like an hour—we'd killed at least twenty-five Germans, and were still picking them off as they ran down the back of that ridge. When we couldn't see any more, I ordered everyone down the other side of the ridge, about twenty or twenty-five yards. I figured the Germans would pour some hot 88s on us, now that they knew where we were. Just to keep everyone busy and their minds off what was happening, I had them dig holes to at least get their shoulders in. I sent Stutzman back up to the top of the ridge to act as lookout. Then, we awaited the arrival of the company.

About ten minutes later, Lieutenant Studebaker came running up the ridge, followed by the rest of the first platoon. All I said was, "Where the hell have you been? You missed all the fun!"

He ordered the platoon to go to the top of the ridge and dig in deep for the counterattack. He said that Company K had run into a mortar company, too and had taken heavy losses, but were digging in on their ridge. Company I was coming up on our right and would dig in to our right on this ridge; they hadn't made contact with the Germans at all. He added, "After everyone's dug in, we'll have a continuous line of about two miles, just like the brass planned and with no fighting."

That miffed me, and I told him that this had been as good a fight as we'd ever had, and we'd been alone. "Don't give me any bullshit that there was no fighting up here. Go down and count the dead Germans lying down there! Hell, if you'd've looked, you'd've seen 'em! And DeSola's attending to my wounded now. Where the hell do you think those wounds came from, self infliction?" He was pretty sheepish after that, and only said he'd see that we received credit for what we'd done. With that, I went over to DeSola and had the wound on my right leg wrapped. He took all the names down of the men who'd been wounded. Each man would receive his Purple Heart.

My squad dug in, in the middle of the platoon, two men to a foxhole. After about an hour, the lieutenant came up and told us that since we'd made the patrol and assault, he was putting us in reserve; we could move back behind the line. I told him he was too late. We had our holes dug and we'd be damned if we were going to dig others back down the ridge somewhere. Let some other rear echelon squad go in reserve. He knew I was still miffed and said okay. I didn't see him again for quite some time.

The Greek came up with supplies. All we needed was water, but I told the guys to load up on bandoliers and fill their ammo belts. We also opened the box of grenades and each of us took three more.

We had been up here now for nearly two hours, and I really hadn't had a chance to look over the valley in front of us. We could see the big ridge in the background when we'd been approaching this one. It was about two or three miles away, and behind it was still another ridge, even larger than the one in front of us now. I said to myself, *Don't they ever run out of mountains? They keep promising us that the Po Valley is just across the next ridge. And there's always a "next ridge."*

We settled back. I decided I would go back and apologize to Studebaker. I crawled out of my hole, told Stutzman to keep his eyes peeled and to holler out if anything happened. I went back to the Lieutenant's foxhole. He was eating a C ration, and he had his Coleman stove going. I said, "Lieutenant, could I talk to you a minute?"

"Sure, come on in. Have a cup of coffee."

"No, thank you. I just wanted to apologize for talking to you the way I did a little while ago. I was hot under the collar."

"I understand," Studebaker said. "I knew just how you felt. I also knew about the fight. We were watching it with our field glasses, but Battalion wouldn't give us the order to move. And, by the way, the only choice I had in the matter was which squad to send. The other squads're good, but I know that when there's a tough job to be done, I send you. You had every right to blow your top. I'd've done the same."

Later in the day, DeSola came around to see if our wounds were okay. He checked each of the other four guys, then looked at my leg. He said I was seeping blood and should get back to an aid station to have a doctor put a stitch in it; otherwise, the skin would grow back over the bone tender, and it'd bother me the rest of my life. I asked him where the aid station was, but he didn't know, so I said I'd take my chances and stay right here. At least I wouldn't have to go wandering around, not knowing where to look. He said okay, but just as soon as he found a doctor he'd let me know.

It was getting near 1400 hours now. The sun was really beating down. There was no breeze and we were staying very low in our foxholes. I was wondering how those Germans felt in their hot uniforms; they didn't seem to wear anything but those heavy uniforms. They must be roasting. We wore the heavy O.D.s ourselves, but we could take our jackets off and carry them. The fellows down in the tanks were lying in the shade, but one guy was up in the turret of each tank with his headphones on. Stutzman was snoozing real good now, even snoring. I noticed a man who is a bit relaxed will snore, but a guy with trouble on his mind will not. I wondered how some of these head doctors would explain that; they probably had some answer; they seemed to have answers for everything. It's really funny what comes into a man's mind when he's sitting by himself, waiting for God only knows what to happen.

Levin came up to my foxhole and wanted to know how the new men had performed. Like veterans, I told him. There wasn't a man I wasn't proud of, including DeAngelo. I advised him that the whole squad had acted beyond the call of duty; if one man deserved a decoration, then the whole squad did. He said he'd talk to Studebaker. Levin left and I returned my attention to the plain in front of us, looking for that counterattack. I felt in my bones it was coming very soon.

Chapter 22

It came, all of a sudden. Shells were bursting everywhere. They were hitting the top of the ridge. I knew someone had to get hit. There seemed to be everything the German Army had. Artillery of all sorts, even rockets—those rockets were enough to scare a man to death with their screaming. There were explosions all over the ridge. I glanced over to where Company K was; they were getting it too. We hit the foxholes and stayed down. Between the bursts, I could hear guys screaming, and the call, "Medic!"

I kept my head down for quite a while. I knew damned well that while we were taking this barrage they were moving troops and probably panzers up. Finally, I had to take a peek. I just couldn't lie down in that foxhole not being able to see what was going on. I pulled out the field glasses, but before I could get myself up, Stutzman barked, "Where the hell are you going?" When I told him, he said I was nuts. "Let someone else look. It's a helluva lot safer down here."

I stuck my head up about an inch above ground level, and raised the glasses to my eyes. Sure enough, there were ten or twelve panzers with clusters of infantry around each. It looked like about a company of men with each panzer. They must be coming with a regiment; and behind them was another line — six panzers, again with a cluster of men around each. The panzers were firing as they moved up, and there was a lot of other artillery fire in addition to theirs. The first assault line was about a thousand yards out yet; the second, maybe fifteen hundred yards. We had some time, but not much. They'd keep us pinned down until that first line was maybe two hundred yards from us. Then their infantry would set up mortars and machine guns and try to keep us pinned while their riflemen made the final assault. They had quite a long haul; the ridge was steep on their side, but they could make it if we didn't interfere. We had to get some firepower down on them, this I knew.

I called out to Studebaker to come running. He crawled up to my foxhole and jumped in, almost landing on Stutzman who was still in the bottom of the hole. Studebaker didn't have to look twice. He had a walkie-talkie with him. He immediately called for the captain and gave him the story. By this time, the Germans had gobbled up another two hundred yards. The lieutenant called out along the line to his three squads: "All right, men, heads up and asses down. We're going to have target all over the place in about three minutes."

The barrage hadn't let up. If anything, it had intensified, and the guys were reluctant to stick their heads up. I gave them a call, and one by one the heads came up. I looked over at Brooklyn. He was ready to go — anxious to go. Al called over to me from two foxholes away to tell me that Dollar had been killed; he been in a hole with Fienberg. Fienberg was okay, not even wounded. Poor Dollar. He'd just come

209

overseas, and now he was dead.

The Germans were now only about six hundred yards away. I could see them setting up their big mortars. There must have been ten or fifteen of them. I told Brooklyn to open fire on them now, kill as many of them bastards as he could before they had a chance to fire up here. He started shooting everything in his way. I hollered to him, "Hit the goddamned mortars, you shithead! Let the infantry get the riflemen!" He nodded and let go on them.

All along the line now firing had opened up. You could see Germans falling, but those panzers kept firing right into our positions. They meant to take this ridge back and kill as many of us as they could. They meant to keep us out of the Po Valley. We knew we had a fight on our hands. We'd need more ammo, especially hand grenades before long. Reds and I had grenade launchers. I quickly attached mine to Stutzman's M-1 and gave him my carbine. I stuck on a grenade and let it fly. It landed about five hundred yards out. I saw several Germans go down. Hot dog, these things work! Keep firing! I called to Reds to do the same thing, but he'd already thought of it and was firing with good results.

Our mortars were at work now, too. The Germans were almost at the bottom of the ridge. Everyone was firing. Their barrage let up. The only artillery firing against us now came from their damned 88s on those tanks. I turned to see what our tanks were doing, and noticed that they'd started to move out, three abreast. If they could get around to the front of this ridge without being spotted, they might be able to knock out several of the German panzers.

Meanwhile, we were knocking off their infantry like kingpins now, but we were losing men, too. I told the squad to start using their grenades. I took the launcher off Stutzman's M-1 and handed it back to him. He gave me back my carbine and told me to keep it; he liked the M-1 much better. So did I.

A shell hit right below us. I couldn't see, hear, or think for a moment. I thought maybe I'd had it; maybe I was dying. But little by little I came back to my senses. Stutzman looked like he was drunk, but he was recovering, too. Al and Homer were lying outside their foxhole. I thought they were dead, but after a while first Al, then Homer started to move. They were holding their heads. I told them to get back into their foxhole and start firing that BAR. Al looked at me and said "What hole?" He was right. There wasn't any hole. It had been completely blown away. How those two guys weren't killed, I'll never know, but they picked up where they'd been, lying flat on the ground firing. Brooklyn was calling for more ammo and one of his ammo carriers skidded back to bring some more up. He was doing a real job on those heavy mortars back there.

The tanks were all out now and they put on the speed as soon as they saw the German panzers. They fired a volley, a second, then a third before the panzers even knew they were there—five panzers bit the dust. They manuevered closer to the other panzers, which were in an awkward position, and before they could get turned around to fire, two more of our volleys hit them: Three more panzers were on fire. That was eight of sixteen.

The artillery fire eased up a bit, giving us a chance

to toss our grenades down below and keep firing. The panzers from the second line were coming fast and hard at our tanks now. We would surely lose some of them this time, but our tanks held the line. The other three panzers still in the first line stayed with the infantry and kept firing up at us. Suddenly, our tankers held their fire, and the panzers held theirs. They were only about three hundred yards apart now. Then our tanks fired a volley. Three panzers immediately stopped in their tracks and started burning. The panzers fired a volley and two of our tanks immediately went up in flames. I didn't see anyone get out of them. The second volley from our four remaining tanks stopped two more panzers. The last of that group wheeled around as fast as he could and got the hell out of there. The Germans inside would have a story to tell their grandchildren, I was sure of that.

Meantime, three more panzers were still firing on us, but the enemy infantry had had about enough now and were beginning to pull back. We didn't let up. We poured fire and grenades into them until our supplies were exhausted. Everywhere along the line guys were calling for more grenades. Most of the heavy mortars were out of action, and what were left were packing up and starting to pull back. The second line wavered when they saw five of their six panzers burning. They never did mount an attack; they just started to take off toward the big ridge. Our mortars were pouring it into them now, and they were hitting home. Bodies were starting to mount up. The three panzers, seeing their infantry waver, must have decided they'd better head for home, too. Our four remaining tanks were coming up on them and they saw they'd have to fight their way out to get back to that ridge — or wherever these devils were holed up. The four tanks were within about four hundred yards of them now, and the panzers turned and headed out, firing wildly. Their shots didn't do any damage, and our tanks fired two more volleys. Another two more panzers bit the dust. The crew of one of them crawled out, and one of our machine-gunners let them have it.

The Germans had lost fourteen panzers — and how many men, no one would probably ever know. Germans were running helter skelter all over the field now, trying to get away from our fire, but what the riflemen and machine-gunners weren't shooting down, our mortars were cutting up pretty badly.

The German artillery was starting to come in hot and heavy again. There weren't many targets left for us, so we slithered back down into our foxholes and let the artillery do its worst; we couldn't do anything about it anyway, except to pray we wouldn't get hit, and that was what most of us were doing.

Our four tanks were following the German infantry and firing their guns mowing them down like hay. It was just plain murder. Why, oh why, did the Germans waste their men like this? Our tanks apparently received the word to break off and return to our lines. They took up positions in the ravine again between us and Company K.

No infantry attack had been made on Company K. They'd received just artillery fire. Why, no one knew. The enemy knew they were there. They had drawn fire first, and they'd been fired on for two or three miles up on their ridge, but for some reason they weren't attacked. If there was a reason, it was probably that the Germans had thought they could break through us, go up the ravine, and cut Company K off. As it was, they'd attacked the strongest part of our line—two companies, but whatever they'd had in mind, it hadn't worked. They'd lost fourteen panzers, and probably at least five or six hundred men. I could see now that this was the last big fight the Germans would put up, and that if they lost here they'd run. The Po Valley would be ours. So they'd fight like tigers now to keep us from advancing. I looked my squad over and said to myself, *How many, oh, Lord, will see those Alps? How many will die tomorrow and the next day? Will I live to see another day?*

The German artillery was letting up a bit now. Their infantry was almost out of sight, but I kept my field glasses on them; I wanted to be sure. I could see now that there was a small ridge in front of the large ridge; as soon as they crossed that, the last two panzers disappeared.

The enemy artillery had all but ceased now—just a shot once in a while to aggravate us, so I looked to my squad. Fienberg was sitting and holding his head, as were Al and Homer. They'd all received concussions from a shell that had landed almost next to them. I asked them if they wanted to go back and all three said no. I called DeSola up and he gave them some pain-killers and told them to lie down and not to move for an hour or so. Al said they had to dig another foxhole; theirs had been destroyed. I told him that I'd get someone else to dig one for them while they rested. I asked Black and Russ to dig it. They didn't like it much, but they dove in. Some of the other platoons had heavier casualties. All in all, the first platoon had five men killed and eight wounded—enough that they had to be evacuated. That left us thirteen men short. Just twenty-eight of us would be crossing the plain down there.

We improved our foxholes, brought up more ammo. We were damned near out of everything. We'd expected one helluva lot of ammo, more than anyone expected us to. About thirty mules were brought up, each loaded with water. The mules were being handled by men in Italian army uniforms. They'd be with us all the way now, just as long as we had to use pack animals for supplies. The Greek came back and let us know he'd been relieved of his mule job. He wasn't happy, but he was a good soldier and did what he was told. We put him in a foxhole with Miller, who somehow could make out what the Greek was saying.

The litter bearers took away the wounded. Then they came back and picked up the dead. After that, they started down the ridge and looked for any Germans who might still be alive. A couple of squads from Company I were sent down with them just in case any German had any ideas about dying for the Fuhrer and taking an American with him. Ambulances had been brought up behind the ridge and six or eight men were put in each. They disappeared back down the ravine.

The litter bearers were bringing in wounded Germans now. They were receiving the same treatment our guys received. Some fellows resented that and I could hear the men cursing about it. They must have brought in at least a hundred wounded Germans. I also noticed that they stuck the dead Germans' rifles in the ground and put their helmets on them, so whoever had to clean this mess up knew where the dead ones were. Regardless of what else we might have thought of the Germans, they would have done the same thing.

It was nearing 1700 hours now. We'd quite a day, and I was sure we wouldn't get much sleep tonight. Right now, the guys were too keyed up to sleep. Some of the fellows were opening K rations. The cigarettes and candy arrived. I lit up a cigarette; it tasted terrible, but I smoked it, to try to relax. Most of the guys were out of their holes now, but sitting close to them.

The shock of losing Dollar was about over, and some joking was going on again: The wishing, talk about girls, hoping all those rear-echelon troops wouldn't drink all the booze so we could have some the next time we went back for a rest. Food seemed to be the main subject, though. Everyone wanted a steak, smothered in onions with fresh fried potatoes and lots of iced tea, all they could drink. It was hot now, the hottest day we'd had in Italy so far.

Lieutenant Studebaker called all three of the rifle squad leaders back behind a little hill. He told us we weren't going to move again tonight. We'd stay here, but we could probably expect another counterattack. We would put two outposts out about four hundred yards in front of the ridge. Two men from each squad went out as soon as it started to get dark. Each post had a walkie-talkie and would stay out there until dawn. Six more tanks came up during the night, and we would have seventy-five pack mules with us on the next attack.

I sent Stutzman and Miller out for guard post. Even though Miller was the newer man, I think Stutzman was more nervous.

All night, I kept checking my squad. I was three men short now, and checked them to see that someone was alert in every hole. Levin came up and crawled into my hole a couple of times during the night. We just talked, and between every sentence, we listened. It was quiet. Not a sound except an occasional cough, or the scrape of metal on metal. Otherwise, it was quiet. The lieutenant came up once to tell me that everything was okay down in the outposts. When he left, it was 0130 hours. We would know in about an hour what our schedule for the day would be. I knew what it was before they ever issued any order: Advance and take the objective.

Chapter 23

At about 0230 hours, the lieutenant called all the squad leaders back to his foxhole and gave us the complete plan. We would attack just after dawn. Companies L and I would cross the plain; Company K would come off their ridge into the ravine and follow us up about three to four hundred yards behind—they would actually be in reserve. Each platoon would have two bazooka squads with us, in addition to our light machine guns and the mortars behind us, about a mile out from the ridge. The seventy-fives would be brought up here on the ridge and take up positions where the infantry now was. Each company would have three tanks about one hundred yards behind, and three would be kept in reserve and move out behind Company K. Again, our platoon was to take the point, and my squad had the dubious honor of being the point for the platoon. Air reconnaissance had reported heavy defenses ahead, but the second ridge back was the main defense point, the last one in the gothic line, and that was where we'd have our toughest fight. The brass wanted both ridges before nightfall. Their schedule called for entering the Po Valley the day after next. I asked the lieutenant if they expected that this job could be done with just one battalion, and he said that if need be they'd throw in the rest of the regiment, who were sitting up above us on the left. And that we'd receive a lot of airpower with this attack. Still they were asking for the impossible—asking a battalion to do the job that should be done by a division. We were good, but I wondered if we were that good. I couldn't see why they couldn't have brought up more troops, and more artillery and definitely more tanks. I asked the lieutenant how far apart the two ridges were, and he said that according to the map, approximately a thousand yards. That meant that after we took the first ridge and regrouped—if we had anything to regroup with—we'd have to cross a thousand yards of sheer hell and then climb up to where the enemy was dug in and kill them. I couldn't see how any of us would make it. Whoever thought this one up must have gone to a butcher school instead of any army training school.

When I returned to my squad I told them what we'd be doing, up to the first ridge, but I didn't tell them we'd be taking the second ridge. They'd have enough worries about the first one without thinking about the second. There would be plenty of time to tell them that after we'd regrouped. I was beginning to know how those German soldiers felt when they were ordered to counterattack; they probably knew it was an impossible job, but they did it anyway. *Ours is not to reason why, ours is to do and die*—that kept going through my mind.

A priest came around and asked if anyone wanted communion before we kicked off. Most of the Catholic boys did. It was the first time I'd ever seen this; must be rough, what the brass had in mind for us.

By 0400 hours we were ready to go. It was lighting up now. The sun was coming up in the east; you couldn't see it but the rays were spread across the sky. The six tanks were rumbling out in front of the ridge, and I could see the men of Company K coming down off the ridge into the ravine. The battalion of 105s had moved down there and were setting up all over the place, well spread out. Everything was to be in order now but the infantry. We hadn't received a command to start moving out. I saw a group of men coming up the ridge, and recognized Colonel Track among them. It was the first time I'd seen him since we returned from our rest camp. He was laughing and pointing, joking with the guys as he passed. Most of the men in the regiment would do most anything for that old guy. He asked me if he could use my foxhole after we left, and I told him I was vacating very shortly and it would be up for rent. He laughed and said he'd take it, that foxholes were hard to find up here especially empty ones. He turned to a captain who was with him and asked which company was in reserve and was told Company K. He told the captain to get a platoon ready; when we started the attack, he wanted to probe the left side of that ridge, where the first battalion area was. He said he'd lead the patrol himself. Everyone looked at each other; this was a colonel, and colonels didn't stick their necks out — they directed the traffic far back of the lines. But no one had had this colonel in mind when that was written. He was a combat man, probably the best in the regiment.

Shortly after the colonel left, the lieutenant came up and gave us orders to move out. Two companies would be abreast. This would give us about a five-hundred-yard front for the attack, and would make the Germans think that there were more of us than there really were.

We hurried down the ridge as fast as we could go, and when we arrived at the bottom. I spread the six riflemen out, I staying a bit to the back, kept the BAR team, only two in number now, behind me and to my right. I told DeAngelo and Black they would get the word when the command came for scouts out; then they were to go, DeAngelo about forty yards and Black about twenty yards. I would then pull up so I was about ten yards ahead of the squad, but still leave the BAR team where it was.

Soon, there was the sound of motors behind us, lots of motors— airplanes. I turned around, and the sight was lovely. The air was full of P-47s and P-38s, and up and behind them B-26s, there must have been at least two hundred planes. I began to believe we would take those ridges and take them today. The P-47s dove down and dropped their bombs on that first ridge; the B-26s went on and bombed the second ridge; the P-38s came in behind and strafed the hell out of the first ridge. Then they all circled around and came again. Flights of four or five planes would go in low and blast the hell out of the ridge. They kept this up for quite a while, so long that we were ordered to sit down and open our straps to our backpacks and relax. The show was good, and we did just that.

By the time the planes had disappeared and the sky had grown quiet, the first ridge was on fire; the second ridge was also burning, but not as fiercely as the first. We were ordered to our feet. We walked about two hundred yards, and our artillery opened up.

We were in platoon formation now, scouts out. We expected to get enemy artillery at any moment. We'd gone about five hundred yards now, and still no German fire. We were passing up a little grade now, and before us was a house—no, two houses and some out buildings. This would certainly serve as a good outpost for the Germans. I told DeAngelo to get ready, that there had to be Germans there.

We were within fifty yards of the first house when they opened fire, with machine guns and rifles. We hit the ground and tried to spot them. Small mortars were coming in now. Luckily, we had a nice rise we could lie behind, and so far no one had been hit. The lieutenant came crawling up and looked the situation over. He thought Berg, another of the squad leaders, could get behind that house and silence those gunners.

I said, "Lieutenant, he might do that, but you have another house back there and some out buildings. He'd be walking right into them. Don't you think this is a job for one of those tanks?" He surveyed the area again.

He decided I was right and called back with the situation. Colonel Track came back with an answer and said he'd send in two tanks. The infantry would hold our positions until the outpost was knocked out, then go in with the tanks and finish them off. The colonel didn't say so, but what he was implying was not to take prisoners.

Two tanks came lumbering forward. They went about twenty yards, then both opened fire. They each fired about four or five times, and the buildings just faded away. Then they opened up with machine guns and advanced, and our squad followed. Two or three German heads came up and we opened up with our rifles. They disappeared fast, and by the time we ran into the mess, there were no living Germans there, just dead and mangled bodies. Those tanks had done a good job. I hoped they'd stay with us for a long time.

We re-formed and started moving again. Now we started to get mortar fire, from back of the first ridge. They were big mortars. We kept advancing, but we were losing men. Their mortars got heavier, then our seventy-fives opened up, but I doubted if they could touch the area where these mortars were coming from.

Our tanks were spreading out more now, and the three they were holding in reserve were also coming up to the line. That meant we'd have nine tanks with us. And there were three more with Company K if we needed them. The seventy-fives were peppering the ridge now, thirty or forty shells a minute. But those damn mortars weren't touched. They were still dropping our men.

We were only about two hundred and fifty yards from the bottom of the ridge and moving in fast; still, no small-arms fire. This should be the place where they start hitting us with small arms, but it didn't come and we kept advancing. A hundred yards to go, then uphill. The mortars couldn't find us now. We'd reached a road and crawled across it, then lay in the ditch. The German guns were still harassing the other fellows, and they were still falling. I could see the medics out there trying to do what they could until the litter bearers could pick up the wounded. The lieutenant reached our ditch, then the other two squads. The other platoons, and Company I, were getting up behind the ridge now, too.

The captain gave the command to go forward, and the whole company jumped up and started the ascent to the summit of the ridge. Now the small arms started—machine guns, rifles, and grenades were coming down at us. Some of the guys froze—just lay on the ground. Gardner and the lieutenant were walking around like nothing was happening and kicking these guys, telling them we had to get out of this fire and the only way was to the top of the ridge. Most of them rose slowly and started up. Some just stayed there. Some were dead.

We reached the first row of bunkers. They were open holes. We started throwing grenades when we were within twenty or thirty feet of them.

I couldn't see my whole squad; I was sure some of them were dead. Brooklyn was carrying his machine gun over his arm. He had a belt in it and one of his carriers was carrying the end of it as he fired. Russ pulled ahead of us. He found a spot behind a rock and started peppering the bunkers from that angle. He was hitting them. The Germans didn't know he was there and he was hitting them like sitting ducks. I saw that there was a chance for us to advance as long as he kept firing. I told Al to put that BAR down and keep firing. Brooklyn already was firing and had his machine gun on a tripod. As soon as Al opened up, I ordered all the riflemen to fix bayonets and move up the slope, firing as they went.

I heard a German call out and point toward Russ. I yelled at Russ as loud as I could to hit the dirt, and we

224

rushed the bunkers.

By this time, our other squads were coming up, and so were our other platoons. The German fire was becoming lighter. I don't know how many of them were dead, but there had to be a lot. I saw Levin coming up the slope. He had a tommy gun and was firing all the way. He walked right into an M-34, and that German kept firing at him, but he just kept firing back and walking. He finally reached the bunker and shot three Germans. How he ever kept from being hit by that M-34, I'll never know. His God was with him today.

We reached the bunkers. Some of the fellows were using their bayonets. Some had already jumped into the bunkers and were firing at the summit of the ridge, where the next line of defense was dug in. Russ joined us in the bunkers. He was all smiles. He knew he'd done something great. The next row of bunkers were about forty or fifty feet above us, and fire from them was coming in hot and heavy. Brooklyn was beside me and he kept firing away. I told him just to fire small bursts until we figured out what we had to face. The lieutenant came crawling up behind the bunker I was in. I told him that I thought we could use some mortar fire up there for a couple of minutes before we started the final assault. He looked the situation over and said he'd see what he could do.

Company K was at the bottom of the ridge now, but had not started to come up. Studebaker called over his walkie-talkie, then turned to me and said that the captain would fire our small mortars. And the machine guns of Company M would fire also; they'd keep up a steady fire for five minutes, then we would go. He'd give the order to advance.

The mortars started coming in soon, then the machine guns from M opened up. They kept it up for what seemed an hour. Then, all at once, a white flag went up from the enemy bunkers. I heard the Lieutenant cry out to cease fire, then the same command from the captain. They were both on their radios telling the mortars and machine guns to cease fire.

All at once it became very quiet up there. We all had our rifles aimed at the row of bunkers. Someone called out in German for them to come out with their hands up. One by one, the enemy started to stand up. Some started out of the bunkers still holding their weapons. I heard the command in German to lay their arms. There were at least a hundred of them now, all with their hands up; they were ordered down the ridge. If one stumbled and fell, a GI was there immediately with his rifle. The lieutenant ordered our platoon ahead, to occupy the bunkers. We approached them cautiously, ready for anything. We were near the summit of the ridge, and it was possible that there were more behind the ridge who didn't know their comrades had surrendered. There were Germans in the bunkers, all right, but they would never surrender; they were dead. We rolled them out and took their places.

Strewn over the plain we had crossed and on up the slope of the ridge, dead and wounded GIs lay everywhere. The medics were doing what they could, as fast as they could, but many died before they were attended. I saw many mules coming over the plain now; some seemed to be loaded with seventy-fives. They were probably bringing them up for our next bout with the enemy. We desperately needed supplies; some of the fellows had expended one helluva lot of ammo. One thing we wouldn't need as much of, however, was grenades. The final part of the battle had been close fighting, and very few had been used. Some of the guys were wiping off their bayonets and putting them back in their scabbards. This was probably the first time most had used them. It's the worst of war, fighting hand-to-hand, and with bayonets.

We hadn't been in the bunkers long before the lieutenant came up and said that we had to look on the other side of this ridge. "Crawl up there with me, and bring your glasses. We'll see what's out there." We found a little rise at the top where we could hide ourselves, pulled out our glasses, and scanned the area. There were some houses on the next ridge, near the summit and to the right. That must be Monte San Pietro. We saw no activity, but both of us had the feeling that there were Germans there. The slope of that ridge was slight, and was being used to farm. There were crops of some sort planted there, but I couldn't tell what they were. I did see chickens around the buildings, but no other animals. To the left of the buildings were holes, with piles of dirt around them. They couldn't have been bunkers, but most likely were holes from our mortar fire. Then, below those, the lieutenant spotted what we were sure were bunkers. "That's it—their main defense line," he said. "We'll be getting a lot of their artillery fire as soon as we show ourselves. They'll be cutting loose with everything they have."

From the foot of the ridge we were on, to the summit of the next, was a distance of about a thousand yards. I hoped we'd make it.

We reported back to the captain what we'd spotted, then I returned to my squad to see if we'd had any more casualties.

Black had a small wound, but he could go on, and Stutzman had had the wind knocked out of him from a blow on the back. He had the biggest, blackest bruise I'd ever seen. I was afraid he might be hemorraging, but he refused to go back. When DeSola came around, he looked us all over, re-dressed my wound, then went on to the other men in the platoon. Our squad came through pretty good this time. When I reported back to the lieutenant, I learned just how good: A lot of the platoons had been hit much harder. Company I had a platoon of only two men left.

The heavy artillery were setting up now, their positions staggered and on different levels instead of in a straight line, as they'd been before. Then the order came down to get ready to move out. This time it would be Berg's and Les's squad—the second—that would go over the ridge first, until they drew fire.

My squad had re-supplied themselves. I told everyone to get into their bunkers, that a patrol was being sent out, and I was sure the Germans will cut loose on us. I did not receive any argument. Then I filled them in on what we'd be doing—that we had to take the ridge in front of us today. "This is the last ridge before we hit the Po Valley," I said.

"We've heard that one before," Black growled. He was right. We had.

We could hear the plane engines now. Coming in from behind were those lovely P-47s and P-38s, and way back behind them came the B-26s. The P-47s and

P-38s flew in, strafing and bombing the summit of Monte san Pietro. Everytime a bomb dropped, we bounced about two feet. The B-26s came in slow and low, as if they were thumbing their noses at the German anti-aircraft guns. They let go of their bombs, and the explosions were twice as powerful as the first ones. Man, it was a beautiful sight. I could sit here and watch it all day. After the B-26s finished their run, the P-47s and P-38s came in again, dropping their last bombs and strafing. They made two or three more runs, strafing everything in sight. The buildings on the ridge had now become rubble. Then the second squad was called back; they wouldn't have to go out and draw fire after all that.

Now the 155s opened up. They kept the fires burning on Monte San Pietro. I don't know how many big guns we had back there but they were really pouring it on. Their barrage lasted about five minutes, then the tanks disappeared to the right of our ridge. We couldn't detect any German artillery coming in from anywhere yet. I was hoping that between the planes and the 155s, all the enemy guns had been knocked out, but that just doesn't happen. It would shake their gun crews up a bit, but they'd come back and fire away at us when the time came. We all knew this.

The 155s were now joined by the 105s; the 155s had lifted their aim and were firing behind the ridge now where the enemy would have their concentration of fire, artillery, panzers and heavy mortars. The 105s were hitting the lower part of the ridge, where we'd spotted the row of bunkers. Their barrage kept up for about fifteen minutes, and then we received the order to saddle up and move out.

Company M had brought their heavy mortars and big machine guns up. They would support us while we were moving. Our 60 mm mortars were going with us, as well as our 30 caliber machine guns and the bazooka teams. I saw our tanks coming around the ridge, spread out, and start moving toward the enemy position. There were six of them out now and they were moving, not firing, just moving. I hoped they wouldn't move too far out, I wanted that artillery fire when we started to move, and if the tanks went too far the artillery would stop firing.

Now the German artillery started up. Man, they were pouring it on—not at us but at those tanks. But the tanks just kept manuevering, not moving so much forward, but just moving around drawing fire. Our artillery kept firing, and then the seventy-fives opened up. They would be our walking barrage; they would keep firing in front of us while the big guns tried to keep the enemy pinned down.

The command came to move out in platoon formation and move fast. We scrambled out of the bunkers and headed over the summit, down toward the foot of the ridge. No one had to tell anyone to hurry.

When we hit the foot of the ridge, we moved faster. We were covering ground now; we'd moved a hundred yards, two hundred yards, and still were moving at a good pace. As far as you could see there were infantrymen coming off the ridge and moving forward. The colonel must be using all three companies in a frontal attack. It was a good feeling knowing you weren't alone.

Our other six tanks came from behind the ridge on the right and kept in one straight line about fifty yards apart. They opened fire, then the other six tanks out on the field opened up. Each time their cannons went off, it felt like we were lifted off the ground.

The German artillery was getting heavier now. We were out about five hundred yards away from the other summit and we were taking casualties. I couldn't see who was hit, but I knew my squad was losing men. I had my eye on DeAngelo, and all of a sudden he just disappeared. I don't remember hearing a shell—just seeing a flash, and as I walked by where he'd been, all that was lying there was his legs and billfold. It unnerved Black and he started to hestitate. I shouted at him to keep going. He turned and showed me a terror stricken face. I said, "Look, you bastard, keep going or I'll shoot you here," and he turned and moved out, and my mind started drumming to the explosions: *Why the hell don't they silence some of those guns? What the hell are those goddamned artillerymen doing, firing from their assholes? We can't take much more of this!*

Half of us must be dead by now, and still the goddamned German artillery kept coming in. Some of the guys had had enough and were hitting the dirt. Lieutenant MacLean came around and started kicking the shit out of anyone lying down. "Get behind that ridge up there! There *is* no other relief!"

Lieutenant Studebaker and Sergeant Gardner were shouting, "Keep going! Keep going!"

I saw Levin taking two bazooka teams down on their knees and firing about six or eight rockets into the row of bunkers. That had more effect than the damned artillery.

The tanks were taking an awful beating, but none

231

had been knocked out yet, I was surprised the Germans hadn't come out with their panzers and finished them off.

We'd gone another two hundred yards—two hundred more should put us right in the middle of that German infantry. Then it would be up to us. The artillery and the tanks couldn't help us then. Levin was keeping up with us with his bazooka teams. They would drop every once in a while and fire several shots into those bunkers. If they weren't hitting anything at least they were keeping them pinned down. We went another hundred yards—a hundred to go. The German artillery was letting up a little, but their mortars were coming in like rain. I kept shouting, not knowing for sure that there was anyone to hear me, "Keep going! Don't stop now! Keep going!" I could hear Studebaker and Gardner; at least someone was alive in this platoon beside myself.

We hit the bunkers with our grenades, and got small-arms fire from above. I hollered at Brooklyn— not even knowing if he was there—to set up his machine gun and start firing. I no more had the words out of my mouth than I heard his gun going. He was raking the top bunkers now while the riflemen were cleaning out this lower row. I heard a BAR cut away. Good old Al had made it, too. He was raking the top row also. The small-arms firing was slowing up. There was no more artillery now, but the tanks were using their machine guns.

Just a few more feet and we'd be at the summit. Two of the tanks fired their cannons into the ruins of the buildings from where some firing was coming. I knew, as soon as we reached the summit, that the Germans would cut loose on us with mortars. But by that time, the seventy-fives at least should be shelling the hell out of the back side of this ridge. The tanks were coming right up to the summit. We needed the mortars and machine guns now. Company M should be moving up to cover us.

We hit the last row of bunkers. There were dead Germans all over the place. Our artillery had done a job. So had the tanks and the machine-gunners.

The German soldiers were surrendering now. The command came to gather in the prisoners. The fighting had all but ceased. Now it was time for the mortars to go to work on that back side of the ridge, and they did. I happened to glance over the field we had just come over. It looked like a slaughter house; dead GIs lying everywhere.

The German artillery was still falling out on the field. I'm sure a lot of wounded were being killed, hit again by that murderous fire.

The medics were busy trying to patch up the fallen men enough for the litter bearers to get them out of the range of artillery fire. There were so damned many, though; it was a slow process. DeSola had just told me that he'd seen the Greek dead, when I saw Les run back on the field and start carrying men up behind the rise on our ridge. He was running through artillery bursts like they weren't there! He'd brought up six wounded men and was going out for more. He'd picked up one more and started back, when a shell hit about two feet in front of him. It knocked him off his feet, but he got up, picked up the wounded man and staggered up the slope. When he finally reached the rise, he collapsed on his face.

DeSola was working on the men Les had brought in. He immediately looked at Les. Les was smiling, but he was wounded; blood was running down his leg. It looked like he had been hit in the balls. I went over to him and he looked up at me and said, "That ought to be good for the Silver Star." Then he laughed.

Then he died.

I lost a lot of friends that day.

It was ironic; the man Les was bringing in when he was hit had been dead for some time.

I sat down and lit a cigarette, trying to calm my nerves. I kept lighting up, one right after another, taking three or four drags off each. My composure was coming back.

A litter came over from Company K on the summit and I recognized the man on it, though he was blood from one end to the other. But that bald head was showing, one heavily muscled arm dragging on the ground. It was Colonel Track. His combat patrol had found the Germans on the left side of the ridge, and the Germans had killed most of them. Those who hadn't been killed were wounded. Not one man could walk away from that little skirmish. The colonel had been hit several times with machine-gun fire, and while he was awaiting evacuation, he'd been hit again with mortar fire. The medic bringing him back said he'd never make it.

Some of our tanks had gone around the ridge now, following the stream, and were firing at the German artillery. The German gun crews were pulling out, some taking their guns with them, some just pulling out to save their skins. Their panzers were running too, as was anything on wheels—trucks, half-tracks, and even horse-carts.

The firing began to ease back on the plain. The seventy-fives were setting up and just as fast as they set up, they opened fire. They were inflicting some casualties. They fired at anything moving, as did the tanks. The tanks had gone out about four or five hundred yards and stopped. They were pouring out cannon fire. We had had a lot of casualties, but the Germans had more. I realized then that the whole action had lasted less than half an hour. But in that half an hour a lot of men met their maker, both American and German.

I was looking down on the field, when I saw the Greek. I thought I must be hallucinating. I looked again. Yes, it was the Greek. He was walking up in our direction and calling out. He was wounded. I was about to go down and bring him up. He was carrying something, and he kept dropping it, then he'd bend and pick it up and start walking again. I took a better look. What the hell could be so precious that he'd carry it up here? Jesus Christ! *It was his guts!* He'd been wounded and his guts were spilling out, and he was picking them up and walking up to us. Both Reds and I ran down, grabbed him and carried him up to the rise. I thought sure he would die any time. I'd never seen such a mutilated man, dead or alive. He couldn't possibly stay alive. DeSola looked at him and said he didn't know what to do. He called for a litter bearer, and we loaded him aboard. DeSola just laid a bunch of bandages over him. They took him away. I thought I would never see the Greek again.

I started looking over the rest of my squad. I knew we had a lot of casualties, but I didn't realize until after I took count—the whole damned squad was a casualty. DeAngelo, Homer, Fienberg, and Miller had been killed, and all the rest of us had been wounded. Reds was hit in the left arm; Al had been hit on the back of his right shoulder. Stutzman was bleeding from a small hand wound. Russ was holding his head. He said something had knocked his helmet off and given him one helluva headache. He also had a slight cut, but it was bleeding like hell. The Greek, who was as good as dead, had been evacuated. Black had multiple leg wounds and would have to be evacuated. And I'd got hit in the same leg, just above the other wound.

The lieutenant came around to see what our casualties were. When I told him, he said "You still have the magic squad. The second squad is completely gone, and Nielson has two men left. My runner was killed, so there's just Gardner and Levin and us. Eleven men in all, and we started this drive with forty-one."

We practically didn't exist anymore. We were almost completely wiped out.

I asked him what we were going to do, thinking they would certainly take us off the line now. He said we were going up to the ruins to dig in. A counterattack was not expected, but we had to be ready in case it did come. There was no one to replace us, so we would stay until we get replacements. Then we'd hit the Po Valley, probably day after tomorrow.

I couldn't believe it. After all we'd been through, how could we go on? It was just a matter of time before we hit the Germans again. What the hell were we suppose to attack them with? Ten men and one officer? Why the hell didn't they let someone else have some of the glory? Why should we have it all?

When we finished digging in to the rubble that had been Monte San Pietro, we had quite a fort. It was pretty dusty down below us. I supposed that was the valley, the promised land. The seventy fives were firing right on it.

Later, they brought the 105s up on the slope behind us, and their observers came up to where we were dug in. They started firing, too. The Germans weren't fighting anymore. They were running, taking anything they could with them and leaving the rest.

It was hot. Man, it was hot. We weren't used to this heat. And we still had winter clothes on. There were no trees up here to speak of, and since our bombs and artillery had destroyed the houses before we'd arrived, there was no way we could get out of the sun.

It was getting toward late afternoon, when we saw troops coming over the area we had just covered. They had tanks, trucks, and all kinds of equipment. As they drew closer to us, we could identify just about every American division in Italy. They were all coming through our break in the gothic line. They would fan out after they reached the valley and start their walk across. Some uncomplimentary remarks were thrown our way. They weren't too happy with us, and I didn't understand why. We'd opened the whole damned Po Valley for them! I'm sure I never will understand the reason for their epithets. It hurt, it'll always hurt. Wherever I would go after the war and someone would tell me he'd been in one of those divisions in Italy, I would always be a little suspicious of him.

We watched these guys marching by for a couple of hours. There were some British units, Brazilian, Japanese Americans, and some Canadians who were in a special service force attached to our division. They weren't moving down into the valley yet; they were spreading out on some of the lower ridges and would stay there for a day or two. We would be the first into the valley. We broke the gothic line and our general insisted that we be first into the Po.

The artillery was still pounding the Germans. They would probably keep that up until there wasn't a German in sight. With my field glasses, I could see quite a ways, fifteen or twenty miles. I could see cities to our front and to our left — Bologna and Modena. There were a lot of smaller villages in between and a lot of fruit trees — peaches, apples, cherries. I was hoping they'd be nice and ripe when we finally made our way down. Some fresh fruit would taste good about right now.

The artillery was down to firing at targets only now. It had grown fairly quiet. I was getting hungry, so I opened a K-ration, lit up my stove, and had a meal of I don't know what. We were beginning to relax a bit.

Captain Bear came up to the ruins to say goodbye. Battalion had lost quite a few of their staff, and he was being promoted to major. He said he was leaving the company, what was left of it, in good hands. Lieutenant MacLean would be taking over. He also said that we would be getting replacements either later today or early tomorrow morning, and he hoped we would have a full complement before we started out across the Po Valley. He said he would see us from time to time and appreciated everything we had done for him while he was commanding. I asked him about a medal for Les. He said he'd seen the whole thing and was putting in a report about it, recommending the Congressional Medal of Honor. The lieutenant was also writing a report, and the captain said that if I also would submit a report, it would help strengthen his recommendation. I told him I would. Captain Bear shook each man's hand and wished us all luck. He'd been a good field officer. Today, he's as good a college professor. The lieutenant called Reds and me over to talk in private. He said he was putting Reds over in Les and Berg's old squad, as the squad leader. He wanted to know who I would put in Reds' place. It was between Stutzman and Russ. I thought Russ would be the better man. There were times, although he was a good soldier, that Stutzman hesitated; he didn't act on instinct—he'd think things out too much before he acted. I recommended Russ. Al would actually have been the best—he was a fast thinker, knowledgable, and quick to react—but I knew he wouldn't take it. I told the lieutenant I'd like to offer it to Al first, then to Russ. And if they both turned it down, then Stutzman. He agreed.

They had unloaded the mules down by the road, and supplies had been deposited there. The mules were going back across the plain and disappearing. We would be supplied by trucks as soon as we were in the Po Valley. The mules that were to carry the seventy-fives were standing by, though. It looked like we would have artillery with us all the way across. I also noticed that they were bringing up mules for Company M, which meant the men wouldn't have to carry those heavy weapons and they would stay right up with us. And it meant more support. We would be a task force all by ourselves.

The tanks were starting to pull back now. Only two of them were still setting down there in front of us. They sure had been a help, and I hated to see them go. We might need them down in the valley; they told me it was real tank country. But at least we'd have the seventy fives, the bazookas, the heavy mortars, and machine guns.

The sun was low enough now that some of the ruins were making shadows. It wasn't very cool, but at least we could get out of the direct sun.

We spent a quiet night. Just some artillery fire from our side and not much of that. We were sent up some C rations, but no one really wanted to eat much. We had our minds on our buddies, now dead or back at an aid station awaiting evacuation to a hospital. I wondered how many of them we would see again. I think most of the guys had million-dollar wounds and would be shipped back to the States. Which of us were the lucky ones?

Chapter 24

Early the next morning our replacements arrived. Fresh from basic training in the States. As they marched across the plain, they looked like a couple of companies. Sergeant Schidt was bringing them up to us.

My squad got the first eight. Now I had twelve men again—four old hands, bandaged and dirty, and eight new recruits with shaving cream still on their chins.

There was Anderson, from Ohio; he wanted to be a scout. God, I thought, this young blond strapping kid probably last saw action on a football field somewhere, and here he is eager to do one of the most dangerous jobs in the infantry. "Okay," I said. "Poof! You're a scout." Barwick, who came from Jersey, said he'd go with Anderson, and he became my other scout. Then there was the skinny kid, Herr, who came from California; and the tough-faced Madden from New York; the wide-eyed Parker from Texas; and the freckle-faced Starke, from my own Indiana. They were all riflemen with Stutzman. The other two worked with Al as his BAR team. There was Ragone, who'd said he was "from upstate."

"Upstate? Upstate what state?"

He looked at me as if I'd just got in from Mars.

"New York. Albany."

I asked him how the governor was doing.

Then there was Owens, who'd been set on a college career playing basketball for Michigan State.

All in all, I thought we made a pretty okay squad. We started training them right away, with grenades, launchers, movement positions. They picked up on everything quickly. I could tell that each of them was ready to see some action.

By now, there was only my squad, plus Studebaker, Gardner, and Levin, with Studebaker's new runner, in the ruins, so we had plenty of room for our Berlitz training exercises.

After we'd eaten and shaved—what a luxury, to be able to shave!—orders came down that we'd be kicking off the next morning at 0600 hours. There would be no artillery barrage; the whole regiment would line up and start down the slopes into the Po. We were to be on the alert—no bridges would be used, in case of booby traps. The infantry would stick to the fields, and the armored division would go along the roads. We were told to watch for signs of snipers, and to assume that the area was riddled with mines.

I watched the faces of the new men as Studebaker gave the orders. The eagerness in some had turned to fear. Anderson's face grew pale, and I half expected him to come to me and ask to be taken off scout duty, but he didn't. Owens shut his eyes; he was probably thinking about basketball hoops and all else he'd left behind for this. I figured that none of them would be getting a lot of sleep tonight, and decided to give them first guard duties; better that way for a new man.

At 0500 hours the next morning Gardner came around and woke us. In half an hour we were ready to go. We moved out in platoon formation. We'd go right over the top of the ruins and keep up a steady pace until the order came down to halt. Our battalion was expected to cover thirty miles today, then take the town that was on the main highway, and cut the Germans off.

When my scouts got to the top of the rise at the summit, they were a little reluctant to go over it. I hollered at them to move their asses, and they were up and over in a minute. All was quiet as we moved down the slope. Heavy artillery was poised behind us, and we walked on toward the Po.

Up ahead, probably four or five miles, P-47s were strafing. They would come over out lines and glide down, then fire. They weren't dropping bombs, but they were strafing the hell out of something up ahead. We found our later that they were hitting German truck convoys carrying infantry and that they'd really wreaked havoc on them.

We kept walking, our weapons at port ready for anything. We were approaching the flats now. I laughed to myself. I was wondering how long it would take us to get used to walking on level ground. I was beginning to think we'd got to be like Kentucky mules—longer legs on one side so we could walk evenly on the hills.

From time to time we would come to a farmhouse. Whenever we did, we'd hit the ground and I would send my scouts up to make sure there were no enemy soldiers in it. I went with them the first two or three times to show them what to look for and how to search a house. There were always Italians there — not like back in the mountain villages where they would all have headed for the hills until the fight was over. They would always tell us that the Germans had gone, that they'd left two days ago. They also told us that the Germans had taken their horses. These people seemed interested only in their farms, their fruit trees and crops, like farmers all over the world. One thing I noticed right away, there was plenty of food here; it seemed these people didn't lack for anything. They lived the good life of farmers, and the small villages also reflected their attitude. After a while, even as old campaigner, I began to have faith in what the farmers and villagers told us.

We had walked for about two hours. The sun was getting damned hot. I couldn't remember a hotter day. I saw fellows throwing their field jackets away — they were too heavy to carry. But the nights would probably get cool yet, and when we reached the Alps we'd definitely need these winter clothes. I took my field jacket off and shoved it in my backpack. We hadn't had a break yet, though we must have walked at least five or six miles across fields. We were catching up to the work done by the P-47s. It was a sight you wouldn't believe. I've seen dead men, many many of them, but I'd never witnessed anything like this. Some of the German convoys had never had a chance to pull off the road. Men were setting in the trucks with their eyes open, but they were dead. On both sides of the road, for about a hundred fifty yards, there were dead men all over the place. I doubt very much if some of these convoys had any survivors at all. It was an awesome sight, one I will never forget.

Among the dead were not only men, but animals—horses, mules, cattle, goats, and sheep. They hadn't been dead very long, but they were starting to swell up already. The place would smell like hell in a few more hours.

Some of the new men were vomiting. I told them not to look but at the same time, they were fascinated by the sight. And the more they looked, the sicker they got. Let them look, I thought. Let them get used to this sight now so they could take it when the time came for us to start dying again. The older guys would just keep going, without a sideways glance. They'd seen all they wanted to. More, in fact.

We were well into our third hour of walking, and still no break, I told the new men to take it easy on the water. We didn't know when we would get more.

We were coming to little streams now—back in Indiana we would call them drainage ditches. Sometimes they had bridges over them, and the new men would always head for them. Then I'd remind them that we couldn't use them, and they would bitch. Though it was hard on the feet, walking in wet boots, the water did cool us off for a time.

There was a beautiful fruit orchard up ahead. The fruit was not ripe, but the trees provided shade and would be a great spot to rest. We were walking right toward it. A road ran alongside the orchard, and as we approached it a panzer stuck his nose out and fired right into our ranks. I saw him coming out, and shouted for everyone to hit the dirt. He fired two or three times, pulled back into the orchard, and disappeared. No one was hit, but it shocked the hell out of everyone and put us all on the alert. Everyone was so wired that

245

I was half afraid to say anything, for fear of startling someone into firing.

The moment after the panzer had fired, the P-47s were coming down at him. After a few more minutes we could hear strafing, then all at once there was an explosion that shook the ground. That was the end of the panzer.

The P-47s were flying over head again just as if nothing had happened.

Our platoon was ordered into the orchard to make sure no other fanatical Germans were in there to strike our backs after we passed. The other troopers were ordered to take up firing positions and await our return. At least the other guys would get a good rest while we went racing through an orchard looking for something we did not expect to find. My squad, as usual, was the point of the search. I had my two scouts out. They really didn't know what to do, so I told Russ to take over the squad and I went out with them. We moved fast. The ground was cultivated and I could see immediately that there were no enemy soldiers in this place. When we'd combed the entire orchard, we returned and learned that our long-awaited break had come.

We settled back, rested, and ate and drank to our hearts' content, then snoozed for a while. We stayed in the orchard for about an hour, then started walking again.

We were walking almost straight east now. The town we were to take was east and south of here, about ten miles away. We should reach it around 1600 hours.

At about 1530 hours we halted and lay on the

ground, keeping our eyes ahead. The mules carrying the seventy-fives passed through us, then the artillerymen began unloading their guns. I could see about twenty guns from where I lay. Next, the Company M mules began bringing up the mortars, the 81 mm guns, and the 50 caliber machine guns. They set up ahead of the seventy-fives. We could not see the town in front of us. There were trees, but not that many—the town had to be at least two miles away.

Orders came down for us to move. We were to keep moving until we hit opposition. We moved out, past the seventy-fives and the mortars. We were out in front again. We had our light mortars and light machine guns with us.

We were moving through a pasture field. There were some small trees, hardly more then bushes, lining both sides of the field. Other troops moved at the periphery of it, along with Italian partisans who knew the area well. I could see the partisans now and then. It was a little startling to see civilians carrying rifles and tommy guns.

We kept moving and the nearer we came to that town the more nervous I became. Shortly after 1600 hours, the river came into view, and on the other bank was the town. If we were to be fired on, it would be now. They wouldn't want us to get across that river.

As if they'd heard my thoughts, mortars started falling. The river had built-up banks, like levees along the Mississippi River. We were only about two hundred yards away. I hollered at the men to beat their asses toward the bank and hit the dirt. I don't know what the lieutenant had in mind, and I didn't wait to hear. All I had on my mind now was to keep these guys from getting killed and to get across that river.

As soon as we'd hit the bank, the enemy cut loose with machine guns, and their mortar-fire increased. But none of my men were hit. I saw other platoons coming up now. Our other two squads were behind the bank now, too, as was Lieutenant Studebaker. He came over to me and ask why I'd done what I had. I told him I wanted to reach this bank and put down a covering fire for the rest of the guys, and he said that was really smart. "Your men don't know what a good squad leader they have."

Right now I wasn't looking for praise. I was looking for a way to stop those mortars and the machine-gun fire. I crawled, with the lieutenant, to the top of the bank. We both took out our glasses and scanned the terrain. There were lots of civilians, but no enemy. Still, the mortars kept coming in, but from where, I didn't know. We could see puffs of smoke when the machine guns fired. They were in the top floors of some of the buildings setting about a hundred and fifty yards back from the river. The artillery observer came up to join us. He also saw the smoke and immediately ordered the seventy-fives to open up. It seemed they must have been aimed and ready to fire, for as soon as he gave the command, the seventy-fives started coming in. Man, they must have all been firing. They were hitting the very buildings we'd pinpointed.

As the seventy-fives fired, we looked for the mortars. They were coming in just as thick as they had been, but they weren't as accurate as before. Lieutenant MacLean came up and said, "There may not be a better time. We're going now, Studebaker. You lead off, and the other two platoons'll be right behind you."

The river came up to our chests by the time we were halfway across. We were getting some machine-gun fire, but not much. The mortars were still firing on the other side of the river, doing no harm at all. They were firing blind; their observer was gone—one way or another he was gone, and they just kept firing. When we got across, we plunged into a swamp. It gave us some cover, but it also slowed us up. Once we crawled out of the swamp, the machine guns started up again. Civilians were running all over the place, hindering our fire.

We hit the first houses. By this time, the other troops were over the river. We threw grenades into the windows, and as soon as they exploded we jumped in with our rifles blazing. There were Germans in there, all right, but there were also Italian civilians. A lot of innocent people were killed that day.

We kept going, house to house. My new men were getting real training now, the kind they wouldn't forget. The seventy-fives had stopped firing now. Our light mortars were firing into the next town ahead of us, but we weren't receiving any mortar fire from the Germans at all now.

Almost every street we hit, we found Germans. The civilians were fewer and further apart now. I don't believe they realized what was happening when we first hit the town. Either that, or they'd believed the Germans had had everything under control.

We hadn't had any artillery hitting on us when we entered the town. Not even 88s from their panzers. This meant only one thing: They'd left an infantry unit here, probably a battalion, to hold us back as long as possible while their mechanized force moved away. But I was sure the P-47s would take care of them.

We had crossed the main road: the buildings were fewer, and there was practically no enemy opposition at all. We were taking some prisoners now, men who were glad the war was over for them. There were some wounded Germans, so we had the prisoners pick them up in litters and take them back to the river, where our troops were gathering prisoners. One German officer drew himself up when I asked him to help carry a wounded man and told me in the king's English that he was a German officer and would not dirty his hands carrying a common soldier. I got so enraged that I kicked out and caught the haughty bastard right square in the ass. He dropped like a stuck hog. I hadn't meant to kick him so hard, but I guess he was lucky that's all I did. Needless to say, he was carried out on a litter himself, cursing and swearing that he'd kill me if he ever saw me again. I assured him that if he wanted to take a chance, I'd give it to him.

The engineers had removed the charges under the bridge, so the tanks and other mechanized equipment could enter the town. We had another company from our battalion moving in behind us, sweeping up any Germans we might have missed.

The battle was over; we moved to the north edge of town along the main route into Bologna and were told to dig in.

Chapter 25

I'd been taking my turn off watch, sleeping in one of the shallow foxholes we'd dug beside the road, when I awoke to someone shaking me. It was Anderson. He and I had been taking watch shifts. No sooner did I look up at his frightened face than I saw flares and heard gunfire. The minute I was out of the hole, I saw the panzers—coming right down the road at us. Then, German infantry, spread out all over. Our light machine guns—at our flanks—and the heavy guns were firing at them. They weren't more than three hundred yards away—a great target for the bigger guns, but hell for us troops.

Fire was coming down on us from the other end of the town now, too. It looked for the first minutes like we were surrounded, cut off.

Our tanks moved in now, firing away at the approaching panzers. Then our mortars opened up. We were all out and firing now, and the German soldiers were falling like ripe apples. I saw a couple of their panzers go up, then another. The troops were backing off, and the fire from behind us stopped as suddenly as it had started.

I could hear our radios crackling and orders coming over for the company that had set up in the town to the south side; they were sending tanks in there, and others to the north end, to ward off more panzers. That was us. Good old Company L, first to beat off the panzers every time.

What was left of the German infantry was only about a hundred yards in front of us now, and the few who were left kept coming. The last two panzers burst into flames, and the moment that happened, every soldier out there with a German uniform on his back shot his hands into the air.

It looked, after closer observation, like the panzers were SS and the infantry was army. When the last panzer was gone, so was the SS. We took about forty prisoners. The lieutenant told me to take four or five men and get out there to see if any of the Germans were still alive. If they were, to send medics.

Something snapped in me. "What the hell is this, a one-squad army? Send some other poor bastards, dammit!" The lieutenant's jaw dropped, and he stared before he found words. "What the hell's the matter with you? You got battle fatigue or something? You never talked to me like that!"

He was dumbfounded, and so was I. Maybe I *did* have battle fatigue and needed a rest, but, by God, every time there was a dirty job to do it was the first squad, and I was getting goddamned sick of it.

I took four men and we walked out among the Germans. I told the lieutenant to keep the flares up, I didn't relish walking around in the dark among Germans who might or might not be dead.

We found quite a few wounded Germans, and called for medics. Litter bearers came out and started carrying them back. They were put in ambulances around our lines and hauled away, to where I do not know. All in all, we found twenty-nine wounded Germans, so our prisoner take was up to sixty-nine.

There was still hard fighting at the south end of town. A German force was trying to get out of a trap behind us set up by the British. When their patrols discovered we'd taken the town, they'd sent a small force around to the north end and made the attack on us as a diversion, while the main force tried to break through from the south. It must have been a very heavily mechanized force; if it had been just infantry, they would've gone around us. But they needed the road and the bridge. The British force holding back the Germans were coming up on the rear of the enemy, so the Germans were now fighting on two sides. But the whole thing meant that our battalion was out here all by ourselves, cut off from the rest. We didn't have any detachments within reach and we were in trouble. We had only one recourse, and that was to fight.

All the armor had been taken away from our flank, to aid the southern part of town. We had only one tank. The heavy mortars were turning around and were bombarding south of the river, and I knew we had some seventy-fives south of the river. Levin came over and asked if we had any bazookas. We didn't. He said he was gathering up all the bazookas he could get his hands on and sending all the men we had who knew how to handle one back to the bridge. They didn't want to destroy the bridge if it was possible to save it, but they weren't going to allow any enemy panzers to cross it, either. Whether the bridge stood or was blown up was entirely in the hands of the Germans, and the guts of the American troops defending it.

We held our positions; I thought sure we would be ordered back to help, but we weren't. The fighting had been going on for quite a while now; they were really doing a lot of firing back there. It must have been quite a large enemy force to fight that hard.

If the British cut them off from behind, they would have no place to go except through us and out into the open country toward Bologna. I was sure the German commander had figured this out a long time ago, but he also should have figured out the war was over and all he was doing was killing people—both his own and ours. Maybe they called this bravery; I called it damned foolery.

When it started to get light, at about 0400 hours, the firing died down a little. There still was a lot of artillery fire, but the small arms had almost stopped.

Levin came back and told us that the enemy hadn't made any attempt to cross the bridge. They'd lost a lot of panzers and self-propelled guns, and probably a lot of men during the night, but had not really mounted any large-scale attack except by the infantry, which we'd beaten back. He thought they were getting ready to surrender. They could not go forward with us standing in the way. While Levin was talking, I heard the radio crackle to life. The Company K commander was giving a two-hour truce to the German commander. Company K had just received an emissary from the German commander, and the company officer was contacting Division Command with the terms of the German's surrender. While we were waiting for the answer to come back from Division, we re-supplied ourselves with ammo, and loaded up on K rations. That was one thing we had plenty of, K rations.

We were fed and loaded and ready to go regardless what the decision would be, when Studebaker walked over. "Ike," he said rather tentatively, "would you please take about two or three men and go out there and count those dead Germans?" I thought, *When the hell had we started counting dead Germans? Hell, I could have counted hundreds, maybe thousands since I joined this outfit.* I looked at him and said, "I'm sorry about that little fracas I put up this morning."

He said, "Forget it, Ike. I know how you felt, and in a way, you were right. But don't forget, in the whole platoon, you have more experienced men than any other squad." He was right, I did, and if I had Reds back, I'd be that much better off too.

I took Al's two men. BAR men never have any excitement, I said to myself. I'd give them a little change. Ragone and Owens were bright-eyed and ready to go. Al had said they'd performed well and without bitching all the time, and he was very happy with them.

Well, this will give them a little experience, I thought. I didn't know for what; I couldn't think of a job in civilian life that would require a skill in counting dead bodies, not even Al Capone's men ever did that. We went out; by this time some of them were beginning to swell, and with the swelling came the smell. We counted; I was even surprised by the numbers lying out there. There were a hundred eighty-nine men, and that wasn't counting the ones who'd been in the panzers. When we returned and reported to Studebaker, I still couldn't get it through my head why they'd wanted the count.

The word finally came down from Division for the Germans to throw down their arms and surrender. There would be no terms. The word was unconditional surrender. As if by magic, about a dozen P-47s flew low over us and headed toward the German column. The emissary took the message from our colonel back to his lines. They had fifteen minutes, then our planes would come in and we'd cut loose with everything we had. We got back into our foxholes.

A little piper cub landed on the road ahead of us and taxied up to our lines. We were up and had our guns ready, in case it was a German trick; we had reached a point where we trusted no one. It was not a good feeling, but it was the right attitude to have here; it could keep you alive. A British officer got out and conferred with Lieutenant MacLean. Then MacLean sent him with a runner toward the south end of town to find the colonel.

Word came down at the last minute that the Germans were surrendering. They started coming over the bridge, a company at a time. I wondered what the hell we were going to do with all these prisoners. After about an hour, they were still coming. In the distance, I could see the British units moving up. They were searching the panzers and other mechanized equipment and trucks.

Finally, the last German unit crossed the bridge, then the tommies came across. They had Scotch whiskey and were passing it around to the GIs; there they also had photographers with them, and they were having a field day taking their pictures.

We had captured a whole German division; we had

taken many panzers, trucks, armored cars; personnel carriers, and plenty of 88s. It was an armored division and it was a good one—one of the best the Germans had in Italy.

Soon, trucks came up the road—at least two hundred of them. They drew up to the bridge, and the prisoners were loaded in.

The prisoner trucks had long disappeared when we were ordered to start moving out. The armor was going down the road again, and we would cut across the fields, the same as we had done the day before. We headed out this time to the northwest. What the hell's the matter with these people! I thought. Don't they know what direction Bologna is in. It's straight up this road! We'd all seen pictures of soldiers liberating big cities—but we had never had that opportunity. We always ended up with bombed-out villages or towns like this one where everyone was afraid of us and wouldn't even bother their heads to talk to us.

Well, northwest was our direction. We'd be going to Modena. A pretty good-sized city. Maybe they'd greet us with open arms, food, wine, and women.

We hadn't been walking very long when someone started shooting at us. We hit the ground. I couldn't believe one German would fire at a whole company, but the firing kept up. Some of the guys were getting uncomfortable; the bullets were coming close. Then I saw them; there were about six or seven civilians to our left. They were partisans. What the hell were they firing at us for? I waved at them, and they waved back. Then they came over to us. I had my finger on my trigger—I still hadn't figured out why they'd been firing at us in the first place. They ran up to a couple of the men who had put on German army jackets—the same guys who'd thrown theirs away when it had got hot yestersay. The partisans wanted to know why we let the Germans have guns. I laughed and explained the situation. Then I looked over at our German-clad guys again and nearly fell over. They weren't wearing any old German jackets—they were SS coats! They got rid of them, pronto.

We walked for several more hours without incident. This time the receptions we got at the farm houses along the way were friendlier. Many of the people were awaiting us with bread, wine, and cheeses. Young village girls started following our march, calling to the men, grabbing us with hugs and kisses. I was beginning to think that this was a helluva lot better victory march than one through a city, after all.

But then, I reminded myself, we were still looking for the enemy; the victory wasn't yet complete.

We must have walked twenty-five to thirty miles before we stopped to dig in for the night. We were beside a small stream that ran north, and we made our shallow holes on its east bank. The night passed peacefully, and by 0500 hours, we were ready to move out again.

When the orders came to move, we saw a convoy of German trucks up the road about half a mile. All of us grabbed our rifles and hit the dirt, until the lieutenant came around and advised us that those were our transportation.

What? I thought. Ride in captured German trucks with those planes buzzing overhead? But my worries were foolish after all; each truck was marked at the top with pink banners, and each squad leader was given a supply of pink smoke grenades, in case the banners got dismantled.

We'd been riding for more than an hour when the trucks pulled over and started down through the orchards. We jumped from the trucks and hit the ditches. German panzers had been spotted—three of them—and our tanks were going after them. We started to hear firing—lots of firing—and saw clouds of smoke climbing toward the sky.

The P-38s came in, flying low, and as soon as they were over the panzers, they dropped their loads; we saw the smoke and the tops of the flames. Another cloud of smoke went up, then another. The planes circled back and then disappeared.

We waited for a while, until the noise died down, then got back into the trucks and were on our way.

We'd traveled only about a mile when the P-38s came over us again. They circled a few times, then flew off, only to return. I saw them coming over the orchard, straight toward us, and with a jolt realized what they were about to do. Frantically, I got my hands on the pink smoke grenade and lobbed it out of the truck, but the planes were on us by that time and they were letting go with all they had. I jumped from the truck—hollering for everyone to dive out. All the time I was letting those damned pink grenades go, but they didn't do a bit of good; the P-38s kept buzzing us, firing.

By the time they'd figured out the mistake, we'd lost twenty-one men in that luckless convoy.

But we got back into it, and moved on. Needless to say, every time we heard a plane, the trucks jerked to a halt and we all hit the dirt. Some way to travel. Next time, I'd walk!

We camped that night at the south end of a fairly large city. We were on a main road, and had to post guards through the night. A patrol had been sent out — not us this time — and checked out the city and the road during the night. At dawn they came back, with reports of a number of German vehicles by the side of the road — mostly burned and overturned.

The captured German trucks that had brought us here turned around and headed back early in the morning. Then other convoys began to pass us, going toward the Po River. The river was ahead of us about six miles. We received no orders until late in the afternoon — then it was our turn to move again. We started walking out, toward the river. Ahead of us were the other battalions, and ahead of them, trucks carrying the boats that would ferry us across the Po.

According to orders, we would just dig in behind the bank of the Po and wait our turn to cross. Some of the other battalions would make the beach head, and we'd follow. It seemed too good to be true.

And it was.

We camped again, half a mile from the Po. And spent the next afternoon there awaiting word. Then it came. We were the first to cross. And our company, our platoon, would be points. We would make the beach head, after all. When the news came up, Studebaker just looked at me and shrugged. "Look," he sighed. "I didn't know, either."

"Yeah," I said. "Many can follow. Only a few can lead." I was getting cynical, I realized, but I was up to my ears with the honor of drawing fire every time, and every time we made honorable attacks, we left some honorable men lying in ditches and gulleys, and I was fed up with it. I suppose I was getting to the point where I didn't give a damn anymore. I tried to check myself before I went back and told my squad the good news.

We ran down to the shore of the river, threw off our backpacks. There were twelve to a boat—six riding, six rowing. The shore engineer gave us a shove and told us not to row until we'd got the word. There were about fifty boats now, ready to go.

Our artillery had begun to fire across the river, and the Germans were returning it, hitting right along the shoreline. Smoke bombs went up, and the water was a haze; we'd be covered in our crossing. Still, the Germans fired their big guns toward the river. The shells fell far wide of us, but they sent up waves, and the boats started rocking. I could see the lieutenant step into his boat, near ours, then stand there for a few moments. He looked, through the smoke, like George Washington crossing the Delaware.

We were still awaiting the order to start crossing when our planes came in and started hitting the big German guns hard and heavy. Then our artillery increased its fire. The current in the river was swift, and we were drifting out to the ends of our ropes. All the men were snapping to go. Then the big gunfire eased up; more smoke bombs came in and added to the haze around us. Suddenly, what must have been a squadron of P-38s and another of P-47s crossed over us and bombed the hell out of the far bank.

The word came: Start rowing!

Chapter 26

We were coming into the bank now. I told the rowers to quit rowing and grab their equipment. As soon as the boat was in close enough and our mortars and artillery lifted, we got the hell out and dug into the sand.

We hit five feet out from the shore and all jumped out at the same time and headed for the sand. Al was firing. He had a target, a machine gun nest, and they were firing down right on us. The guys were digging in, just to get themselves off the surface, but the machine gun had to be stopped. I motioned to Stutzman to cover me, and I made a mad dash toward the nest. As I'd expected, I was drawing fire from other points now, but enough boats had come ashore that we had some more firepower, which made the Germans keep their heads down some.

I was only about fifteen yards from their nest when I let go with a grenade, then another, and a third. I didn't hear the machine gun anymore.

I ran up and found three dead Germans. They had controlled a good sector, and with them out of action, our troops were able to move up to higher ground and away from the beach.

The planes were bombing and strafing further back

now. They were hitting artillery pieces; and I could see the dust from either panzers or trucks—and they were running.

Our entire platoon was up on the heights now. Although we were holding our own, it would only be a matter of time before the Germans would counter-attack, and unless we had some tanks and anti-tank guns over on this side of the river, we'd be right back in the water—or dead.

They were bringing the heavy-weapons company over now, and more and more men had got over. They'd hit the beach, under cover of the artillery and mortars, then head for the bank. We'd have to move pretty soon; it was getting crowded here. The planes kept their strafing and bombing up. It was a bloody battle now. The Germans were starting to get our range up here on the bank, and just about every time they let go with a shell, they caused casualties. We were losing men, and I thought to myself that we should stop bringing men over until we can protect what is over here.

The medics were putting the wounded men back in the boats and transporting them back to the south shore, but the casualties were starting to get ahead of them. Our heavy-weapons platoon was pounding the area right in front of us and doing a great job; and Company M had their mortars working a little further back. We had good protection now, but I was worried about panzers; they could sweep down on us and there wasn't much we could do. What we needed were tanks—*get those damn tanks over here you guys!*

Then they came—the panzers. At least twenty of them. They were spitting death from their machine

263

guns and firing those damned 88s, hitting right at the top of the bank and on the beach.

We had to spread out. We had at least a regiment over here now and the men were practically shoulder to shoulder. Why don't those silly bastards give us an order to move out? We couldn't be any worse off than if we were just sitting here! We were up against terrible odds with those panzers, plus the Germans who were dug in.

Now the panzers were forming up into a line and getting ready to attack us with infantry. There were all kinds of orders being yelled out down on the beach, but I doubt if very many people knew what they were doing. Lieutenant MacLean came up to our position and looked the situation over. He immediately radioed the colonel and told him we would have to hold this position, and that as soon as the Germans started to pull back, if they did, we'd have to follow them or we'd never get out of this trap. I heard the colonel say, "Will there not be a lot of casualties?"

The Lieutenant said, "Yes, and if we stay here, there'll not only be a lot of casualties, but we won't accomplish a thing.

The colonel told us to hold and destroy the offensive. By that time, he'd have two other companies ready to take the offensive.

Back on the river, the engineers were building a pontoon bridge—a bunch of boats were strung together and a roadbed was placed on top of them. It was almost halfway across. We hadn't seen it before because of the smoke, but the smoke was clearing now and we could also see the troops massing to come across, waiting for their turns in the boats. Still, what we needed now were tanks not men. I looked again, and I saw guns coming across. Big, beautiful anti-tank guns, seventy-fives, and 105s. They'd lashed several boats together and were bringing them over.

The panzers were about to move. We could handle the infantry, but I was really worried those panzers would get to this bank and pour fire down on that river. If they did, everything we'd done up to now would be wiped out, and with it one hell of a lot of good men's lives. There was no way they could get us off here if the panzers broke through. If they kept building that bridge at the rate they were, we should have tanks over here by noon, or even before. Once we had them we could move, and the Germans should start pulling back.

In the meantime, we had an attack mounting against us. The enemy artillery was really hitting us now. I hoped this was not the only spot where our army had crossed the river. If it was we could very easily be whipped in this battle. The Germans had us at a disadvantage, and if they sustained their attack, they could defeat us and definitely drive us back.

They were landing the guns now. The seventy-fives rolled right up among the infantry and opened up immediately. The anti-tank guns were also rolled up on the bank, but they were not yet fired; they would hold them until the panzers actually attacked. There were lots of German infantry standing around; they were about a mile away, but I could see them good with glasses. Our artillery was falling among them, but it didn't seem to bother them too much. It indicated to me that they were seasoned troops and would fight hard.

More and more big guns were coming over now, and the bridge was progressing. Every once in a while a shell would hit the bridge and kill some engineers, but as soon as the smoke cleared, others were hard at it again.

It was 0900 hours; at the rate they were going, the bridge would be in before noon.

At about 1000 hours, the German artillery increased. They really pounded us. I don't think I'd ever been in such a barrage. It seemed that every spot on that beach and bank was being hit with a shell. Our planes started diving down on the panzers. I put my glasses on the panzers, and sure as hell, they were coming. There had to be at least a brigade of them. They were concentrated in a two-mile front, and firing.

The anti-tank gun guys were primed and ready to go. The seventy-fives had been firing, but now they were firing as fast as their crews could load them, and the 105s down on the beach were really opening up, too. We were also receiving some help from artillery on the south side of the river. And the planes were dropping bombs like mad now. But I did not see any panzers getting hit, although some of their infantry was going down.

The Germans kept coming; they would not quit. This could be their last fight, one way or another, and they knew it. And if they were the seasoned troops we suspected them to be, they didn't know the word surrender. We'd fought this type before, and they would just keep coming until they were either dead or captured. They were closer now, and we could be in the battle of our lives.

The bridge was almost across now, but every once in a while a German shell would hit the bridge and put a hole in it, then the engineers would have to repair it.

The German advance was now only about half a mile away. We had enough artillery on this side now that it was starting to do some damage. I kept my glasses on the advance when I wasn't ducking down. Some of those German shells were falling very nearby, but as far as I could see, none of my squad had been hit. They were staying very cool; they were ready for anything, but no one was saying anything. I know they had their own thoughts, and I'm sure quite a few of them were wondering if they would be alive when the sun set tonight.

Gardner and Levin were working themselves along a fairly deep ditch out toward the enemy with their bazookas, I also noticed that they'd picked up two more bazooka teams, and they were loaded down with rockets. If they could find themselves a good spot, they could do some damage.

By now the bridge was within twenty feet of the shore. At the far end, a tank had entered it and was coming slowly across. Other tanks were lining up now, too. They would probably give the tank in front plenty of room, so they wouldn't bunch up and make a bigger target. They were beginning to lay down a smokescreen again, as well.

The Germans were still pouring in their artillery, just as heavily as ever, and we were still taking heavy casualties. But for the first time, knowing those tanks were coming over, I felt we had a chance to hold this beach head and expand it.

We could not see the bridge through the smoke at all now, but I did see one of the tanks hit the beach head.

The enemy were within five or six hundred yards now. I hoped they would put that tank right to work. Maybe by the time they reached us, we'd have three or four tanks over here and could at least make a battle out of it.

Our heavy machine guns started firing, then our heavy mortars. They were doing a good job on the infantry, but still not touching the panzers. One of the anti-tank guns was hit and its crew killed. It was a helluva mess. We pulled the gun down and called for another, but there was none to replace it. They finally put a 60 mm mortar where it had been standing. The planes continued strafing and bombing—and all at once two of the panzers went up in flames. Only eighteen to go.

The German infantry was taking a beating now, and we hadn't even opened up on them with our small arms. They were still too far away for us, but the heavy stuff was really getting them. The other panzers kept coming, although our air corps was still hammering away at them. I don't know for sure how much infantry they came to us with, but they were losing it faster than I'd ever seen.

I took a glance down on the beach and was surprised to see three tanks and two trucks loaded with ammo. One was pulling an anti-tank gun. The lieutenant saw it, too. He ran down and directed the truck up to where we had lost the other gun. The tanks were taken down to the right of us, to a road, and the last I saw of them, they were climbing up toward it.

The advance was now only about three or four hundred yards out. Our small mortars opened up as did our light machine guns. The riflemen were ordered to wait. It was hard to do. The Germans were well within our range and we were itching. We didn't want them so close that we had to use bayonets—and I'm sure the Germans felt the same way. That's a dirty way to fight.

The anti-tank guns were opening up now, and they were getting some hits, but not stopping the tanks. You could almost see their shells bouncing off that German armor. I could not see Gardner or Levin with the bazooka crews anymore; they'd disappeared behind a curve in the ditch.

The planes had stopped firing, so the battle was completely up to the land forces now. The enemy infantry was going down all over the place; none seemed to be getting any closer than about three hundred yards, but those panzers were practically right on top of us. There were five of them within eyesight now. One had stopped and the crew was crawling out of it to see what happened. As they did, they just fell off the panzer. Someone was shooting them. Then I saw Levin. He was letting go with his tommy gun. No wasting a bazooka rocket on a panzer already stopped—just get the crew. Right behind that panzer, another was approaching. They slowed down just a bit as they came in line with the halted panzer, and that was their mistake. Two rockets hit it at about the same time. When the smoke cleared, it was just a burning mass. It had also set the other panzer on fire and it was exploding all over the place. Beautiful. Four down and sixteen to go. The German infantry had small mortars with them, and they had begun pounding us with them. We received the word to fire away, and all our pent-up energy let go. We hit those Germans with everything we had. I thought Al was going to burn his BAR out, and I told him so. His answer was to slam another magazine into it and begin firing again. He wasn't just ripping away—he was firing carefully, and just about everytime he fired he was bringing down a German. He never let up. We'd killed so many Germans now, they were actually beginning to pile up in front of us. The panzers had stopped and were firing their 88s right into us, so we were dying, too.

More of our tanks were landed, and as fast as three of them were grouped on the beach, they would take off. At this point, our tanks outnumbered the panzers. Little by little, we were gaining the upper hand.

The medics were running all over the place, trying to keep up with the wounded. I saw a lot of German medics running around out there, too.

More panzers were getting hit. I didn't know who was knocking them off; all I knew was that when one was hit, it didn't fire at us anymore.

The air corps resumed its bombing and strafing, but further on back. That could only mean there was another line of Germans behind this one.

The big thing now was supplies. I called the lieutenant over and told him we were running low on ammo. He said okay, and not long afterward, a couple of people came running up with boxes of ammo. I told them we also needed BAR magazines, and they said they'd be right back. They did come right back and they brought a box of BAR magazines. This made Al very happy, and he cut loose again, knocking off more Germans.

At about 1330 hours, we counterattacked. They were very weak at this point; practically all of their panzers were knocked out. I couldn't see any that were not. The only thing they had going for themselves was their artillery. It was possible we could move under that and then we could effect a breakout and the Germans would have to fall back—if they didn't have another line of defense set up back a little further.

Our tanks advanced up into the open. The infantry charge had been broken, and if the Germans had in mind sending in a second wave, I'm sure our planes had changed their minds. There were so many dead Germans lying out there it would take days to count them. Some of the Germans were running back through our artillery toward the north while others just stood there with their hands held high. They had had enough, and they just wanted to live. It was not our job to take prisoners now. We just pointed to them to head for the river with their hands up, and other GIs would take care of them.

We were in platoon formation again. We did not have many men missing. It was unbelievable what we had just gone through and still had most of our men intact. The German artillery was still coming in, but not as hard or steady as it had been before. We could see dust trails blowing up in the distance. They seemed to be coming from vehicles heading north. This had to mean the Germans were pulling out. Our tanks had also organized and were giving chase, while our artillery was still giving its all, landing back where the dust trails were coming from. There was German equipment lying everywhere. Mortars, machine guns, rocket launchers, even bazookas. I had never seen a German bazooka before. They weren't all that different from ours. It would just take a minute or two of study and we could fire them.

We had gone only a short distance before we came to a road, a fairly good road. We walked along it for maybe a mile, then were ordered into the fields on both sides. It looked like this was a battalion operation again. We had some armored personnel carriers with us, but I didn't see any tanks. I would imagine the armored division was re-organizing and would fight as a unit again. This was real tank country, and, apparently, the Germans had a lot of panzers yet. These had to be destroyed as soon as possible. We did not want them to reach any of those roads loading through the Alps; they could hold us up for days in those narrow passes.

The Alps were becoming an obsession with us now. They were all we could think of. We had it all figured out—just as soon as we were on the north side of the Alps, the war would end and we could go home.

More and more equipment was coming over now. We began to see other division patches, too. It looked like they had crossed the river where we had blazed the trail again. What history gave us for that was a mention in the official archives of World War II. We lost a lot of good men back there.

We were heading due east now, crossing fields, while the armored cars and armored personnel carriers were going down the roads. The tanks were nowhere in sight now; they must have been chasing down the last of the panzers; at least, I hoped they would be the last of them. We had walked along for quite a while, possibly two hours. It was getting on toward evening. I hadn't had anything to eat all day. In fact, eating was the last thing I had had on my mind.

We came to the edge of a small city, a city of maybe fifteen or twenty thousand people. The flags were out and the people were there to greet us. I think we must have been the first troops in. The wine and food came out, and the pretty girls were all over us. It was hard to keep going. We had to get to the other end of the city and dig in. There were still bands of the enemy roaming around. When we got through the city, we marched another half a mile and were directed into a field on the north side of the road. After another half an hour walk, we dug in.

It was getting dark, but I could see how the defense was laid out; we had lines all the way around this city — all the way back to the road we'd come down, to the river. We had a perimeter defense set-up, with the river as our south barrier.

The morning light awakened me. I'd taken my watch from midnight to 0300 hours, so I'd had a very good sleep. I felt like I could walk to the moon if they asked me to today. I also was hungry. Some of the other guys were stirring now, and the line was coming alive. I saw Reds sitting over by his foxhole. I took a K-ration and went over to join him. He told me he had hot water boiling in his foxhole, if I wanted to make coffee. I took him up on that offer. We just sat there and drank coffee and munched on our K-rations. We were getting a little tired of them by now. We'd had them morning, noon, and night for so long now, they were starting to get to us, especially when we'd see those armored force guys lining up at their field kitchens and eating decent food.

I asked Reds how he felt, and he said those four guys from his squad who'd been killed back there on the truck were still on his mind. I told him he had them on his mind because they were the first who'd been killed in the squad after he took it. There was absolutely nothing he could have done about the incident; it had happened before any of us could have done anything. He said, "*You* knew what to do!"

I said, "All I did was to yell to get off the truck. They were going to shoot at us, and before I had the last word out of my mouth, they *were* shooting at us."

Reds said he hadn't even thought of that, and he didn't think he should be a squad leader. He was going to tell the lieutenant to take his stripes away today.

"Hey," I said, "who do you think would be better than you?"

He fell silent, but he must have changed his mind. He didn't go to Studebaker that day, or any other day, to turn in his stripes. I'm sure Studebaker would not have taken them anyway.

The day went by lazily and calmly. We could hear motors, trucks, tanks and other vehicles back around the city, about half a mile away. In the meantime, we had had C-rations brought up, heated to perfection, and hot coffee; even our candy and cigarette ration caught up with us. We had about a week's worth of stuff coming and supply was extra generous. The fellows who were addicted to the weed smoked and smoked; I thought they would soon blow up, or burn their lungs out. I smoked a couple of cigarettes myself, but after two I didn't have any taste for them anymore and I gave the rest away. You would have thought I had given those guys gold, the way they thanked me for them.

Lieutenant MacLean came back around 1900 hours. The first thing I noticed about him was that he was now a captain: Captain MacLean. Then Lieutenant Studebaker came down to the platoon; he was wearing first lieutenant's bars. It looked like all the officers were getting promoted today.

The lieutenant gave us orders for tomorrow. We would be moving out before dawn. We had about thirty miles to go. We were going to Verona; we were on the right flank again. The other two regiments of the division would be on our left, and the other two battalions of our regiment were also on our left. On our right would be some armored units which would not co-ordinate with us, and the British, who also would not be co-ordinating their movements with ours. It sounded like we were a bastard unit again. But I was beginning to think we fought better that way. The brass expected quite a lot of opposition; Verona was a main railhead and an important road junction, but we'd have only our own support—seventy-fives and several tanks from our own tank company.

The trucks we were to use tomorrow morning came rolling into our area before dark. They were American six by sixes. At least, we'd be riding American equipment this time.

Our orders called for posting only one guard from each squad tonight. That meant that almost every

275

man could sleep through the night. I was well rested, so were Stutzman and Russ. I said to them, "What say, let's let the other guys sleep tonight. We'll take all the watches."

They agreed. It didn't get dark now until nearly 2100 hours, so most of the guys just sat around talking; I had noticed this bunch hadn't started a poker game yet. Maybe they were too young, or maybe card games just bored them. Athletic prowess seemed to be their thing.

Shortly after 2100 hours, they wandered to their foxholes, one by one, and went to sleep. They would need that sleep for what was coming up.

At about 0230 Willie came along. I hadn't seen him for quite a while. He told me to get ready. We'd be loading very shortly. If any of the guys were hungry they could eat on the truck.

It wasn't quite dark yet. The trucks were not using lights. The tanks went out first.

Our convoy proceeded down the road to the east, clipping off miles at a good pace. We came to a larger city. MPs were directing traffic, and our convoy was directed to make a left turn at the north end of the city and proceed north. The sun was showing signs of coming up now. It was going to be another hot day, but we would not have that far to walk, and if the fighting was not too ferocious we should be on the main east/west road before the 1200-hour deadline.

We had ridden at least twenty-five or thirty miles and had passed some artillery, which was firing. Then the trucks slowed and pulled off the road, then back into a field, where we were ordered to dismount. I made sure each man filled his canteen. From here on in, I didn't expect any supply for quite some time.

After a lot of nonsense, yelling and a lot of general confusion, we began to form up. Company L would take the point; we would go in by the main road, followed by a platoon of Company M with their heavy equipment. The other two companies would go in, one on each side of the road, spread out for about half a mile on each side of the road. The seventy-fives were setting up where we had dismounted, which was about two miles from the outskirts of the city. Three tanks would go down the middle of the road with our company to protect us from any German panzers which might show their ugly heads. By the time we had formed up and started walking it was 0600 hours. We had six hours to get to the main east/west road.

Madden piped up and said, "This is the place where Romeo and Juliet came from," and Ragone came back with, "I think they're dead." Owens said, "If she ain't, the Germans have probably raped her by now. She was a pretty good-looking chick." Everyone laughed.

We started receiving artillery fire, but couldn't tell where it was coming from. It was not too close, but we were sure it was meant for us, it could have been heavy mortars. It definitely was not 88s, so apparently they were laying back with their panzers or they had already removed them from the city and they were back in those beautiful Alps just waiting for us.

When we entered the city, the shells got heavier, and they were landing closer. We were on a main street; on one side were houses and the other a river. Over the river were several bridges which had not been blown or bombed by our planes. I think they were the first bridges I had seen in Italy that were not destroyed, except the Ponte Vecchio in Florence and some of the bridges in Rome. I was sure they were mined. They were beautiful bridges — ancient, arched, real works of art. I hoped we could save them, I'd like to come back here someday and really look them over.

We began searching the houses. There were some citizens here, not too concerned because we had entered the city, but no Germans. One old lady, who could speak perfect English, said the Germans had left the day before, after making sure they had taken everything of value — paintings, statues, tapestries. I asked the lady where she had learned such good English, and she told me she was American; she had married an Italian count fifty years ago and had lived in Verona since then. She said she had been born in Virginia. She had always lived in Verona, the most artistic city in Italy next to Florence and Rome, and she wished to die here. She lived in a large villa and said if we were to stay in Verona, she would like us to visit her here. We told her we would, but I thought we would be on our way very shortly from Verona.

As we worked our way up the main street, searching every building and villa, the other companies were doing the same thing in their areas. We were still getting a lot of shelling; they were definitely mortars, and we still could not spot them. They would fire a few rounds then pull back somewhere else before our planes could find them.

We had worked our way up into the city and were getting close to the marshalling yards, where we expected to receive some opposition from the enemy. If they had trains ready to pull out, they might just give us a good fight to make sure they got them out into the country before we had a chance to stop them.

Behind us came a large explosion. It shook the hell out of us, it was so close. We could feel the air rushing past us. It was nothing like a bomb or a shell—it was a bridge, the first one we'd seen when we entered the city. I don't know how much TNT they'd put under it, but it went sky high. When the smoke and dust had settled a bit, there was nothing there. It had even affected the current of the river. You could see little whirlpools all around. We had passed two other bridges in addition to that one, I hoped these weren't mined, but I suspected they were. We reached the main piazza; the next thing we would tackle would be the railhead. Company I was coming up from the south, and we would cover them from the piazza. They were to enter the railhead and take it. We did not know if there were Germans there or not; up to now, we had had no encounters with them except for their mortars.

The thing I was afraid of now was that the time bombs would start going off. We took over the buildings facing the piazza and back up toward the railhead. Our mortars were set up and we entered the buildings that overlooked the railhead. They were three and four stories high so we had a pretty good view of the whole area. There were a lot of rail cars sitting in the yard, but no engines. We supposed the Germans had used all the engines they had to pull out what they could, and left the rest of their equipment and supplies behind. So many railway engines had been destroyed by our air corps, they were in short supply. I knew that the Germans would not leave loaded cars without booby trapping them.

Shortly, we could see Company I men approaching the south end of the railhead. They had three tanks with them and quite a few bazookas. I would imagine bazookas would be good weapons to have against these cars if a fight developed. We had our bazooka men well placed and loaded in case we had to fire. The tanks stopped at the edge of the railhead, but the infantry entered it. They were ready for anything. They did not touch the cars.

The infantry came right on through the yard. They had not fired a shot, and were now approaching the north end. We relaxed a bit. Soon we could resume our own advance toward the main road and get ready for the next move. Even if we did have a little fight now, at least we had been lucky, I had not heard one small arm fired in all the time we had spent in Verona up to now.

The Company I guys now had reached the north end and were filtering out into the north end of the city. The tanks were coming through the yard. We were ordered back down into the piazza, where we reorganized and continued our advance. We didn't have that far to go now.

We had entered what appeared to be a factory area. I told the guys to be very alert here. Some of these places had very thick walls and would make one helluva place to harass us from. It wouldn't take many of the enemy to set up a couple of mortars and a squad or two of riflemen and really give it to us. The streets were fairly wide here, probably for the trucks that traveled through in peace time.

We didn't have any trouble; we just kept going.

Some of the squads searched the buildings, but our whole platoon was just told to keep moving.

After we passed the factory area, we came to some more houses, which we searched, but again found no enemy—just frightened civilians whom we assured we would not hurt. They were very cooperative and assured us they had not seen any Germans since the day before; they had all pulled out during the night. When we asked them which way they went they told us they went west. We also found out they didn't have many tanks, just a lot of trucks and some large guns, and that the trucks had been loaded down with everything they could get their hands on. These sounded more like rear echelon troops, possibly artillerymen. It sounded to us like they had moved all of their panzers and combat troops long before yesterday. They would be in those Alps just waiting for us. This we were quite sure of. And we weren't far from wrong.

We saw the road up ahead, about two or three blocks away. It certainly looked good. It looked like we would reach our destination without even seeing a German.

We reached the road and hit the dirt on the south side.

We were lying there, slightly relaxed, when the sound of motors came to us from the east. We looked and could hardly believe our eyes. A German convoy of about ten or twelve trucks was coming right at us. They had no guards on the trucks, but the trucks were loaded down with just about everything you can imagine. The lieutenant yelled for us to stop them. I gave Herr a yell to hit the first truck with his bazooka.

The truck came to a stop and several Germans tumbled out of it on fire. They were immediately shot, and the rest of the platoon came out firing.

The Germans jumped off the trucks. Some were still moving, and held their hands high. The lieutenant ordered a ceasefire.

We rounded up the Germans—forty-one prisoners. They were transportation troops, and had no taste for fight. They had been ordered to Trento, they said. They talked their heads off; they thought for sure we were going to kill them. We'd found a lot of British and American equipment on their trucks. They said they had taken the equipment from a warehouse in Verona, where all the enemy equipment was taken when it was captured.

We didn't know what to do with these prisoners. We knew we were a task force and had no rear echelon troops with us, so the captain said we would turn them over to the partisans; they would take them back for us. I often wondered how many of them really did get back to be handed over to the MPs at a compound.

We didn't know what to do with their trucks. They were loaded with a lot of paintings and statues, and other things which must have been very valuable. The captain said he would ask Battalion what they wanted to do with them. He was on the radio for quite some time, and when he came back he said Battalion was turning the trucks over to the Italian police, since most of the loot was probably taken from the homes right here in Verona.

It wasn't very long before several truck loads of Italians drove up and took the trucks away. I hoped the paintings and statues the American lady had lost were on these trucks and that she would get them back.

After the trucks were gone, our platoon was ordered to go on patrol, north to a little town about three miles away. The lieutenant ordered my squad to the point, so we put our scouts out and spread out. We also took two machine guns and two mortars with us, plus our three bazookas.

The three miles were all up hill, and when we finally reached the village, we were fairly high and could see a good part of the surrounding country. Verona itself was beautiful from here. You could see the river winding its way through the city and right up to where we were standing. We were greeted by the people as liberators, and the food and wine again came out, but before we took any of it we searched the village. Here again we found no evidence of German troops, although the villagers told us some had been there the night before and had pulled out early this morning before dawn. They were on foot and had headed straight north into the mountains. The Alps were not far from here, five or six miles at the most.

We noticed that the people had a lot of livestock here. I suspected they were collaborators, which should be one reason the Germans had let them keep their animals; on the other hand, as we had come north we had found more and more livestock. Possibly, because the Germans were moving so fast they just couldn't take them with them. One thing missing were horses and mules.

After we had satisfied ourselves there were no Germans in the area, we went back to the village square and took off our backpacks and sat down for a rest. Actually this was the first rest we had since we entered Verona hours ago. The villagers brought us meat, cheese, and wine. The lieutenant drank some but told us he did not want to report back to Captain MacLean with a bunch of drunks.

We stayed there for another half an hour, before we left. We returned in platoon combat formation, the same way we had come up. We reached the road and the rest of our company at 1100 hours. We had secured the road long before deadline. The other troops told us that another bridge had gone up while we were gone, and a bunch of engineers had gone up with it. The only bridge still left over the river, except the one on the highway, was a railroad bridge, and they were trying to find hidden charges under it now. Our orders were to hold the road until we were relieved. So we just sat there and took it easy. No one knew what was to happen next. Trucks started arriving from Verona. When they hit the east/west road, they turned east, toward the British sector. They kept coming for hours; it had to be a whole division.

No further orders came down. We just sat there. There was no artillery fire, no enemy in sight. Outside of a smoke haze hanging over Verona, the day was beautiful, just about as far away from war as we had been in weeks. We had taken food from the village with us when we'd departed and were eating it. Just about every guy now had a bottle of wine, but no one was drinking too much.

Russ and I went back to the company supply point to pick up our water and C-rations. We each put a case of rations on our packboards and together carried the water. We met Reds back there. He seemed to be taking life a little better now. He joked a little like he used to, and even said he would like a drink about right now. I was glad he was beginning to come out of his melancholy over losing those four men back there. I know it's tough, but you can't bear that cross the rest of your life.

When we returned with what we thought would be good news about having C-rations instead of K's, the men were not overjoyed. They were eating too well now, getting used to the Italian food. I began to think this was Mussolini's secret weapon—feed them to death.

It was starting to get dark, so I thought I would check just one more time with the lieutenant to see if he knew of anything that might come up. He told me he hadn't received any news at all, nor had Captain MacLean, so we definitely would be staying here tonight. I returned to the squad and gave them the news. It was now about 2100 hours and dark. I decided to crawl in. I really wasn't too tired, but I thought this might be a good chance to really get a relaxing sleep and be ready for what might come. Most of the other guys felt the same way; as soon as I had crawled in, the talking quieted down as each guy drifted off to his hole and crawled in.

I had no more than lain down when it started to rain. Dammit, now I had to get up and pull the shelter half over me and I'd worry all night about getting wet. Anderson did the same thing; we could have pitched the shelter halves together over the hole, but we were both too lazy at this point to get up and do it. We would just lie here all night and get wet.

I was just falling off into a miserable sleep when I heard the lieutenant calling for all squad leaders. Damn, I knew it was too good to be true. We'd be pulling out, and in this damned rain, too. I crawled out of the hole, grabbed my carbine, and headed for the lieutenant's foxhole. We had just received orders to move. One of our regiments was in trouble along the bottom of Lake Garda, and needed all the help it could get. Although most of our own regiment was already there to back the troubled regiment, they wanted the bastard battalion too, so we had to go. It was only about twenty or twenty-five miles, and we'd be taken there by truck. The trucks were coming up to get us now. They'd take us to a small town on the banks of the lake, and we would receive our orders there as to what our mission would be.

I went back to the squad and alerted everyone. It wasn't easy, but I finally had everyone ready to move. All the backpacks were packed; each man was carrying a rocket for our bazooka in his backpack as well as all his own equipment. We were loaded down with grenades, too, which I was pretty sure we would appreciate shortly. Now, all we had to do was sit and wait for those trucks. The whole battalion was up and by the road. There was a lot of bitching. Some of these guys had dug vertical foxholes under the road-bed and had been very comfortable; now they were sitting here in the rain awaiting trucks.

The regiment that was in trouble had been sneaked into an Alpine lake in the hopes that we could get a jump on the Germans up there. Someone had thought it would be possible to get into their backyard and break up their base. Apparently, the Germans saw them coming, let them get up the road about five or six miles, then laid into them. Before they could get their men to safety, the Germans, being on higher ground, cut them off. Now we had a trapped regiment, and the nearest we could get to them was about four miles. We could not run armor up there because the Germans had everything mined, and they had anti-tank guns dug into the sides of the mountains. They were pounding hell out of this regiment, and if they did not get relief soon, there wouldn't be anyone left except the dead. It seemed like a pretty desperate situation, and I doubted that one more regiment could do much good.

The third regiment of the division was on the other side of the lake, and it was agreed they could not be pulled back, because if they could get up as far as the trapped regiment on their side of the lake—the lake was only five or six miles wide at that point—they would bring up armor and artillery and blast the Germans from that side. What we were to do was to relieve the trapped regiment, then take over the advance against the Germans. I hoped we would not end up in the trap with the other outfit. No one knew how many Germans were in these mountains.

The brass hoped we could relieve the trapped regiment no later than 0800 hours.

They sure as hell didn't expect much from us, I thought. I did admit, we'd had it fairly easy coming across the Po Valley, and our ranks were fairly full, while our other regiments had had some pretty hard fights coming up and probably had depleted ranks.

The trucks came at 0200 hours, it would be dawn in another two hours, and we were supposed to start the attack then. We still had about twenty-five miles to go. It was raining, the trucks had no canvas over the beds, and we rode with the rain beating down on us. We would be in fine shape to start an attack—stiff, sore, wet, and mad.

We had loaded fast. The trucks had their dimmers on, and the road was straight, so we made good time. I reassured myself with the thought that the division that had gone through us in Verona was now fighting up the main road toward Trento. If we could get the enemy out of the lake area, we would be a good way through the Alps and heading for the Austrian border.

We arrived at the south end of the lake at about 0330 hours. It was a big lake, all right. The waves were being kicked up by the wind and it looked like the ocean out there. The rain had let up some, but had not completely stopped. There were quite a few tanks sitting around now—our own tank company, several self-propelled guns, and lots of artillery. I also noticed mules again. Our buddies the mules were back, and they were loaded down with seventy-fives and ammunition. It looked like we were really back in the mountains again. I even recognized some of the mule-skinners as being from the same bunch that had been with us when we'd come out of the mountains on the other side of the valley. There were also quite a few troops from the trapped regiment. This was their third battalion, which had been in reserve when the entrapment came. They had been able to get back and spread the alarm.

At 0430 daylight broke, but still no orders came to

move. I saw the colonel come walking along with Captain MacLean, and I figured he was getting orders now. I was right. Just as soon as he disappeared toward another company, Captain MacLean called all the squad and platoon leaders back to him. We studied maps of the area and got our orders. The lake was approximately thirty miles long, with roads on both sides of it. There were many tunnels, probably from Roman times. The mountains came right up out of the lake, and the Romans had built a road out of sheer rock, tunneling through where it was impossible to get a road across. He said there were also some bridges, which they expected the Germans to blow before we arrived, if they hadn't already. They had not been able to get decent pictures from our observation planes, and really didn't know what to expect—which was why the regiment got trapped up there; they were sent in blind. The roads up ahead were mined, and the engineers had gone ahead and found most of the mines on the road; we would have another company of engineers going with us, and their sappers would try to make it safe to pass. The mules were bringing the seventy-fives up, and they would be in line with us, as well as a platoon of heavy mortars and machine guns from Company M, which would be with us. After we had moved out and were about half a mile out, the tanks would try to go as far as they could, but if they couldn't get through a tunnel, or if a bridge was knocked out, that would be the last we would see of them this time. The mountains weren't actually that high, but they were treacherous—steep and rocky.

My first squad would lead off, staying close to the

mountainside.

I hoped the operation would go as well as the brass had it figured. But like most battles I'd been in, I didn't think it would. How right I was.

Chapter 27

Levin was calling to one of the engineers who would be going with us. It was his brother. They hadn't seen each other since we had left the mountains. Both were laughing and crying to see that each had made it this far. He had a mine detector, and said that his squad was leading off. They talked for a minute, then he was gone. I saw tears in Levin's eyes. It was the first time I ever saw him get emotional. I had a pretty good idea how he felt.

We let the engineers get out in front of us about one hundred yards. They would start looking for mines about two miles up. It had stopped raining now, but the sky was very overcast. I hoped it would stay that way until we had engaged the enemy. We could see much better if there were no shadows. It was almost 0530 hours; we were just about an hour and a half behind schedule, when we started off along the lake. The road was fairly straight here and we could see the troops strung out behind us. We had walked about two miles, when we began to pick sounds of gun-fire—machine guns and rifle fire, but no heavy stuff. The Germans were probably just trying to keep our guys pinned down. As we went on, the cliffs became steeper. The sappers were working, and our progress was slow—slow but sure; at least the roads should be safe for us. In the background we could hear the rumbling of our tanks. Our mules were coming right along with us, bringing the seventy-fives. Company M had a couple of heavy machine guns set up on carts. All they would have to do would be to turn them around and start firing.

About three more miles up, and the road became curvy. From the description given us, this was about where the third battalion of the other regiment had turned to go back to the town where we had met them. This would mean we should start running into Germans at any minute now.

As if someone was reading my thoughts, several mortar shells hit the road near us. We all hit the small ditch near the cliff. The tanks stopped, and I could see their guns swinging up the cliffs. If anything was spotted, they would open fire, and that should help clear the area real fast. More mortar shells came in. We could not tell where they were coming from. They could have been coming from the top of the cliffs, and in our location we couldn't get to them with small arms.

We got up again and sped up. The engineers had also taken cover, and we passed them and kept going. The mortar shells were coming in closer. The tanks had not moved, and I doubted if they would before the engineers began their work again.

I glanced back and saw that the whole column of infantry was moving at the same pace we had set; mortar shells were falling back there, too, and they were taking casualties. But they kept moving.

We had not received any small-arms fire yet, but I

expected it at any moment. They had to be among the boulders ahead.

We had come approximately half a mile since the first mortar fire hit us, and I moved up with the scouts, telling Russ to run the squad. My scouts were good, but they'd never had any experience of what we were running into now, and at this point I wanted to keep going. There must be a safe place up ahead where we could halt long enough to look the situation over and make some definite plans as to how we would operate. Lieutenant Studebaker came up with me. He was a damned good officer, sticking his neck out like this when he didn't have to. Between us, we decided we would just keep going until we received orders otherwise. I told him I couldn't understand why we weren't receiving small-arms fire, and he said he couldn't understand it, either. From the reports we'd had back at the town, we should be fighting our way through at least two miles of enemy territory; and if they had mortars up there, they must have riflemen, too. Would they be leading us into a trap? Would we round one of these curves and walk into a solid wall of lead?

He said he thought they had seen the tanks and artillery and may pull their infantry out, rather than make a fight here. It didn't make sense to me. They had us in a trap if they decided to close it and could sit all day picking us off one by one. This was the most dangerous territory I'd ever seen. For the first time I thought I might not come out alive.

We were still moving, but not very fast, and were just about to round a curve when I grabbed the lieutenant, motioning everyone to hit the dirt, and quietly. I could hardly believe my eyes. A German patrol was just ahead, coming down from the cliffs—five men, and they were laughing and telling jokes. I raised my carbine and fired, and killed two of them. The other three threw up their hands before I could fire again. I was in no mood to take prisoners, but the lieutenant yelled at me, "We need prisoners. For God's sake don't shoot any more." He was right, I really almost screwed that detail up for a fare-thee-well.

We motioned to them to come back toward us, after they threw down their weapons and bags. They were SS. They came over to us, and we had them lie on the ground. The lieutenant called for Willie to come up and interpret. He came crouching and running up.

The prisoners were only kids, probably seventeen at the most, and they were damned scared after they saw two of their friends come to such a quick end. They were ready to talk, and talk they did. They'd been sent out to take from the American dead all the papers they might have on them. But they thought they would help themselves to anything else of value—money, watches, rings, cigarettes, candy, gum and any other valuables they thought they might like. They had no idea we were as close as we were. They had heard the mortars starting up after they left their lines, but thought we were still some distance away. They had put their loot in the bags they were carrying.

The lieutenant told Willie to have one of them retrieve the bags. Willie spoke to one of them, then pulled his pistol out; the German shook his head yes and took off. He gathered the bags and ran like hell back to us. When we opened the bags, we found what the Germans said we would find, plus field glasses and a .45 colt automatic with a plaque on the pistol handle inscribed *A. E. Henderson, Colonel, USA, on his thirtieth anniversary, 1944.* We asked the Germans if the man they had taken this off was alive, and they said no. They had not killed anyone; they only took things from the dead bodies. We asked them how many were out there, and they replied over a hundred. Colonel Henderson had been the commander of the regiment we were trying to rescue.

We asked the Germans where they were holed up; they pointed to a cliff right in front of us and said this cliff was honeycombed. They had anti-tank guns, artillery, and tunnels from the other side into which they could bring tanks. There was also at least a company of infantry, well-armed with automatic weapons, the best in the German army. Had we gone another one hundred yards, we would have walked into a death trap.

Willie took the prisoners back to Company Headquarters for further interrogation. We had a lot of thinking to do before we made our next move. The mortars were still coming in, and they were getting closer to us now. I was worried they might open up from the cliff in front of us. It was only about three hundred yards away, and if they had artillery and infantry in there as those prisoners said they had, they could do us a lot of damage, and there wasn't much we could do about it except pull back.

Captain MacLean came up to see what the holdup was, and after we gave him the whole story, he looked the situation over with his glasses. None of us could figure what we should do now, and after a while of going back and forth over the possibilities, MacLean went back to notify Battalion and let them decide. That meant we would just have to sit and wait until the brass thrashed this thing out before we did anything. It was a very nerve-wracking situation, this sitting and waiting, knowing you have to do something, but not knowing exactly what. Well, the Germans were keeping us entertained with their mortars; we ourselves were in no immediate danger. But the troops behind us were right in the path of those mortars, and I know they had to be taking casualties.

The sun was trying to break through the clouds. We would have the heat again, but at least we would have a chance to dry off. It was getting fairly late, and we were way behind the schedule that had been laid down for us, but I would rather be late and alive than early and dead. The regiment up ahead was still taking casualties; we could hear firing. I wondered how much ammo those guys had left.

The squad was behind us about twenty-five yards, spread out for about another twenty yards. I could see All looking over the top of the cliff behind which we were hiding. He was very good at seeing things other people could not see. The slightest movement would catch his eye, and once he caught sight of something, it was not very long before he could identify it. He motioned to me to come back to where he was. He told me he'd been observing the cliff above us and had spotted four Germans so far. He believed they were hiding in holes behind those boulders, and every once in a while they would take a look down at us. He wanted to shoot. I told him I'd talk to the lieutenant and let him know. I went back up with Studebaker and told him what Al had told me. He said that if he was sure they were Germans, let him fire. "Hell, they know we're here. I don't know what *they're* waiting for." I motioned to Al to go ahead and fire if he had a good target. "Don't take a chance of just wounding a man. Make damned sure you can kill him before you fire!" He waved, aimed, and fired.

Captain MacLean came running up to us, and said Battalion had okayed the plan to hit the cliffs with bazookas. We were to use the three bazookas in our platoon and to fire as low as possible, to make the Germans think they were being fired on by tanks. He said to wait about fifteen minutes before we opened up; he wanted the whole company dug in before we opened fire.

I ran back and told Herr to gather up about six or eight rockets and get his team up with Studebaker. Then I told Reds and Neilson to get their bazooka teams up there with the same amount of rockets. When I returned, the lieutenant was showing the bazooka men where to fire.

Before the first bazooka was aimed, Al opened up again. He fired three shots, and two Germans tumbled out of the cliffs. I said to the lieutenant, "Can't we get some mortar fire up on that cliff now that we know where they are? Those Germans were only about fifty yards away! We could do a good job with our mortars, the 60 millimeters from our heavy weapons platoon."

He said he would talk to the captain, to hold everything up until he returned. I watched him run like the wind back to where the captain was dug in.

They conferred for a couple of minutes, then I saw the captain on his radio. A couple of minutes later, Studebaker came running back up. He said that not only were we going to use our 60s but the 81s as well, and they would set up several seventy-fives to fire first. When they opened fire, that would be our signal to open up with the bazookas. "I think your friend Al solved this whole problem for us. Why the hell doesn't he have some rank?"

I said, "Al won't take rank, that's why. But he should be decorated for figuring this thing out when the whole damn brass in the rear couldn't figure it out with their maps and glasses."

The seventy-fives opened up. They had fired so high to make sure they didn't fire short, that they didn't even touch the cliff. The next volley was down a little further, but could come down more. The third volley was just right. Now the 81s could zero in and the 60s would come in last. The lieutenant called Herr up and placed him so he could see over a boulder. He put the number two bazooka over to Herr's left almost out on the road. The third bazooka, he put on the right of Herr, fairly high. The seventy-fives and the mortars were all going good now. They were dropping shells all over that cliff. There was so much smoke and dust now we could not see too much, and our riflemen had not opened up.

It was noisy! We were lying in a low spot, and we picked up every little sound that came along. There must have been at least twenty or twenty-five shells exploding a minute right above us. When the bazookas started firing, half the cliff came tumbling down on the roadbed. They must have had charges planted there and we had hit one. That didn't stop the Germans, though. They opened up now, firing almost where we were sitting. This was too damn close for comfort, but this was the purpose of our firing those bazookas. If it was true what the prisoners had told us, the enemy had lost their advantage now. We spotted the anti-tank guns—firing right at us. Behind us, we were taking casualties. The lieutenant had all three bazookas loaded and ready to go again. He told them to fire at any target they could get. They concentrated on the left side of the cliff, nearest the water. The cannon fire seemed to be coming from that angle. They fired away, reloaded, and fired again. The Germans were still firing, but had slowed up. I think we had hit some of their guns.

All at once, behind us, the riflemen opened fire. I think the whole platoon was firing. We looked back to see what was going on and could see the guys firing up on the cliff, and up there was a sight for sore eyes. There were Germans all over the hill. They were running and climbing, trying to get the hell off that cliff. The guys were popping them off like ducks. The lieutenant told the bazooka men to keep firing. It looked like we'd moved those bastards. Now we had to keep them on the run.

MacLean came up and told the lieutenant we were going to rush the cliff. It was a good two hundred and fifty yards, if not a little further, and when the Germans opened up with their small arms, they would murder us. When he came up he brought three more bazooka teams and two mules loaded with rockets. They would add to our covering fire while we moved.

We would go out fast, running to get under the cliff, a whole platoon together. Once all of Company L was there, Battalion would decide if it was necessary to bring any more troops over. Captain MacLean was going with our squad. He came up and crouched beside me and said, "Are you ready Ike?"

I said, "Yes, let's go," and we shot out. I don't think I ever ran so fast in my life as I ran then. The whole platoon was out in the open now. I had worried about Captain MacLean keeping with us, but he was so far out in front, the devil himself couldn't have caught him. We were about halfway to the cliff when the German small arms opened up on us. They hit us with everything they had in the book, and I think a few things we hadn't read about. You could have walked on their bullets, they were so thick. The captain landed against the cliff and almost bounced off. I hit it the same way. I looked up and I could see rifles and machine guns sticking out of holes in the side of the cliff. We would have to use grenades to get the bastards out. Our whole platoon was over here now. We were below the fire, but they could still throw grenades down at us.

The next two platoons arrived. The Germans were getting zeroed in on us now and everytime we sent another bunch of men across the field of fire, we would lose some. The medics were out there patching up the wounded and trying to get some of them to a safe place, and I'll give the Germans one bit of credit, they were not shooting at them.

The whole company was under the cliff. The captain was on his radio, and was arguing with someone. Finally, he slammed the receiver and just sat there. He spoke with Studebaker and I heard that the captain wanted a company to go up over the cliff which the artillery had just cleaned off. This would divert some attention from us and we would be able to go around the road near the lake and possibly get behind the cliff. He had talked to a captain at Battalion, who had not thought it was a good idea; he would have to call a meeting and discuss it first. MacLean then had asked to speak to the colonel, but the captain said he wasn't there, he didn't know just exactly where he was, but he would leave a message for him. MacLean said we would sit here for a few minutes, but if grenades started down on us, we would move and try to cut the Germans off down the road behind this cliff. "If Battalion don't like it, they can sue me!"

The mortars and artillery were still hitting the cliff where we had flushed the Germans out, but the firing had decreased to a point where it would be just an aggravating fire, not really effective. No troops had yet moved up on the cliff; we just sat right under the enemy's nose. The German guns would appear, fire a few rounds, then disappear. Their cannon fire had almost ceased, and I was beginning to wonder what they had up their sleeves. Germans do not quit easily unless they have an alternative in mind. I suspected they would soon make a concerted effort to get us out from under this cliff. After a few minutes, when Battalion still hadn't got back to us, MacLean called all the platoon leaders together now and started giving orders. He knew he would be in trouble if he did anything on his own now, but he also knew we had to get out of there.

He decided one platoon—ours, naturally—would

go up over the cliff. It was about six or seven hundred feet high here. The other two platoons would inch thir way around the road. If everything worked out okay, we would wait on the backside of this cliff, which according to the maps, had the road winding back away from the lake and into the tunnel where the other regiment was pinned down. The platoons going around the road could at the same time survey the road damage and possibly estimate how soon we would be able to get armor up with us.

We would be climbing the cliff without ropes or any other assistance, and on the way, dropping grenades into any holes that might be airholes or gun ports. Without my bazooka team, I had only nine men, plus myself. I reminded all the guys to make sure their backpacks were packed so that the loads would not shift while they were moving; that could throw them off the side of a mountain. Their ammo was in good shape, and everyone had grenades.

The lieutenant grabbed a rock above his head and said, "Let's go," and we were on our way.

We climbed the first fifty or seventy-five feet straight up, then the cliff eased off and we were able to crawl. We made good progress, but had not found any holes to drop grenades into. We kept going up until we reached a plateau and were able to stand. We could see the other cliff now—American infantry was climbing all over it. Someone at battalion had awakened and decided that Captain MacLean knew what he was talking about and decided to execute. This would help a lot; they would cross that cliff and we would cross this one, which would mean we had two companies of infantry overlooking the tunnel. If we were careful now we could sneak up on any Germans below us and get them before they knew what had hit. The regiment would be relieved, and we could get on with the war.

We were supposed to be at the north end of that lake before dark, and it was still at least twenty-five miles away. It was 0900 hours; we would have to hurry.

Below us, the bazookas had opened up again. There was no danger to us unless the Germans had another large charge planted somewhere and one of those bazooka rockets happened to hit it.

We could really see now; we could see miles to the south of us, and we could see across the lake. All along the road behind us were trucks, artillery and tanks. As far as we could see, the tanks still had not moved up any further than they had when we were down on the road.

We kept climbing. We had about two or three hundred feet to go to reach the top. That would be about where the Germans would hit us if they were going to, but we had boulders and large rocks to dive behind, and they were thick enough that we could advance from one to another and still put down a pretty good fire. I automatically looked to see where Al and his team were; they were to my right about thirty feet away, and although Al was chugging along, he was ready for anything, and from his looks, I thought that if the Germans were smart, they certainly wouldn't start anything with that boy. We had to depend on Al's BAR for automatic fire; we hadn't brought the machine-gunner along.

The lieutenant called a halt, told everyone to get

behind a boulder but to keep his eyes open. He motioned for me to meet him. I slipped back down to where he was.

"Ike, I hate to send the whole platoon up there blind. We have to know if there are Germans up there."

I said, "Yeah. I know. You want me to go with my squad."

"No. Just two men. You and me. How about it? I hate like hell to ask you, but I have more faith in you than anyone else, and we have to be damned sure."

I agreed to go, but I wasn't crazy about the idea.

Gardner was left in charge of the platoon; I put Russ in charge of the squad. And the lieutenant and I started up the cliff. We stayed about twenty feet apart. I knew we were so close to the top of this cliff, that if anything happened—if there were Germans waiting for us up here—grenades would do a good job. I pulled one from my belt and removed the pin. I put the pin in my mouth in case I had to replace it. I saw that the lieutenant had done the same.

We moved slowly, deliberately. When we were only about twenty feet from the top, we both stopped and caught our breath for a minute or two, then started moving again. I could see rocks piled up ahead. Damnit, I thought. They were here, what the hell were they waiting for? The lieutenant saw the rocks about the same time I did, and we both let go with our grenades. Before I hit the ground, I'd pulled the pin on a second one and from the prone, let it go. Nothing happened. The lieutenant let his second one go; still nothing happened. We both jumped up and rushed the pile of rock, firing as we went. We threw ourselves over it, still firing—and to our surprise found nothing. Not one German, no evidence that they were ever here. We looked at each other and started laughing. I'm sure if anyone would have seen us at that moment they would have put the straight jackets on us and sent us back. We signaled the others to come up, and while they were moving to the top of this cliff, we observed the surrounding terrain. It was rough-looking. We could see the company on the other cliff; they had reached the top and were setting up a defense line. In front of us and below, about a thousand feet, was the mouth of a tunnel which had been partially closed, probably from rockets hitting it. We supposed this was where the regiment was trapped. We looked the other way, but couldn't see the other two platoons of our company. They should have been around that cliff by now, unless they hit something and were engaged in a fight. There was no sound of firing coming from that direction, so they must have gotten around somehow.

Behind us, as far as we could see, the road was clear of troops. Every once in a while we spotted a mule, but we couldn't see what they were carrying. I did not understand why they did not bring those tanks up and blast the hell out of this cliff.

I told the lieutenant that we should do something. The problem was, we didn't have a radio with us, so we could make no coordinated moves with the rest of the troops—and we didn't even know where the rest of our company was.

I looked over the north side of the cliff as far as I could without falling off. I could not see anyone, American or German, but I swear I saw holes below us with some type of gun popping in and out. I could not hear shooting, so I had the idea someone was zeroing in on an area. And I suspected they were the same bunch we had been fighting on the other side of the cliff. They had moved their operation, or at least part of it, to this side. If any American troops tried to come around that road along the lake heading for that tunnel, they would cut them down. That had to be it—how else could they have trapped the other regiment in that tunnel? I doubted that they knew we were here, or if they did, that we were only a platoon, lightly armed, very much at a disadvantage. This cliff, once our troops reached the north side of it, would be isolated. No way for the Germans to get out of it except surrender.

We still couldn't see the rest of our company. I began to suspect they were pinned down somewhere, and that the troop movements on the south were to give them some relief. There was quite a lot of artillery fire, but it didn't seem close. I doubted it was concentrated on this cliff. I kept watching those guns popping in and out below us. An idea came to me. I didn't know if it would do any good, but at least it should shake the hell out of someone, especially if they didn't know we were up here.

I asked the lieutenant if it was all right to take a look on the back side of this cliff to try and figure out what was going on. He said he had no objections, so I took Anderson and we scooted down. We didn't have to go too far, before we could see all the way to the road level. I could see the bazooka men still lying behind that wall. If I had been a German there would have been some dead bazooka men; they weren't trying to protect themselves at all. In fact, it seemed as if everyone was a little lax down there, guys sitting around smoking, eating, drinking; and the tank crews outside their tanks. In fact, the only activity seemed to be in our division's Company K. They were moving up, and with them they had mules, some loaded with seventy-fives, and some loaded with other supplies. I presumed these were rockets, mortar shells and ammo for our small arms. I presumed most of the other troops sitting there were from the battalion that had escaped. Company M, at least some of it, was moving up behind Company K, and it did look like they were getting ready to go into combat. I also noticed, as they approached the cliff, that they stopped and clung against the wall of the road. They were not advancing past that fortress, which would indicate the Germans were still there and were still potent. That answered one of my questions, and from what those prisoners had told us, this cliff was honeycombed, so the guns popping out on the other side had to be the same bunch.

We went back to the lieutenant and I told him what we had discovered. The thing I couldn't get out of my mind, though, was who was really trapped. These Germans were definitely surrounded and I could not see any possible way out for them. Between this point and the tunnel up ahead, where the trapped regiment was supposed to be, the only Germans were these. I began to wonder if that regiment was trapped or just afraid to come out. There was no way we could communicate with them in these mountains. Radio was just not that good. The only way we could talk to them would be to go to them.

The idea in my mind was taking final form. We were above the Germans — why not let ourselves down, and when we came to a hole, toss in a grenade? It would only take two or three of us, and before they discovered what was happening, we should be able to do a lot of damage.

Damn, if we just had some communication with someone else — anyone — we could coordinate this movement with something else.

Still, I decided to approach the lieutenant. After all we were more or less cut off now, and he was the only man who had the authority to say yes or no. The first thing he said after I told him of my plan was, "How many grenades do we have?"

I told him I had eight myself, and there must be a total of at least sixty or seventy in the platoon. Each man, if we sent three or four, would need about ten grenades. The lieutenant said this was no answer to the big guns they had in there. I agreed, but if we started with the grenades, they might come out fighting on this side, and if they did that, our whole battalion could advance and move on that tunnel. We could see Company I, they still had not moved; they seemed to have dug in defensively. The lieutenant looked at me and said, "Why the hell do we have to lead the parade all the time?"

I laughed at his mocking. "You know, Lieutenant, that's the question, the sixty-four-dollar one."

He considered for a moment. "If we just had some contact with the company. If we just knew where the hell they were and what they were going to do, I'd feel a helluva lot more like doing it. I'd hate to break into someone's plans and screw them up."

"I know what you mean, but we are out here for one purpose and that's to get those damn Germans out of that fortress. I don't see that we have any alternative but to slip down there and drop in those grenades." I assured him it was my idea and I would execute it, just to give me two men with ten grenades and turn us loose. If we got in trouble he could help shoot us out of it.

Finally, he agreed. I took Russ and Anderson. Anderson was getting pretty good—definitely leadership. He'd probably get the next stripes in the squad.

We gathered up thirty grenades, and I explained to Russ and Anderson what we would do. Anderson was eager to go. It was as if I'd passed him the ball and told him to make the winning touchdown.

We took all our equipment off except the grenades and our ammo belts. We slung our rifles—we wouldn't need them on our mission, but might on our withdrawal—then crouched and ran to the point of descent. We were about seven or eight feet apart. We looked over the edge of the cliff—it was not too steep here; we could almost crawl down. It would have been nice if we had a rope, but we didn't.

We had slipped down the cliff about twenty or twenty-five feet when we found the first porthole. It was about ten or twelve inches in diameter, big enough for a grenade. I signaled the other guys. They stopped moving and I pulled the pin on the first one, then shoved it through the hole. It went off, shaking the whole area. I thought for a minute it would shake me off the cliff. Russ had slipped down below about five more feet, and he let go with one—same reaction. So far, we could not tell if we were doing anything or not. Anderson slipped over about four feet and dropped one in a larger hole. That did it. The whole side of the cliff went. The last I saw of Anderson, he was flying through the air toward the road below. If the explosion hadn't killed him the fall did.

Russ and I were hanging on for dear life. The whole cliff came alive with small-arms fire. We could see the guns now, and just as fast as we saw one, we headed for it and dropped in a grenade. I was out of grenades now and signaled so to Russ. He understood, and we started to climb back to the top of the cliff. I could see Studebaker right above me. The Germans were firing away with small arms, but didn't know what they were firing at. Their fire seemed to be directed out and down toward the road. I believe they thought they had been hit by mortar fire.

After we reached the top of the cliff, we could hear heavy fire behind us. Several of us ran back to see what was going on. The tanks were advancing now, firing as they moved. I could also see those bazooka men firing away, and clouds of smoke were rising all over the south side of the cliff. I decided this was no place for us and went back. The lieutenant was pointing down on the road near the lake. The rest of our company was coming around. At least now we could get reorganized and get on with this war; all we had to do was get down to them. Studebaker told us to stay where we were. He suspected the company would be coming up here. He figured we would probably spend most of the day up here moving along these ridges in front of us instead of going ahead on the road.

I still couldn't get it through my head that the Germans would let themselves be trapped like this. It was not a very large force—maybe two hundred men with heavy equipment. They were probably in that fortress when the trapped regiment went by and just stayed there for the exact purpose of holding them up as long as possible. It could be that they couldn't get the equipment they had in there out, and decided they would use it to their best advantage. Our own company were still inching their way around the bottom of the cliff. They had not yet made any contact with the enemy. I could see what would happen if they kept coming the way they were—they would soon be right underneath the part of the cliff where the guns were.

There was another large explosion on the south side of the cliff. I didn't know if our guns had hit another cache of dynamite, or if the Germans were beginning to blow things up in preparations to leave. We may have done more damage than we thought we had. But our company was still advancing right into those guns. I begged the lieutenant to let me go down there and warn them before it was too late. He thought that was a good idea, but wanted to know who I'd send. I told him I'd go myself, and he said no, let someone else do a dangerous job once, you don't have to carry the whole thing all the time. The lieutenant decided we would send Reds. I knew Reds had the moxie and could do the job.

Reds climbed down fast. When he was only about three hundred feet from the company, he started shouting. I saw rifles turn in his direction, but he was recognized. I saw a big man running toward him. It had to be the captain.

The whole platoon was on the edge of the cliff looking down. I glanced over toward Company I, and noticed some activity, but no movement. They seemed to be getting ready for something, though. Our company was still about four or five hundred feet from the portholes, and holding. I could see the captain looking at what I presumed was a map; he had several other people with him.

Then I saw Reds going on the run along the road. He ran past under the portholes and disappeared into a ravine to our right. He apparently was coming back up here and would have orders for us.

The next thing I saw was a tank coming rumbling around the road. I found out later that the engineers had brought up a couple of bulldozers and cleared the road enough that we were able to get some armor around. Now we had armor on both sides of this cliff. There was absolutely no way out for the Germans. Surely, they would surrender now and we would be able to give relief to the trapped regiment.

Not once since we had arrived up on this point had we seen any sign of the trapped regiment. I would have thought that they would have outposts or patrols out, but there was no sign of anything. I was beginning to wonder if they had been taken prisoner and the tunnel up ahead was full of Germans just waiting until we were closer. Of course we hadn't seen any Germans up there, either. From our vantage point up here we could see for quite a distance, probably several miles, but nothing was moving except those tanks down there on the road. There were three of them now, and two weapons carriers. They were ready to blast hell out of that cliff, and from the sound on the south side, they were blasting away, too. Then, without any warning, German infantry came out of the mountain, thick as flies. They were firing as they moved. I don't think they had any particular targets in mind; they were trying a breakout. Our company was firing back, and with definite targets, they were knocking off those Germans like ducks. The Germans were finding hiding places among the rocks now and going for definite targets. I thought this was the time for us to go into action, and we did. The whole platoon cut loose on them from above and really pulverized them. That gave our company down on the road a chance to move up. They moved fast, and were among those rocks throwing grenades and firing their rifles in a minute.

Reds came chugging up the ravine and hit the top of the cliff. He did have a message. We were to stay up here on the cliff and work ourselves up the ridge, staying above the tunnel. Company I would be on our right, and somewhere on the other side of the tunnel the rest of Company L would also come up. The battalion that escaped was going to stay on the road after we had passed through the tunnel, and our battalion would keep to the high ground. The schedule had not changed, we were still to be at the north end of the lake before nightfall.

Below us, the battle was just about over. They were taking prisoners now, and a platoon was entering the main tunnel into the cliff. Shortly after that, we saw engineers entering the cliff, and the platoon of infantry came out. About fifteen minutes later, the engineers came out. Our company pulled up ahead, about a hundred yards, and hit the rocks. There was an explosion; the ground shook for a long time. When it stopped shaking, a big cloud of smoke and dust was coming up from the cliff. I heard later they found a lot of German munitions and guns, and that the brass had decided they would destroy the guns once and for all.

Company I was beginning to move out now; they had at least one platoon going out almost straight ahead while the rest of the company seemed to be going higher. They could not go much higher; they were near the summit now.

Apparently, from what we had heard, another division was over this ridge coming up the main road to Trento, where the Germans were expected to make their last stand in Italy. After they were cleaned out there, the next big battle would be at the passes going into Austria—Passo di Ressia and the Brenner Pass. The whole idea now was to cut off as many Germans as possible in the lake country so they could not get to Trento. So far, we had not cut off any Germans, but if we were to get to the north end of the lake, we would cut off at least two main roads—roads the Germans needed to pull back what armor they still had. It sounded very simple, but a lot of dead bodies, both German and American, would be lying along the road to Trento.

Company I had slowed down. They had one lead platoon out on our side of the ridge, and the other two spread from them over the summit and on the other side of the ridge. They were moving, but very slowly, very cautiously. We started to move forward, too, but still we could not see any sign of the trapped regiment or any more German soldiers.

The rest of our company was starting to climb up the ridge now. At the bottom it was almost straight up and would call for some climbing. After about seventy-five or a hundred feet it began to slope and the men could crawl. A little further up, they could stand and walk.

When we were only about three or four hundred feet across from the mouth of the tunnel, we could see the damage that had been done. We would need the engineers and their bulldozers to open it up again for the armor, but we could get infantry through. There still was no sign of life. We began to suspect the worst, that the entire regiment had been killed or taken prisoner, and the Germans were just waiting for the right moment to open up and finish us all off. Our whole company was up on the ridge now and moving toward the tunnel. The troops on the road were in combat formation and approaching the tunnel. Still, no one was in sight at the mouth of the tunnel, we all crouched behind rocks and aimed our rifles down now, expecting all hell to let go. The first troops on the road entered the tunnel—still no fire and no Americans. We received orders to advance.

We kept moving above it, and the tunnel did not blow. As we moved along, a small village came into view below, on the other side of the tunnel. No one was in sight, but there must be Germans down there somewhere. As we passed over the other end of the tunnel, we saw a lot of our other troops marching in combat formation toward the village. We kept advancing until we were right above the village. Then we were ordered to dig in or get behind rocks. They expected the Germans to put up one hell of a fight to hold the village; after the village, we would have smooth going for about five or six miles, with no place for the Germans to set up an ambush.

The same thought was on the mind of everyone in the company: Had we relieved the trapped regiment?

We sat behind our rocks and watched the troops on the road approach the village. When they were about two or three hundred feet from the village, they laid down a small-arms barrage which lasted for about a minute. We thought they had spotted something up here on the ridge but they had not. After a moment, a German officer came forward from the village with a white flag. One of our officers walked out to meet him. They talked for maybe five minutes. The German saluted the American officer and returned to the village. Then about thirty-five or forty Germans—well dressed, definitely not infantry—came out with their hands held high; following them was a car with two Germans in the back seat and driven by a third. When the German troops reached the American lines, they were taken into tow; but when the car approached the American lines, the American officer saluted the man in the car and crawled into the front seat beside the driver. The car was driven into the tunnel. That was the last we saw of that action. But we understood that a German general had been captured, and was being given the privilege of his rank.

After the Germans had surrendered, the troops on the road entered the village and searched. They did not find any more Germans. We must have captured a headquarters.

Was the fight over? Would we just walk to the north end of the lake now?

Still, we had not gotten an answer to the question of the trapped regiment. When we had first seen the north end of the tunnel we'd also seen a lot of GIs standing around—hundreds of them. Had that been the regiment? If it was, why had they said they were trapped? By what? One old man and forty or so troops in the cliff? And why hadn't they had an outpost back there at the south end of the tunnel? There were a lot of questions here, and I sure wanted to hear the answers. The lieutenant said he was hearing rumors now, but would not pass them on until he knew them to be facts. I agreed with him to a certain extent, but on the other hand, I think everyone had his own idea as to what happened, and most of these fellows could put two and two together. We had a scandal brewing in the division. I believed that if the regiment had wanted to, they could have fought their way out of that so-called trap. Their dereliction had cost some lives.

Chapter 28

We were advancing and feeling pretty cocky after the capture of that General, like the war was over. We felt now as if all we had to do was to march the rest of the way to Berlin—hell, they'd probably make us march in step pretty soon. That would be very impressive for consumption back home, our victorious troops marching on the road to Berlin. They're sure to make us shave—and I was just now getting to like my beard and it was getting to like me. It didn't itch anymore.

We were ordered to advance, slowly. We could see up ahead now for miles—the lake, the road running alongside it, and bridges. I could see two bridges from where I was standing. Right after the second bridge, about half a mile, was the mouth of another tunnel.

These mountains were steep, and if a man didn't watch his step, he could end up a few hundred feet below, and he wouldn't fall gently, either.

I noticed the armor had taken off ahead of the infantry now, and was driving for that first bridge. If we could get some armor over these bridges, at least we could be that much closer to the north end.

Three tanks were tearing down the road, and all at once they started drawing artillery fire. I swore they were 88s, but had no clue where they were coming from. There was a lot of firing from the other side of the lake. But the tanks just kept going. They were about a mile and a half ahead of us now, and getting very close to that first bridge. A second group of tanks had taken off now, they were tearing down the road, too, and with them were three weapons carriers, probably loaded with tank ammo. If we could get those tanks over those two bridges, we should be in fairly good shape. At least, if they were going to make a stand at the next tunnel, we would have some artillery with us. Apparently, the Germans on the west side of the lake had spotted us now and began pouring shells on. They weren't 88s—whatever they were, they seemed to break up more and would shatter a whole area with tiny pieces of shrapnel. I heard a man who'd been hit, crying to put out the fire. It sounded like phosphorus. I had never heard of this type of shells being fired on troops, but when you're down to the last, I suppose you'll do anything. The Germans were peppering the whole hillside now. Practically everyone was lying down behind a rock and trying to put out a fire, they were literally burning us up. The medics were doing what they could, but they were not equipped for this type of wound. In fact, none of us had ever been instructed in this type of shell. It scared the hell out of us, I can tell you that.

But the first group of tanks had crossed the bridge and was heading hell bent for the second one. The second group was right behind them. Our officers were trying to get us up and get moving. We had to get out of this fire or we'd all just lie there and be killed. In addition to the phosphorus shells, they had begun firing 88s into us, and some of the units were taking casualties. We *had* to move out.

The second group of tanks was across the first bridge now, and the first group was approaching the second bridge. They had slowed down some, it was possible they had spotted some mines, or they were going to test the weight of the tanks against the strength of the bridge. The first group made it okay. They were now within half a mile of the tunnel. They pulled off to the side of the road, protected by large boulders, and brought their guns down on the tunnel area. The second group approached the second bridge, and one by one they crossed it. They also took cover, a little ahead of the first group, and sighted their guns down on the tunnel. We were still about half a mile behind them. It would be another fifteen or twenty minutes before we could get into position for an attack on the tunnel. The troops on the road were crossing the first bridge now, not too far ahead of us, and they were becoming very cautious. There had been no small-arms fire yet, but every indication was here that the Germans were waiting for us and at just the right moment would hit us.

The infantry below came to the mouth of the tunnel, and still nothing happened. They seemed hesitant to proceed.

We stayed up above, just sitting, awaiting orders. The troops below entered the tunnel, not hesitant anymore. One by one, they disappeared inside that dark hole. After they were all inside, we were ordered to keep moving along the ridge. We were to move until we either received fire or we could see the north end of the tunnel. We could almost walk upright now.

The ground had flattened out, but it was still very rocky. After less than a mile, the north end of the tunnel was spotted. Just north of the tunnel opening was another village, a fair-sized place, probably a resort for the rich before the war. Our troops on the road below were emerging from the tunnel and finding places to set up a defensive line until enough troops had come through the tunnel to make a movement on the village. From our vantage point, we could see for possibly another two or three miles. It looked like another tunnel was beyond. As far as we could see there were no bridges on this stretch of road, but the road itself was built up above the lake on a man-made ledge. If the Germans decided to blow this road, our armor would be stopped and it would then be up to the good old infantry to go in by itself.

At least a company was out of the tunnel now. They were in a primitive defense line, waiting for orders. I put my glasses on the village and could see no one. I don't know where the people had gone; they weren't in the villages and they certainly weren't up here in the mountains. The only thing I could think of was that they went north, and eventually we would run into one helluva lot of refugees trying to get back to their homes.

We had not even seen any partisans up here so far, and this was their kind of country. Most of the partisans we had run into so far had been Communists. Many had worn red stars on their hats.

Orders finally came down. We would attack the village right away. The troops from the road would give us covering fire while we moved in, and the tanks would throw a few shells into the village just to see if there was any reaction.

As we approached it, we could see that we would reach the flat about a hundred yards from the village. This would be the dangerous part of the attack—out in the open. I had eight men besides myself now. The bazooka team had taken two men, and Anderson had been killed. We reached the flatland, and I glanced back and saw the mortars were setting up. The machine-gunners were lying on the ground, and had their guns ready to go. The tanks were still firing. They seemed to be firing more toward the south end now, trying to clear an area of any meandering Germans who might have some ideas about killing themselves an American. We had not received any fire yet, and we just kept going in the slow steady pace of an infantryman, ready for anything and expecting the worst. We reached the houses, and my squad started down a street, searching each house as we went. We would put two or three men inside and the rest would set up outside, Al always staying on the outside with his BAR. We had cleared the street and were coming out near the waterfront. The tanks had stopped firing, as had the troops from the road, and the latter were advancing toward the village now. Next, the tanks entered and right behind them, the weapons carriers. Then came two great big beautiful bulldozers, their blades up.

We were ordered to the north end of the village. We were going to take the road over. Our Company took the point, and the first platoon took the company point. I had only one scout now, so I put Parker out in front, second to Barwick. I stayed up with them, since neither of them had had much experience yet in this game of fighting for a living. We spread out in combat formation and proceeded up the road, before another company fell into line. Three of the tanks followed our company.

The first tank just blew up. No warning no sign of trouble, it just blew up. Everyone hit the ditch or crawled behind a rock. We had not heard a shell coming in, and I doubted that a mortar shell could do that to a tank. It must have been a mine. When the dust had cleared, there was quite a hole in the road. I was sure we couldn't get the other tanks past that point.

The engineers brought up their bulldozers and pushed what was left of the tank over the side of the road. There was no use looking for bodies—the explosion had taken care of them. Then they tore rock out of the side of the mountain and filled in the hole. Some engineers came up with us and started looking for mines, which slowed us up.

About one half hour later we were approaching the tunnel. We were within four hundred yards of it, and hadn't been fired upon yet. Two tanks caught up with us and took their place alongside the road, with their guns trained on the tunnel opening. We were ordered to stop and hit the ground behind anything that would protect us. Then we waited again. But now we had some news to mull over while we waited. When we were back in the village, we had been told that Mussolini had been captured and executed this very day by the partisans, somewhere near Milan. He had left this lake earlier in the day, trying to get to Germany, but the partisans in this district had captured him. There was also a rumor that Hitler had killed himself and his girlfriend, Eva Braun, and that the Germans were about to surrender.

So if that was all true, I wondered why we were still here, staring into a hole in the Alps.

Two tanks came out on the road and fired at the mouth of the tunnel. They fired at least ten or twelve rounds each, then pulled back behind a rock with their guns trained on the hole. If there were any Germans in that tunnel they had to be dead, or at least deaf, from the sound of those shells exploding inside it. We were ordered up and started to advance. We reached a point about forty yards from the mouth and the order was given to run. We ran. It was only a short distance, but by the time we hit the open tunnel we were all in, trotting along. The tunnel was straight, and we could see the light at the other end. We trotted on right out of the tunnel and into the sunlight—and what faced us? Damn, another tunnel! We hit the dirt, crawled behind rocks, and laid our rifles on the tunnel opening. This one was only about three hundred yards away.

Since we'd had no opposition so far, we didn't think we would run into anything, so we approached in a low crouch, running slowly. Suddenly, several burp guns cut loose on us. We hit the dirt and crawled as fast as we could to a retaining wall and set up a defense. The whole squad was there, but we were out here all by ourselves and I began to worry about mortar fire. There was no place we could dig in. The surface was all rock. Then also so was the road. No, the only way we could dig a hole here would be with a trip hammer. Well, we had that retaining wall, and we had the whole company behind us, so we didn't worry about an attack, but those mortars did worry me. The enemy kept firing at us every several minutes just to keep us off balance. We could not tell where the firing was coming from. It had to be around the tunnel ahead, but we could not pinpoint it. Two of the tanks opened fire on the tunnel, but to no avail. While our company was looking for the enemy doing the shooting, the other troops—at least two companies of our battalion and I don't know how many of the other battalion—were in the tunnel. There was no room for them outside. I heard a cannon going off from the direction of the tunnel in front of us—the shell went right into our tunnel, and before the smoke cleared, two more shells went into it. We could hear the screaming from inside. They kept up their firing, and I decided this would be a good time to get the hell away from that wall. I told the guys we would run all together, heading for the rocks outside the tunnel mouth held by our company. I said I would count to three, and on three everyone would get up and in a crouch, run like hell back there. I counted, and everyone but Starke jumped up and ran back to the company. Starke just lay there, frozen. I didn't miss him until we regrouped. Then I saw him. He was lying like he was dead, and for a minute I thought he was. Then I saw him slowly turn his head and look back at us. He was in shock. I called out to him to stay put and to keep down. "Don't even move your eyeballs! Maybe the Germans'll think you're dead."

When the confusion was over and counts were taken, we had fifty-seven men killed and over a hundred wounded in the tunnel. This did not count the men who'd lost their hearing.

We also started getting the story of what had transpired back in that first tunnel.

When the battalion that had not been trapped hadn't been able to communicate with them, they took it for granted that they were trapped and decided to pull back, and alert their Division Command. Division Command decided to put our outfit back onto the line—otherwise, we would have been able to spend several days licking our wounds and resting up in Verona.

In the meantime, the brass was trying to get things organized again so we could get this fight over and get to our destination. The best thing was to hit the mountains above the tunnel, get on the north side, and finish off any Germans still in the area. The brass finally decided they would do exactly that. They would use Company L and Company I, we would take to the mountains, climb about a thousand feet, and go around. The other troops would not move until they had received the signal that we had cleared any mines the Germans had up there.

The command came to move. Company L would lead off, and again the first platoon would be on point. Starke came running up as we were about to leave; he wanted to apologize. I told him no apologies were necessary, to get into his regular position and get going. He grinned and went back with the riflemen. I took the lead. We were doing something now I knew my scouts did not have the experience for. The tanks were firing about five or six hundred yards ahead of us, and the heavy mortars were coming in within two hundred and fifty yards. We were well covered.

We had gone about four hundred yards when one of the German gunners spotted us. He cut loose, and a couple of other guns opened up too. They were splattering the side of the mountain with their fire. I swear, I could feel the wind from those bullets passing us.

We were about five hundred feet up now. Trails ran all over the place. They probably were used for hiking before the war. Our units started to spread out. Company I was above us, but we stuck pretty much to the main trail. It was fairly quiet now. The mortars had stopped firing, but the tanks were still firing ahead of us. We came over a rise in the trail, and there it was, the beautiful view in front of us, and in the distance our destination. We could not see the north end of the tunnel yet, but I saw something that sent cold chills down my back. The road about a mile ahead was blown in four or five places. The engineers would not be able to fix it so we could move armor before nightfall—there were just too many holes.

The lieutenant came up, and with our glasses we perused the area, looking for Germans. We looked for quite a while, but could not find any.

We moved out immediately, half walking, half sliding down the mountain. We only had about four hundred feet to go, and there were plenty of rocks we could fall behind in the event we were fired upon. I felt confident. I really didn't think there were any Germans left down there.

We had scooted down the side and were ready to hit the road. Still we did not see any Germans, not even any trace that they had been there. We dropped to the road, and ran to the tunnel mouth. It was a straight tunnel and we could see all the way through it. We also found the gun that had done the damage — an old cannon, probably a seventy-five, mounted on an old truck. Apparently, the Germans had left it there for the exact purpose they had used it for. They knew they had no chance of moving it out, so they left an old and decrepit gun that was just about worn out anyway.

We raced through the tunnel. By now our whole platoon was at our heels, possibly the whole company. We didn't find one German, they were all gone. But before they'd left they did their job — they held us up for over an hour and finished blowing the road up ahead.

Chapter 29

We were advancing again. Although the mountains were getting higher and the road ahead seemed clear, we still advanced in combat formation. We were close to the first gaping hole which the Germans had blown in the road when several men came out from the rocks of the mountain. By their caps with the red stars, we knew they were partisans. Still, they were damn lucky they hadn't got shot coming off the mountain without any warning. We still had some trigger happy guys with us.

The captain came forward to see what they wanted; we figured they wanted to give us some information about where the Germans were. Then they'd disappear into the mountains again. That was the way they generally operated, but these fellows seemed to be more excited than usual. One spoke English well enough that the captain could understand him. He said that the Germans had taken one of their leaders prisoner and after much torture, he had given them the names of all the partisans in the area. The Germans had brought in men in civilian clothes who were systematically killing all the partisans on that list, and their families, as well. They had killed over fifty people when these fellows had left the village ahead of us, and were now going house to house, killing and torturing. It sounded like the *sicherheitsdienst* — the SD, or Secret Police. They were trained to do just the job these partisans were describing.

They also told us the Germans had a concentration of armor at the north end of the village, but did not know how many, or what type. They told us that we could be there in just over two hours. We explained to them we had no artillery with us now that we had run into these blown-out roads; all we had were small arms and some bazookas, but they said this would be enough. Before we set out again, they told us about other German forces who were moving through the area. It was valuable information. They said they would stay with us until we were near the village; then they wanted to make sure their own families were all right. They had hidden them in the mountains before they came out to find us. They were all on the SD list.

We moved forward with the partisans. The tanks pulled up as close to the first hole as they could. They would be accurate to within about two miles of the village.

Our platoon was at the point again, setting as fast a pace as possible. The partigiani said all of the Germans had gone north from here, and that we could get into the village without a fight, but we were not going to take any chances. We could begin to see the village quite well now. The sun was starting down below the mountains, which completely surrounded us, and it would be dark within an hour. We probably would not reach the village before dark. We kept pushing on. We were past the holes now and back on the road.

Across the lake, our troops seemed to be moving up, but slowly. They apparently had a lot of armor to contend with, but they also had a lot of armor going with them. A whole brigade of armor was with them now, trying to close that gap before nightfall. They were only about two miles below the road junction now, so if we could be there when they arrived, the trap would be shut and the Germans at Trento would have to alter their plans.

We were only about a mile south of the village now, going like sixty, when all of a sudden we heard plane engines. They weren't our planes. They came out over the village, flying low over the water. I didn't think they could see where we were. If they tried to hit us, surely, they would fly into the mountains. But they were flying *over* us. There were three of them, and they were dropping their bombs — not on us, but just emptying them out over the countryside like a final insult to Italy. They were falling at least half a mile from us. We were in no danger. Just then, the Germans decided to clear their machine guns, too. They didn't know where they were shooting nor did they care, but they sprayed the whole area. Some of the bullets came our way.

When the planes had stopped and we were walking again, we came to a fork in the road. The lieutenant told me to take the left fork around the lake. Company I would go straight ahead and pull up at a town about three miles north. Company K would dig in at the bottom of the mountains here and would be available to both companies in the event that either of us ran into anything we couldn't handle.

It was just dusk now. We could still see, but not

very far. The partisans had left us back at the bend and had gone further north to enter the village from that direction. It was still about a quarter of a mile to the village, and we started to receive mortar fire, just enough to keep us on our toes and slow us up.

To the south, on the other side of the lake, a very ferocious fight was going on. Our side was trying to push through before it was completely dark, and the Germans were doing everything they could to hold that road junction. It appeared that the Germans were losing, and little by little, our side was coming up that road.

We kept going and reached a beach about fifty or seventy-five feet from the water. If we could get to those houses right up ahead of us, we should be able to find plenty of cover and protect ourselves from the mortars. They were picking up now, and we were slowing down. I tried to keep the guys going as fast as possible, but it was reaching a point where it was dark and we had to watch where we were going. We reached the houses. There was street after street of three-story houses, and we dived in to get out of the mortar fire. In some of them we found civilians, mostly women and children, but some were men of fighting age. We finally found a house which commanded the main waterfront road. We figured that if the Germans would make a panzer attack, they'd come down that main road. I put part of the squad on the second floor of the house and part on the third floor. The mortars were still firing, but they were hitting behind us. They were firing a pattern, thinking we were still bringing men into the village. From the third floor, I could see six or seven panzers sitting up on a hill above the village to the north. They were taking turns firing. Their shells were falling in the area where Company K had dug in. The battle to the south had subsided some now, but the Germans were giving ground very slowly.

Around midnight, we heard German voices out on the main road. Obviously they had no idea there was a whole company of infantry holed up in these houses. The German soldiers weren't anxious to come into the area, and their sergeants were really giving them hell. A patrol came right under our window. There were six of them. One of the guys on the second floor dropped a grenade on them. It killed some, but the rest started shooting in our direction. There was nothing to do but to finish them off. Soon it was quiet down there again.

When morning came, it was confirmed, we had killed all six. We hadn't been the only ones dropping grenades.

At dawn, I decided to contact the company, so I took Al and his team and went looking for Americans. We walked down toward the lakefront. It was going to be a beautiful day, if we just didn't have to fight. People were out already; they were carrying litters. We looked at their loads to make sure they weren't carrying weapons. They weren't. On each was at least one dead body. They were bringing them to the village piazza, where they laid them out side by side. Later in the morning, there were over a hundred bodies there. The work of the SD. They had done their job, and done it well, there would be a lot of widows here this summer. We had done everything we could to get there before they finished their job, but we were too late for these people.

Many did get away. This country was a land of partisans, with sympathizers everywhere.

The lieutenant had received orders to run a patrol to the north end of the village, up in the hills, to see if the area was clear of Germans. The other regiment with the brigade of armor had reached its destination, but a lot of Germans had slipped through and had raced toward Trento. Our platoon started out, again in combat formation. We had walked about half a mile north from the village when we came to a small complex of buildings. They looked like barracks, but as far as we could see, were completely vacant. We set up two BAR teams, a machine gun crew, and two bazooka teams to cover the riflemen as we searched the buildings. Two or three men entered each building. There was nothing here except bunks with rolled mattresses. There was also a mess hall, in perfect order. Pots and pans hung in place. Firewood was stacked by the stoves. The only thing missing was the food itself.

After we had searched the barracks and found no one, we continued for another quarter of a mile, to the top of a little rise. When we reached it, we all recoiled in horror. Eight GIs were lying dead, lined up with their hands tied behind them. They had all been shot in the head—they had been executed. From the identifications we found on them, we found they were from the regiment that came up the west side of the lake. So sometime yesterday they had been taken prisoner and then brought here and shot.

The madness came over me and I looked around for

a German to kill—I'd kill one if I had to hunt all day, maybe two or three. I even hoped they'd have their hands up in surrender when I shot them! I didn't have to wait long. Up the rise from the west came four Germans, their hands in the air. I raised my carbine and was going to let go when the lieutenant said, "No! Ike!" I collected myself, brought my carbine down. The Germans came up to us with half-smiles on their faces. A little more smiling and I'd forget myself again. They were searched, and we found Lucky Strike cigarettes, American candy and gum, and a sewing kit with instructions in English.

Then I had to help the lieutenant fight off the rest of the platoon—they didn't want to shoot them, they wanted to tear them apart. We asked them where they had gotten the American stuff they had, and they told us they had taken it from dead GIs. We showed them the bodies, and they acted very surprised, and said, "SD."

We returned to the village and made our report. That afternoon the civilian victims of the SD were buried. Their place of burial was high up on a rise overlooking the lake, a beautiful spot to spend eternity, but some of the executed partisans were as young as 16, and among them were their children. After the burial ceremony, tanks and self-propelled guns came rumbling into the village. Trucks, lots of trucks, came with them, and among them were the kitchen trucks from our regiment. We'd finally get a decent meal tonight.

The people were warming up to us now. Though we hadn't got here in time to save those hundred lives, we were able to give a kind of condolence to many of the mourners. Some of us still have friends in this village.

It was still early in the afternoon when we received orders that we were pulling out again. Hell, we'd thought we would at least have the rest of the day to take our boots off, dry our socks, or put clean ones on and just sit around giving ourselves a decent rest. No such luck for this outfit. We were trained to be out in front, and out in front is where we were going. Both Companies L and K moved out. Company I was still up north in the village they had taken without a fight the first night we were here. Several other units were with us—units from the division, a company of engineers, the artillery, probably about two batteries, and some headquarters troops. We also had five tanks moving with us. It was a fairly self-contained task force, so it looked like we would be looking for Germans, probably moving toward Trento, maybe all the way. We might be the units to try to make contact with the Germans and start that last battle. Our assistant division commander was looking us over as we pulled out. This was the first time I had seen him. He was a colonel now, but slated for a promotion to brigadier general.

I noticed that our colonel was riding in a jeep, something I very seldom saw. But, after all, he was an old man—38, and I suppose that at that age you begin to have aches and pains.

We'd marched a ways and I was trying to force myself into a soldiering spirit again, when I realized we had reached the barracks we'd discovered on patrol this morning. I could barely believe it! We were brought to a halt, and the lieutenant announced that for the immediate future this would be our home.

It was only half a mile to that lovely swimming beach on the lake. We would have our own company kitchen. We had running water. We could shave in hot water again. We had our own bunks—and the barracks were less than half full. And there would be no duty for two days.

Other units were north of us now. We were not on the front line anymore, and we wouldn't be. We were rear echelon, living like kings.

Chapter 30

It was almost 1800 hours, and I'd wandered into the
mess hall. They were keeping the kitchen open until
2400 hours, and we could eat all we wanted — after all,
we had to be fattened up for that assault on Austria. I
saw Lieutenant Studebaker sitting by himself at the
officers' table, and he motioned for me to join him.
He asked if I had seen the *Stars and Stripes* that had
arrived today. I hadn't, and he said that the battle of
the tunnels had been written up, and written very
well. Our unit had been named.

He went on to say that it was true about Mussolini
and Hitler. There was a lot of confusion right now as
to who the allies could negotiate with in Germany, but
it looked like the war was over. He doubted if we
would ever be in another battle.

I looked through the *Stars and Stripes* and saw the
story about the rumor that Germans and Allies had
been meeting in Caserta, down near Naples, to
negotiate a surrender.

It was the 29th of April, 1945. As I walked back to
the barracks, I thought about Studebaker. I would
miss him, and MacLean. Neither shunned his men.
Some of the other outfits had some real beauts for officers. They would be remembered by their men, too,

of course . . .

Back in the barracks, I saw that some of the fellows had been down in the village and had had their fill of booze. They were coming in singing and having a good time. I was wide awake, and decided I'd go down to the wash house and do some very grimy laundry, and take a shower and shave. I had a clean shirt in my pack—had been carrying it for months now—so I hung it up to get some wrinkles out of it. I'd wear it tomorrow. When I hung it up, I decided to put my combat badge on it. For as long as I'd had it, I had worn it only once, when we were in the rest camp about a hundred years ago.

When I had got rid of about ten or twelve days of beard and had taken a shower, it was 0300 hours, 30th of April, 1945. I decided to hit the hay. I could sleep as long as I wanted on that nice soft mattress, and best of all, I could sleep with my boots off.

I fell asleep immediately and didn't awaken until almost 0800 hours. I couldn't believe I had slept that long without someone calling me to do something, like kill six Germans before breakfast. I crawled out of my bunk. There were still quite a few of the guys snoozing.

My memory played back to some of the other guys who had gone through this squad since I had joined it. Most of them were sleeping down near Florence; some were in hospitals from here to the States.

After breakfast, I decided to go down to the village with Levin. The bars and restaurants were open again. Levin want to see the beach, and I thought I might be able to find a gift for my mother. We had gone back to our barracks and picked up our carbines and helmets and were walking toward the village, when there was a loud explosion. It sounded like a shell exploding in the village. A column of smoke went up near the water's edge. Levin said he thought for sure that was a shell. It must have been a dud lying there that just decided to let go. As we approached the village, we saw litter bearers loading some bodies on a jeep. The jeep was taking off toward the larger town where our medics had set up an evacuation hospital. We asked a GI standing there what had happened, and he told us that a shell had come in from the north. Only one, but it landed on the right side of the new assistant division commander who was standing there with some of his staff officers. They were killed instantly, and several more were wounded so bad that the medics didn't think they could save them. The colonel's promotion to brigadier general came in several days after he died.

It took all the joy out of the day, and I went back to the barracks.

I had heard so much about that colonel long before I'd ever left the States, and just yesterday had seen him, and then there I was, watching them take his body away. I couldn't have felt worse if he had been one of the men of my squad. I guess a lot of the guys standing around had thought I was nuts when I came to attention and saluted to the spot where he fell, and said, "He was an Infantryman."

I lay on my bunk for about an hour or so before the lieutenant came in and asked if I could start to round up the platoon. We had to go on a short patrol. Germans had been sighted by partisans in a town about three miles north, and they wanted us to check it out to make sure it was not a large force.

I found everyone, got my squad ready to go, loaded for bear, grenades and all, backpacks, full complement of ammo. By the time we had assembled, they had also got the second platoon out. The captain was going with us. We took off down the road and walked in platoon formation for about two miles. Then we got into combat formation and hit the fields. We approached the town on two sides: from the south and from the east. When we got over the last ridge, we could look down on the town. It was a beautiful little Alpine village, with a church steeple in the middle of town, and buildings made of wood. I hadn't seen a wooden building for so long, I wasn't sure one could stand up.

We swept into the village and were greeted by the people as long-lost friends, they fed us and offered us wine. We said no to the latter. No one wanted to get careless from drinking now, not when this damned war was about over. We asked about the Germans, and were told that they had been there this morning, but all had left except three, who were in the local bar waiting to be taken prisoner. They had thought they would be safe from the partisans as long as they stayed and had surrendered their arms to the local police. The local police brought out their weapons. They were old, worn-out rifles. Then the German prisoners came down the street with their hands held on their heads. We took them in, searched them, and asked their unit. At this point they were willing to give us all the information we wanted and spilled everything.

They'd been cut off by our advance and decided to come through the mountains on foot and try to get to

Trento. There were over twenty of them, but they were tired, they knew the war was lost and they just didn't want to go to Trento and fight us again and maybe get killed.

We put the prisoners in the local jail. They were happy enough there. We left the guard duty to the local police, which I think consisted of one man who lived at the jail. The captain radioed back to Battalion and we were instructed to stay overnight in this village and return first thing tomorrow morning.

The mayor told us that the people would put us up tonight. Each family would make sure we were fed and housed. That sounded like a pretty good deal—even better than we had back at the barracks.

At about 1830 hours, Willie made the rounds of our billets to give us a message. As of 2400 hours, May first, 1945, the Wehrmacht Group C would surrender. It was the entire German army in Italy. After that, neither German nor American troops would move, except behind their own lines. The war was over. All we had to do now was seal up the borders, then go home.

Willie left and we just sat there. We didn't speak, we didn't move. Finally, Al brought out a bottle of cognac from his pack. He poured out three drinks, and Russ, he, and I drank to our health.

Several decades later, Al was ordering another round of beers, at the Ale Hoffbrau in Colorado. He asked me whatever had become of that pretty little German girl I'd been chasing all over Italy during the weeks before I'd come home.

I told him that she had come to the United States,

and she'd gone to school near my home. We'd seen a lot of each other in that time.

Al persisted. "Yes, but whatever happened to her? Is she still in the States or did she go back to Europe?"

I said, "Al, why don't you ask her?" I turned and motioned to the beautiful woman who had just come through the door and was looking around the room. "Gentlemen, I want you to meet my wife, the former Erica Von Hoffman, the mother of my three sons."

Afterword

The story was based on the exploits of the Tenth Mountain Division, of which the writer was a member in an infantry unit and saw many of the events portrayed.

I have read many stories of other units, their exploits and bravery, but never a factual story of how a man in the *ranks* felt about what was going on. I tried to portray this feeling here—not from the standpoint of a general planning his battle strategy, or a regimental commander putting it into action—but the thoughts of how a lowly, foxhole-dirty, scared dogface felt about what he was ordered to do, and how he did it.

Our officers, as a group, were fine men. Today, at the reunions, they are respected and in most cases just one of the boys. There is never any rank distinction shown for anyone. But there is respect for everyone.

I had served in several units before I was sent to the Tenth, but never had I seen the *esprit de corps* which existed in that unit, and that *esprit de corps* is carried over today with their association, the monument to their dead, and the fine work we are doing for the youth of various communities.

Men of the Tenth went forward to distinguish

themselves after the war. One is a United States senator and once ran for Vice President. Others distinguished themselves in all phases of society — in business, medicine, education. And several will always be remembered for their ski resorts. And many kept right on skiing and made the sport what it is today. Some, although they are now reaching the age of retirement, still have their skiing weekends.

Our general has passed on, as has at least one of our regimental commanders; other of the officers nearly always show up for the reunions.

I have, and I always will be very proud to call myself a member of this organization.

THE INCREDIBLE STRATEGIES, STUNNING VICTORIES, AND AGONIZING DEFEATS OF THE SECOND WORLD WAR!

THE SGT. #1: DEATH TRAIN   (600, $2.25)
by Gordon Davis

The first in a new World War II series featuring the action-crammed exploits of the Sergeant, C.J. Mahoney, the big, brawling career GI, the almost-perfect killing machine who, with a handful of *maquis,* steals an explosive laden train and heads for a fateful rendezvous in a tunnel of death.

THE SGT. #2: HELL HARBOR—
THE BATTLE FOR CHERBOURG   (623, $2.25)

In the second of the new World War II series, tough son-of-a-gun Mahoney leaves a hospital bed to fulfill his assignment: he must break into an impregnable Nazi fortress and disarm the detonators that could blow Cherbourg Harbor—and himself—to doom.

THE SGT. #3: BLOODY BUSH   (647, $2.25)
by Gordon Davis

In this third exciting episode, Sgt. C.J. Mahoney is put to his deadliest test when he's assigned to bail out the First Battalion in Normandy's savage Battle of the Hedgerows.

ORIGINAL SCIENCE FICTION ANTHOLOGIES
EDITED BY ROY TORGESON

CHRYSALIS 3   (432, $1.95)
An odyssey into the future from the top science fiction writers of today—and tomorrow: Charles L. Grant, Robert Bloch, Chelsea Quinn Yarbro, Robert Thurston, and many more. Introduction by Theodore Sturgeon.

CHRYSALIS 4   (449, $1.95)
Great science fiction stories by established and new masters: Spider Robinson, Octavia E. Butler, John Campbell Award winner Orson Scott Card, and the dean of science fiction himself, Theodore Sturgeon.

CHRYSALIS 5   (518, $1.95)
Fourteen fantastic, never-before-published stories by award winning authors and new discoveries: Nebula Award winner Charles L. Grant, John Campbell Award winner Orson Scott Card, Barry Malzberg, Alan Ryan, and more.

CHRYSALIS 6   (567, $1.95)
One of the greatest anthologies of original stories from the pens of the most talented sci-fi writers of this generation: R.A. Lafferty, Ward Moore, Thomas F. Manteleone, Stephen Goldin and many more.

OTHER WORLDS 1   (558, $2.25)
Visit thirteen imaginary worlds created by the modern masters of fantasy: Jayge Carr, Orson Scott Card, Avram Davidson and many more top talents of today and tomorrow.

Available wherever paperbacks are sold, or order direct from the Publisher. Send cover price plus 50¢ per copy for mailing and handling to Zebra Books, 475 Park Avenue South, New York, N.Y. 10016. DO NOT SEND CASH.

SPECTACULAR ADULT WESTERN SERIES!

A SPECTACULAR NEW ADULT WESTERN SERIES

SHELTER #1: PRISONER OF REVENGE   (598, $1.95)
by Paul Ledd

After seven years in prison for a crime he didn't commit, ex-confederate soldier, Shelter Dorsett, was free and plotting his revenge on the "friends" who had used him in their scheme and left him the blame.

SHELTER #2: HANGING MOON   (637, $1.95)
by Paul Ledd

In search of a double-crossing death battalion sergeant, Shelter heads across the Arizona territory—with lucious Drusilla, who is pure gold. So is the cargo hidden beneath the wagon's floorboards. And when Shell discovers it, the trip becomes a passage to hell.

SHELTER #3: CHAIN GANG KILL   (658, $1.95)
by Paul Ledd

Shelter finds himself "wanted" by a member of the death battalion who double-crossed him seven years before *and* by a fiery wench. Bound by lust, Shelter aims to please; burning with vengeance, he seeks to kill!

SHELTER #4: CHINA DOLL   (682, $1.95)
by Paul Ledd

The closer the *Drake* sails to San Francisco, the closer Shelter is to the target of his revenge. Shell thinks he's the only passenger on board, until he discovers the woman hiding below deck whose captivating powers steer him off course.